HELEN BEEBE
SPEECH AND
HEARING CENT
220 Commerce Drive
Fort Washington, PA 19034
(215) 619-9083 • Fax (215) 619-9087

The Assessment of Learning Disabilities:
Preschool Through Adulthood

The Assessment of Learning Disabilities:
Preschool Through Adulthood

Edited by
Larry B. Silver, M.D.
Clinical Professor of Psychiatry,
Georgetown University School of Medicine,
Washington, D.C.

A College-Hill Publication
Little, Brown and Company
Boston/Toronto

College-Hill Press
A Division of
Little, Brown and Company (Inc.)
34 Beacon Street
Boston, Massachusetts 02108

© 1989 by Larry B. Silver

All rights, including that of translation, reserved. No part of
this publication may be reproduced, stored in a retrieval system,
or transmitted in any form or by any means, electronic, mechanical,
recording, or otherwise, without the prior written permission of the publisher.

Chapter 6 is reprinted from "Learning Disabilities: A Series of Challenges" by
William Cruickshank, *Learning Disabilities Focus*, 1986, 1, 5–8. Copyright 1986
by the Division for Learning Disabilities. Used with permission.

Library of Congress Cataloging in Publication Data
Main entry under title:
The Assessment of learning disabilities.

 ". . . an expanded product of a conference . . . held in
Washington, D.C. in January 1988"—p.
 Conference sponsored by TRI-Services' National
Institute of Dyslexia.
 "A College-Hill publication."
 Bibliography: p.
 Includes index.
 1. Learning disabilities—United States—Congresses.
2. Learning disabled children—Education—United States—
Congresses. I. Silver, Larry B. II. National Institute
of Dyslexia (U.S.)
LC4705.A84 1989   371.9'0973   89-2784
ISBN 0-316-79112-1

Printed in the United States of America
EB

Contents

Preface   **vii**

Introduction   **viii**

Contributors   **x**

Chapter 1   Diagnostic Criteria for Entry and Exit from Service: 1
A National Problem
James C. Chalfant

Chapter 2   Specific Learning Disabilities in Preschool Children   27
Jeanne McRae McCarthy

Chapter 3   Assessment of School-Age Children   73
Joanne F. Carlisle and Doris J. Johnson

Chapter 4   Special Considerations in the Development of   111
Models for Diagnosis of Adults with Learning
Disabilities
Susan A. Vogel

Chapter 5   The Gifted Learning Disabled Student   135
Priscilla L. Vail

Chapter 6   Challenges for the Future   161
William M. Cruickshank

Author Index   **167**

Subject Index   **173**

Preface

The dilemma of the public schools—to meet increasing demands for special services with limited resources—is especially formidable in the field of specific learning disabilities. There are three main reasons for this.

First, the locus of learning disabilities is in the brain and is thus invisible. The absence of visible symptoms often makes it difficult for teachers and parents to accept the validity of the handicap.

Second, there is no unanimity among school personnel or other professionals about the diagnosis or the tests and measures on which the diagnosis is based. Therefore, the critical question of whether a student indeed has specific learning disabilities is often a matter of controversy.

Third, diagnosis is most difficult in the case of the intellectually superior student, who is the most challenging to identify and highly challenging to teach.

To address these issues, a major professional conference was held in January 1988 by TRI-Services' National Institute of Dyslexia. This book is an extension of that conference.

The contributors to this book, all experts in their specialties, offer information designed to assist school professionals, undergraduate and graduate students in education, and parents. It is hoped that this publication will help clarify the issues involved in the diagnosis and placement of students with learning disabilities.

L.B.S.

Introduction

The most recent Department of Education report notes that 4.7 percent of public school-aged children are diagnosed as learning disabled. Many feel that this figure represents, at best, half of the children who should be so identified. Why are so many not diagnosed? Others, however, express concern that too many children are identified as learning disabled and are misplaced in special education programs. Why might this be true?

Public Law 94-142, the Education for All Handicapped Children Act, established a definition for learning disabilities. Since that time, several professional and governmental groups have proposed modifications of this initial definition. In practical terms, the major defining characteristic of a child or adolescent with learning disabilities has become the discrepancy between his or her current academic achievement and the child's intellectual ability as measured by standardized tests.

Today, each state uses its own methods and formulas for identifying such discrepancies. Not surprisingly, different formulas and methods yield significantly varied prevalence rates for learning disabilities. Until there is a national standard for determining what constitutes a severe discrepancy between IQ and achievement, this considerable variability will continue.

Equally disturbing is that some policy makers have sought to control an increasing demand for services for students with learning disabilities—and their state's corresponding increased costs for special education—by tightening the discrepancy requirements for entry into or exit from the special education system. They have required a larger discrepancy between IQ and achievement as a criterion for eligibility for services. From the other side, parents and advocacy groups resist these changes and seek to expand their state's discrepancy formula—that is, to require a smaller discrepancy for a child to qualify for services.

We have a tug of war. What should be a clinical or educational diagnosis of learning disabilities has become a political diagnosis of learning disabilities.

This book focuses on what is currently known about diagnosis. Each author was asked to do an extensive review of the literature as well as to summarize the current status of assessment for specific age groups or special groups.

James C. Chalfant, Ed.D., reviews the current procedures in the United States for identifying children with learning disabilities and the criteria for entry and exit in each state. After reviewing the history relating to these issues, he identifies four tasks that must be accomplished: (1) a clear description of the learning disabled population as distinct from children who are underachieving or failing in school; (2) the development of more valid and reliable diagnostic procedures; (3) a better match between special education techniques and specific kinds of disabilities; and (4) an action plan for searching for the most effective policy to cope with the mild behavior and learning problems often labeled "learning disabilities" in our schools.

Jeanne McRae McCarthy, Ph.D., points out that the question of definition and diagnosis is an even greater problem with the preschool child. So, too, is planning for interventions. Yet passage of P.L. 99-457 emphasized the need to address this group. She discusses assessment and marker variables for each developmental stage within this age group and describes specific diagnostic instruments, current curriculum, and methods of instruction.

Joanne F. Carlisle, Ph.D., and Doris J. Johnson, Ph.D., review the assessment of children and adolescents with a focus on each age group: early childhood, middle childhood, and adolescence. For each age group, they describe the assessment models for social skills, cognition, language, reading skills, written language expression skills, and mathematical knowledge.

Susan A. Vogel, Ph.D., reviews the approaches for defining learning disabilities in young adults. She describes the process of assessment for college-bound students and for vocational rehabilitation. The issues of eligibility for services and for types of special services needed are presented for each group.

Priscilla L. Vail, M.A.T., reviews the special characteristics and needs of the gifted student. She then addresses the special issues for the gifted student who is learning disabled. A discussion of how they are recognized and diagnosed is followed by an overview of appropriate curriculum models and interventions.

William M. Cruickshank, Ph.D., was asked to offer his personal reflections on current issues and future directions.

It is hoped that this book will be helpful to students training to work in the field of learning disabilities and that it will be a stimulus to those in the field to move toward a possible consensus on the definition and diagnosis of learning disabilities.

Contributors

Joanne F. Carlisle, Ph.D.
Assistant Professor of Learning Disabilities, Northwestern University, Evanston, Illinois

James C. Chalfant, Ed.D.
Professor of Special Education and Head, Division of Special Education and Rehabilitation, College of Education, University of Arizona, Tucson, Arizona

William M. Cruickshank, Ph.D.
Professor Emeritus of Child and Family Health, School of Public Health, University of Michigan; Executive Director, International Academy for Research in Learning Disabilities, Ann Arbor, Michigan

Doris J. Johnson, Ph.D.
Professor of Learning Disabilities and Program Head of Learning Disabilities, Northwestern University, Evanston, Illinois

Jeanne McRae McCarthy, Ph.D.
Professor of Special Education, Division of Special Education and Rehabilitation, College of Education, University of Arizona, Tucson, Arizona

Larry B. Silver, M.D.
Clinical Professor of Psychiatry, Georgetown University School of Medicine, Washington, D.C.

Priscilla L. Vail, M.A.T.
Learning Specialist, Diagnostician, and Teacher, Rippowam-Cisqua School, Bedford, New York

Susan A. Vogel, Ph.D.
Director of Research, TRI-Services National Institute of Dyslexia, Chevy Chase, Maryland; Adjunct Research Professor, George Mason University; Editor, *LD Focus*

CHAPTER 1

Diagnostic Criteria for Entry and Exit from Service: A National Problem

JAMES C. CHALFANT

> In Chapter 1 Dr. Chalfant reviews the history of diagnostic criteria for learning disabilities and then presents the current status in the United States regarding the diagnostic procedures used to identify children with learning disabilities. He outlines the criteria used for operationalizing this definition and the strengths and problems associated with each model. He concludes the chapter with specific recommendations to improve the current situation.

This chapter reviews the diagnostic procedures used to identify learning disabled children in the United States and the criteria for determining their entry to and exit from special education programs. Because diagnostic procedures and criteria in learning disabilities differ from state to state and change constantly, it is necessary to discuss the current status of the field within a wider context. Therefore, this chapter (1) highlights the origins of diagnostic procedures and criteria; (2) discusses the criteria currently being used to make decisions about eligibility, placement, and termination from services for the learning disabled; (3) reviews the current administrative procedures used for implementing the diagnostic process; and (4) concludes with a final statement of status and needs. This context should provide a better understanding of where the field of learning disabilities began, where the field is now, and the forces acting on the field that may affect future decisions about the diagnosis and educational placement of learning disabled children.

ORIGINS OF DIAGNOSTIC PROCEDURES AND CRITERIA IN LEARNING DISABILITIES

Three major forces have shaped the evolutionary development of diagnostic procedures and criteria in identifying and serving the learning disabled: (1) the contributions from neurologists who diagnosed and treated patients who had lost functions because of brain injury; (2) the development of psychological tests for the individual assessment of behavior; and (3) the parent movement that resulted in legislation, rules, and regulations to serve the learning disabled in the public schools. Each of these three forces focused on different types of behavioral symptoms and emphasized different diagnostic objectives and procedures. These forces still influence current diagnostic practices in learning disabilities. Knowing the past contributions of neurological, psychological, and educational approaches to individual diagnosis helps one to better understand the changes that have occurred with respect to the target populations of concern, the types of diagnostic procedures and criteria being used, and how current practices have evolved over time.

CONTRIBUTIONS FROM NEUROLOGY

Neurologists were the first to diagnose and treat adults who had suffered brain damage and lost functions such as speaking, verbal comprehension, reading, writing, or doing mathematical calculations. By conducting postmortem studies of brain-injured patients, neurologists began to relate the loss of specific functions to damage in specific areas of the brain. One of the first areas of dysfunction to come to the attention of neurologists was language disorders.

In 1802 Gall related the loss of the ability to communicate orally (aphasia) to brain injury and was the first to attempt to localize different mental operations in different areas of the brain (Head, 1926). Broca, in 1860, studied the brains of 15 former patients who had lost the ability to speak because of head injuries. His studies concluded that the left side of the brain functions differently from the right side and that disorders of speech and language were localized in the third frontal convolution of the brain (Penfield & Roberts, 1959). Wernicke (1872) found that disorders of verbal comprehension, understanding sounds, and associating sounds to written language and writing seemed to be localized in the left temporal lobe of the brain. In 1915 Jackson identified different kinds of aphasia such as the loss of the ability to speak, write (agraphia), and read (alexia). He grouped them as disorders of symbolic thinking (Taylor, 1958). Head (1926) found that damage to different parts of the brain produced different disorders: (1) grammar and word order disorders are due to lesions of the upper convolutions of the temporal lobe; (2) disorders of understanding, symbolic significance, and intention are due to lesions in the supermarginal gyrus; and (3) the loss of the power to remember is due to lesions in the posterior portion of the angular gyrus.

Reading disorders also were first diagnosed and treated by neurologists and ophthalmologists. Hinshelwood (1917) found that few of the children referred to him for reading problems had visual defects. In a classic case study, Hinshelwood worked with a 58-year-old man who suffered a brain concussion. Although the man's visual acuity was intact, he had lost his ability to read. When the patient died, Hinshelwood obtained the brain and found a lesion in the angular gyrus of the left cerebral hemisphere. He postulated that a lesion in that area would result in the loss of the ability to read. He called this condition *alexia* or *word blindness*. He also postulated that children who had an injury or underdevelopment of the left angular gyrus would have difficulty learning to read. He called this condition *dyslexia* or *congenital word blindness*.

Orton (1928) disagreed with Hinshelwood's conclusion that reading difficulties were localized in the left angular gyrus. Orton believed that if one side of the brain is dominant, a person will have less difficulty learning to read. When neither the left or right hemisphere of the brain is dominant, children tend to stutter, reverse letters and words, and have difficulty reading. He called this condition *strephosymbolia*, meaning "twisted symbols." The clinical studies of neurologists added to the knowledge about the results of brain lesions and cerebral dysfunctions on speech and language mechanisms (Penfield & Roberts, 1959); theories of brain functions and behavioral systems associated with brain dysfunctions (Luria, 1966); and the development of neuropsychological tests (Halstead, 1947; Reitan & Davidson, 1974).

To summarize, neurology has made three major contributions to the diagnosis of learning disabilities. Neurologists were the first to identify the disorders that are of concern to diagnosticians today. These include (1) disorders of reception, such as understanding the speech of others or comprehending the meaning of what is heard or read; (2) disorders of association between what is seen or heard, such as establishing associations between sounds and letters, spoken words and printed words, and objects or events; and (3) disorders of expression, such as being unable to express oneself through oral speech and language, or using writing or arithmetic as forms of expression.

Second, neurologists have distinguished between (1) persons who have learned and lost particular functions such as understanding spoken language, speaking, reading, writing, and arithmetic; and (2) young children who experience difficulty learning these functions because of congenital or developmental problems.

Third, neurologists made the distinction between central processing disorders and peripheral disorders, which helps explain why an individual can have normal visual and auditory acuity yet be unable to understand or comprehend what is seen or heard. Many of today's diagnostic procedures are related to or stem from these three concepts.

CONTRIBUTIONS FROM PSYCHOLOGY

Most of the diagnostic procedures and testing instruments used today with learning disabled students came from psychology. To understand learning disabilities one must understand learning abilities (Kirk & Chalfant, 1984), and it was the field of psychology that contributed to our understanding of learning and cognitive abilities.

In 1905 Binet (1911) began developing a set of objective tests to measure the intelligence of children on a comparable basis. This test gave a single score as a measure of intellectual ability. Spearman (1927) hypothesized that there are two factors operating in intelligence: an overall general intelligence factor, and the specific intelligence factor for a particular ability. In the 1930s Thurstone proposed that intelligence was made up of seven factors, which he called the "primary mental abilities": memory, word fluency, reasoning, space visualization, perceptual speed, verbal comprehension, and numerical ability (Thurstone & Thurstone, 1965). Wechsler (1974) differentiated between the verbal IQ, the performance IQ, and a full-scale IQ, which combined the two.

The concept of intelligence consisting of multiple abilities and the different kinds of learning problems found among children and adults led to the development of many specialized tests designed to assess specific cognitive abilities. These include specialized tests in (1) language development and psycholinguistic abilities; (2) visual motor abilities, visual and spatial perceptions, lateral dominance, and motor proficiency; (3) auditory discrimination, auditory comprehension, auditory association, and auditory memory; (4) visual discrimination, visual memory, visual comprehension, and visual association; (5) learning aptitude; and (6) conceptual development. Tests in all of these areas have been used in the diagnosis of persons with specific learning disabilities (Cruickshank, 1966; Johnson & Myklebust, 1967; Chalfant & Scheffelin, 1969; Lerner, 1984).

CONTRIBUTIONS FROM THE PARENT MOVEMENT

The parent movement stimulated federal, state, and local educational agencies to provide services for the learning disabled. Although the parent movement generated public school programs, it also inadvertently changed the direction of the field. Before the parent movement, practitioners in learning disabilities were concerned with the diagnosis and treatment of rather severe "clinical" cases of patients suffering from brain injury, suspected brain injury, or minimal brain dysfunction (Clements, 1966). A learning disability was viewed as a dysfunction in one or more of the psychological processes that affected the ability to learn. Prior to the 1960s most learning disabled children were served in clinics, private schools, or classes established by parent groups, because most public schools did not support services for this population. By 1963 parent groups joined together to take political action, formed an organization, and named it the Association for Children with Learning Disabilities.

Soon federal and state agencies began to respond to the association's efforts to encourage public education to serve learning disabled students. Federal funds were made available to support the training of personnel and research in learning disabilities through Public Law (P.L.) 88-164 under the caption of "crippled and other health impaired."

The Specific Learning Disabilities Act of 1969 (P.L. 91-230) provided a separate appropriation for children with learning disabilities. Soon state governments began legislating provisions for serving the learning disabled. Over 50 terms were created to describe the population in question. Thirty-eight different definitions were reported (Vaughn & Hodges, 1973), and definitions were written by individual states, school districts, and professional and parent organizations. In 1975 P.L. 94-142 was enacted. The term *learning disabilities* was included in the new law, and the category of "learning disabilities" was included in the definition of "handicapped children."

At that time there seemed to be little or no agreement about how learning disabled children should be identified and served. States, school districts, and teachers developed their own terminology, definition, diagnostic procedures, and instructional programs. The enactment of legislation, the allocation of funds, and the need for accountability by federal and state agencies created the need to bring some kind of order to the divergent approaches being used to serve the learning disabled. In 1977 the *Federal Register* published the rules and regulations under which the programs for the learning disabled would operate.

Now all states use the federal definition or a modification of it except Massachusetts and South Dakota, which have noncategorical legislation. Twenty-three states and the District of Columbia use the federal definition verbatim. Thirteen states have modified the federal definition by adding, excluding, or expanding portions of the federal definition. Eleven states have adopted their own definitions that reflect most components included in the federal definition. One state uses the National Joint Committee definition in conjunction with the federal definition (Chalfant, 1984).

Despite the impact of the federal definition and rules and regulations, school administrators and diagnosticians are still experiencing difficulty in determining which students are learning disabled and which students are failing because of other reasons. The heterogeneity of the population and the lack of precise criteria for making eligibility and placement decisions are at the heart of the difficulties in identifying these children.

THE CRITERIA FOR IDENTIFICATION

The key to identifying learning disabled students is selecting precise criteria used for decision making. Federal, state, and local educational agencies have used various theoretical constructs, knowledge, and procedures contributed by neurology, psychology, and legislation to establish guidelines and rules and regulations for identification. This section summarizes the results of the National Task Force on Specific Learning Disabilities with respect to the criteria being used nationwide for entry to and exit from services. The survey included 50 state educational agencies, the District of Columbia, and 50 local educational agencies (one local educational agency from each state) (Chalfant, 1984).

An analysis of all the definitions used by state educational agencies revealed that each definition included from two to five component parts: (1) the failure to achieve component, (2) the etiologic component, (3) the exclusion component, (4) the psychological process component, and (5) the significant discrepancy component (Chalfant, 1984).

FAILURE TO ACHIEVE CRITERION

Forty-eight states and the District of Columbia include "failure to achieve" as part of their criteria for determining eligibility. Difficulty achieving in reading, written expression, mathematics, spelling, and language were the most frequently mentioned. As a criterion for identifying students with learning disabilities, "failure to achieve" in and of itself is not a sufficient condition to identify a student with learning disabilities from those students who are failing because of other reasons. Failure to achieve, however, should be considered in identifying all students who may need some kind of assistance to succeed in school.

ETIOLOGIC CRITERION

References to the etiology of learning disabilities are included in the definition of learning disabilities by 44 states. Most state guidelines mention the need to review a student's developmental history and medical information as they relate to the student's daily functioning. Among the etiologic factors frequently mentioned as being found among learning disabled students are

1. History of brain injury or neurological problems
2. Motor coordination problems
3. Slow speech and language development
4. Immature social and emotional development
5. Hyperactivity or hypoactivity
6. Frequent periods of illness or absenteeism from school
7. Surgery at an early age.

Early symptoms also include infant or early childhood problems in feeding or sleeping, temper tantrums, frequent crying, prenatal or perinatal birth difficulties, low birth weight, or premature birth.

Information or data concerning the physiologic and medical status of a student is in the realm of the physician. However, educators can obtain important information through interviews with parents, reviews of developmental history, and information about conditions that might be contributing factors to learning disabilities. Cooperation with the medical profession may link the student's classroom behavior to etiologic factors. This information, however, is not particularly helpful to teachers who are teaching learning disabled children in the classroom.

EXCLUSIONARY CRITERION

To be eligible for special education services for the learning disabled, the student's *primary* problem should be a specific learning disability. To make this determination, it is necessary to exclude the presence of other handicapping conditions that might be contributing to the problem, such as visual or hearing impairment; motor or health impairment; slow learning rate; mental retardation; social/emotional maladjustment; or cultural, environmental, or economic factors.

The guidelines of 48 states and the District of Columbia include exclusionary criteria in their procedures. Guidelines in most states are rather precise about the criteria for visual and hearing impairments, mental retardation, and motor and health impairments. Criteria are not clearly delineated for slow learners; social and emotional maladjustment; and cultural, environmental, and economic factors.

A brief review of the exclusionary criteria is presented below:

1. *Visual impairment.* Students whose primary problem is due to a visual handicap should be provided with special education services for the visually impaired. Visually impaired students are those whose visual problems after correction (20/70 in the better eye) require special materials and modified or adapted instructional methods. Documentation is usually done by the school vision-screening program and ophthalmologic and/or optometric examinations.

2. *Hearing impairment.* Students whose learning problems are primarily due to permanent or fluctuating hearing losses with or without amplification should not be misclassified as learning disabled. Hearing losses of 20 to 30 decibels in the better ear often require changes in classroom environment or teaching methods, particularly if there is difficulty in communicating with others and educational performance is affected. Hearing disorders are detected by hearing screening programs and diagnosis by audiologists, otologists, and otolaryngologists.

3. *Motor and health impairment.* Many physical problems may affect educational performance. Chief among these are (1) neurologic problems such as paralysis, cerebral palsy, muscular dystrophy, or skeletal problems that interfere with motor performance; and (2) health problems such as malnutrition, allergies, low physical strength, epilepsy, and others. These problems are identified by screening programs in schools and more intensive examination by physical therapists, occupational therapists, physicians, and neurologists. If a student's primary problem is related to motor or health impairments, the student should receive appropriate services for the physical disability and should not be misclassified as learning disabled.

4. *Mental retardation.* Students whose primary problems are due to intellectual and adaptive functioning significantly below average should not be misclassified as learning disabled. Three criteria are commonly used to document mental retardation:

   a. Subnormal intellectual ability ranging from 1.5 standard deviations below the mean on an individually administered intelligence test, or an IQ of 70 or below
   b. Difficulty achieving academically as documented by achievement tests and educational history that might have affected educational performance

c. A defect in adaptive behavior or the degree of personal independence and social responsibility expected of peers of the same age and cultural group

It should be remembered that scores on intelligence tests may be depressed by social or emotional problems, language disorders, cultural problems, physical problems, or other problems.

5. *Slow learning rate.* Students whose intellectual functioning is in the low-average intellectual range learn at a slower rate than their peers. These students are sometimes deliberately and inappropriately classified as learning disabled. This misclassification occurs because slow-learning underachievers do not meet the eligibility requirements for mental retardation or other handicapping conditions, and schools often lack other alternative programs to help nonhandicapped students who are having difficulty in school. Although these slow-learning students need additional assistance, they should not be misclassified and placed in programs for the learning disabled.

6. *Social/emotional maladjustment.* Students who have social or emotional problems that affect their adjustment in school are difficult to diagnose. In some cases social/emotional maladjustment may cause learning problems. In other cases learning problems may cause the social/emotional maladjustment. It can be very difficult to determine whether the primary problem is social/emotional maladjustment or the learning problem. Few objective criteria are available for making this distinction. The two most commonly used procedures are to (1) identify the presence of a specific learning disability in one or more of the psychological processes; and (2) use observations, check lists, interviews, and psychological evaluations to determine the extent and circumstances under which social/emotional maladjustment occurs.

7. *Cultural, environmental, and economic factors.* Students who are failing to achieve in school because of cultural differences, environmental factors, and economic hardship should not be classified as learning disabled unless they also have a learning disability. Differences in the language spoken at home and at school can affect student performance. Environmental conditions such as deprivation, neglect, trauma, poor school attendance, divorce, death, substance abuse, and foster parenting can also affect student performance. The economic hardship of disadvantaged families can indirectly influence student performance at school. Although these problems are documented through interview techniques, social behavior check lists, criterion-referenced tests, and the cumulative file, few objective criteria for assessing these problems exist. Students with cultural, environmental, and economic problems may be underrepresented among the learning disabled population. It is easier to attribute a student's problems in school to these more obvious problems than to a less obvious and more subtle learning disability.

Students who have a handicap other than a learning disability should be placed in programs that meet their needs. Students who have a learning disability and another handicapping condition are multiply handicapped and should receive services in both handicapping areas. When other handicapping conditions have been excluded as primary problems and a specific learning disability has been identified, the student should be placed in services for the learning disabled.

PSYCHOLOGICAL PROCESS CRITERION

In P.L. 94-142—the Education for All Handicapped Children Act of 1975—"the term children with specific 'learning disabilities' means those children who have a disorder in one or more of the basic psychological processes." Despite the inclusion of "psychological processes" in the definition, the federal rules and regulations (*Federal Register,* 1977) omitted the psychological process from the criteria for identification. This omission focused attention on "academic failure" rather than on "specific learning disabilities" and changed the focus of diagnostic procedures. Attention is now being placed on students who are underachieving with respect to their potential. This expands the target population far beyond the original learning disabled population by including many children who are underachieving in school.

Despite this omission, the guidelines of 17 state educational agencies include psychological process disorders as part of the criteria for identifying students with learning disabilities. Another state does not require the evaluation team to document the presence of a processing disorder, but the state guidelines do include a 14-page description of how to assess cognitive abilities including subtest patterns indicative of learning styles common to learning disabled students.

The most frequently named psychological processes used by states in their guidelines were related to attentional disabilities, memory disabilities, perceptual disabilities, oral language disabilities, thinking disabilities, and related social/emotional disorders of the learning disabled. State guidelines included three basic approaches to determine the possibility of a disability in one or more of the psychological processes.

1. *Observing and recording behavioral symptoms.* The guidelines of 18 states include reference to the usefulness of observation for identifying psychological process disorders. Although one cannot observe a psychological process directly, certain behaviors can be observed from which inferences about the psychological process can be made in relation to chronologic age expectancy. Documentation and recording were accomplished using several techniques. Simple check lists were used for some of the more common symptomatic behaviors. Categoric guidelines were much more detailed and included a

definition of each process and examples of typical classroom behaviors for students with a disability in that process. Question formats were sometimes used to direct observations to specific categories of behavior. The task-process check list related different academic tasks to the psychological processes associated with each task, the typical classroom behaviors of students with a disability in that process, and the frequency with which these behaviors are observed. It should be emphasized that standardized tests should be used to support teacher observation. The key behaviors on tests and those observed in the classroom should be mutually supporting.

2. *Informal task-process assessment.* Informal assessment as a means of recognizing a possible disorder in a psychological process was included in 18 state guidelines. Task-process assessments are usually handled as follows: First, select the academic task of concern (e.g., reading numerals). Second, informally assess and exclude other possible contributing factors such as instruction, culture, or environment; sensory or intellectual impairment; physical or health problems; and social/emotional handicaps. Third, break down the academic task into subtasks (e.g., look at the numeral 5; say the numeral name 5). Fourth, determine which psychological processes are involved in each subtask (e.g., visual attention, visual discrimination). Fifth, devise small subtests for each process used (e.g., assess visual discrimination of numerals by having the student match numerals). Sixth, after informally assessing each process of the task, identify those process tasks in which the student was successful and those in which he or she was not successful. This kind of informal assessment should be done on several tasks and confirmed by performance on standardized tests.

3. *Standardized tests.* Eighteen states mention the use of standardized tests in their guidelines. There are two approaches to the use of standardized tests. The first is to use intelligence tests that sample many aspects of verbal and nonverbal mental functioning. An analysis and grouping of subtest scores can give a pattern of cognitive strengths and weaknesses as well as provide a measure of general intellectual ability. A second approach is to use specialized ability tests designed to assess specific psychological processes. For example, these include special tests in the areas of language, auditory and visual discrimination, kinesthetic processing, visual perception, motor coordination, memory, and concept formation. One of the criticisms of specialized tests is that they are not specifically related to academic or school-related tasks, and many educators do not know how to relate the results of specialized tests to day-to-day tasks and behavior in the classroom.

It is not sufficient to diagnose a disability in a psychological process on the basis of one or two test scores. A disability must be validated by having the student perform tasks that require the use of the process in question. If a process disability exists, the student could be expected to have difficulty on tasks requiring that process. If a student has difficulty recalling and repeating numbers heard on a test, then one would expect that student to have difficulty recalling or repeating numbers on tasks in the classroom that require auditory recall. Children who are culturally or linguistically different may require teacher-made tests or criterion-referenced tests to ensure nonbiased assessment.

DISCREPANCY CRITERION

One of the benchmark characteristics of the learning disabled is discrepancy or disparity in performance (Johnson, 1987; Kirk & Chalfant, 1984). Individuals with specific learning disabilities may show discrepancies in one of two ways or in both: a significant discrepancy in the development of psychological behaviors (attention, discrimination, language, visual motor ability, memory, seeing relationships) and discrepancies between general or specialized intellectual development and academic achievement. The rules and regulations of P.L. 94-142, however, specify only the severe discrepancy between aptitude and achievement in one or more of the seven designated achievement areas to become eligible for services for the learning disabled (*Federal Register,* 1977; Reynolds et al., 1984). Disparities in the development of psychological functions were not included in the criteria set forth in the rules and regulations for P.L. 94-142.

Five procedures were included in state guidelines to estimate the discrepancy between aptitude and achievement (Chalfant, 1984).

1. *Informal estimates.* Sixteen states included the use of informal estimates and judgment in determining achievement-potential discrepancies. Informal procedures for estimating achievement usually consist of using graded-level material and studying the student's performance in the academic task he or she is failing. An informal procedure for estimating a student's learning potential is to subtract 5.0 from the student's chronologic age to determine the chronologic-age grade expectancy, or estimating the level of listening comprehension by asking the student questions that most children of the same chronologic age can answer. A rule of thumb suggests that a 2-year discrepancy between chronologic-age grade expectancy and achievement is indicative of an educationally significant discrepancy. Such procedures are subjective and arbitrary, rely on judgment, and are difficult to defend legally. The strength of using clinical judgment in estimating discrepancies between achievement and potential is that the flexibility provided can be used to override questionable formula-driven decisions.

2. *Grade level discrepancy models.* Sixteen states included grade-level discrepancy models as means of identifying whether or not a discrepancy exists. This is handled by comparing achievement with grade-level placement. Cone and Wilson (1981) discuss two variations for determining deviation from grade level. The constant deviation method for determining

deviation from grade level uses a constant level of deviation such as achievement of 1 or 2 years below grade placement. This method does not take into account the number of years a student has been enrolled in school, the fact that a 1-year discrepancy in the second grade is much more significant than a 1-year discrepancy in the ninth grade, and that students of extremely high or low mental abilities may not produce an equivalent score on retesting (regression toward the mean).

The second method uses graduated deviations. The magnitude of deviation increases with grade placement (Lerner, 1984). For example:

Primary grades	Over 0.5 years below current grade level
Intermediate grades	Over 1.0 years
Junior high school	Over 1.5 years
Senior high school	Over 2.0 years

Graduated deviations are sometimes combined with a limit on the intelligence quotient for inclusion or exclusion of services for the learning disabled. Cutoff values range from IQs below 70 to 85. The graduated deviation method is easy to implement and takes into account the increasing range of variability of scores as students progress to the upper grades. This method tends to overidentify slow learning or borderline mentally retarded students who may be functioning at an academic level appropriate to their age and intellectual ability. Students with high IQs are less likely to be identified as being discrepant achievers because of their academic achievement levels.

3. *Achievement level expectancy formulas.* Eleven states included the use of achievement-level discrepancy formulas. These formulas include various combinations of mental age, chronologic age, grade level, and years in school, which are added, subtracted, multiplied, or divided (Johnson & Myklebust, 1967; Kaluger & Kolson, 1969; Harris, 1970; Bond & Tinker, 1973; Algozzine et al., 1979).

In reviewing expectancy formulas, McLeod (1979) and Cone and Wilson (1981) point out that each emphasizes different kinds of variables; these formulas have statistical inadequacies; and they do not address the issues of the following:

a. Errors of measurement
b. Regression toward the mean
c. Group norm comparability
d. A priori knowledge of incidence
e. Increased range of variability of obtained scores for students at higher grade levels

Danielson and Bauer (1978) cited the following concerns about the use of expectancy formulas:

   a. Dependency on scores from intelligence tests
   b. Failure to account for the number of years a student has attended school
   c. Selection of arbitrary severity levels
   d. Lack of teacher preparation to apply the formulas
   e. Difficulty understanding when special education services should be discontinued
   f. Young children and children in the dull-normal IQ range of 80 to 90 were more likely to be identified than older children or children scoring 90 or above

4. *Standard score discrepancy models.* Twenty-three states use a standard score discrepancy model. All scores are converted into standard scores with the same mean and standard deviation. This makes it possible to state the position of a score with respect to the mean of the distribution. The standard deviation is used as the unit of measure. Converting raw scores to standard scores allows for the comparison of scores across tests, subtests, age, and grade levels.

The most frequently used standard score procedure is the Z-score model of Erickson (1975). Reynolds et al. (1984) point out that standard score discrepancy models resolve many of the criticisms directed at age/grade expectancy formulas and offer a more appropriate method for quantifying a severe discrepancy between aptitude and achievement. However, standard score comparison does not take into account the effect of regression of IQ on achievement.

5. *Regression models.* The guidelines of six states included the regression model. The phenomenon of regression toward the mean is the result of imperfect correlation between ability and achievement measures. Children scoring above the mean on ability measures will tend to obtain achievement scores lower than expected. The reverse is true for children who score below the mean on ability tests. A child with a low IQ will obtain scores higher than what should be expected.

It is assumed that the use of regression formulas will reduce the overidentification of children with IQs over 100 as well as reduce the underidentification of children with IQs below 100. Also, standard score procedures emphasizing regressive analysis seem to be more statistically appropriate for quantifying severe discrepancy between aptitude and achievement. Three basic equations have been used for regression analysis: regression prediction expectancy (McLeod, 1979); regression estimates of true discrepancy scores (Linn, 1982, as cited in Mellard et al., 1983), and frequency of regression prediction discrepancy (Cone & Wilson, 1981). For more detailed information, see the reviews of Mellard et al. (1983) and Reynolds et al. (1984).

There are three areas of concern about the use of regression formulas: technical concerns, administrative concerns, and emphasizing reliance on numbers for educational decision making. A major technical concern is that data on aptitude and achievement are viewed as highly suspect because different tests sample different behaviors, and students do not perform well on tests for many reasons. Regardless of how statistically correct a formula may be, if the aptitude and achievement scores are not accurate, the discrepancy determined by the formula will not be either.

With regard to administrative concerns, regression data identify underachievers, not disabled students, and there is concern that regression formulas will increase the number of students identified as discrepant. Parents may use discrepancy scores to demand special services that may not be needed, which will cause enrollment costs to soar. Judges may support quantified discrepancy measures rather than give equal weight to other criteria for identification, which will cause other criteria to fall into disuse.

Parents and professionals often do not want students to be identified by numbers and seem to be more comfortable with behavioral- or educationally based decisions. The lack of statistical understanding of the formula approach also will contribute to resistance to a formula-driven approach.

ADMINISTRATIVE PROCEDURES FOR ENTERING AND EXITING SERVICES

Administrative procedures for exiting special education services are just as important as the criteria used to make eligibility and placement decisions. Efficient administrative procedures for entering and exiting programs must be in place if diagnostic criteria are to be implemented effectively. Four important procedures for implementing entry to or exit from learning disability services are (1) prereferral activities in regular education, (2) formal procedures for identifying high-risk students, (3) decision-making procedures of the multidisciplinary team, and (4) transition and exiting procedures (Chalfant, 1984). This section describes procedures being used to implement these four considerations.

REGULAR EDUCATION PREREFERRAL ACTIVITIES

Every state mentions the importance of the regular classroom teacher in the identification process. The classroom teacher, under the leadership of the building principal, has the responsibility to create an effective learning environment for each student. There are four approaches being used to assist students with learning and behavior problems in the regular classroom.

1. *Teacher intervention*. Teachers are expected to make an initial effort to help students who are having difficulty in school. This is usually accomplished by closely observing student performance and making modifications in the level of instruction, complexity of content, amount of work given, and instructional methods. The early application of direct instructional strategies and classroom management strategies may prevent or resolve early problems in learning before they become too severe.

2. *Teacher consultant model*. The teacher consultant model is used to support classroom teachers who are trying to individualize instruction (Meyen, 1982). Consulting teachers need to be skilled in communication skills, diplomacy, and the dynamics of the consultative process as well as experienced in instructional techniques.

3. *The team teaching model*. Team teaching usually consists of a group of teachers who has the common responsibility for coordinating instructional planning and providing instruction for a specific group of students. For example, elementary schools may have a "pod" of three or four second-grade teachers. A junior or senior high school team may be established along departmental lines in English, math, and social studies.

4. *Teacher support teams*. A teacher support team provides a system within a school that enables teachers to share their ideas, knowledge, and skills in dealing with a large variety of learning and behavior problems. Such teams may be composed entirely of classroom teachers or consist of both classroom teachers and special education personnel. Membership should be based on the purposes and activities expected of the team. Teacher support teams engage in a number of activities such as teacher consultation; informal assessment; generating instructional alternatives; monitoring student progress; providing moral support to colleagues; and referring students to special education when appropriate (Chalfant & Pysh, 1979; 1981).

There are limits to what regular classroom teachers can be expected to accomplish (Minskoff & Minskoff, 1975), but it is important that classroom teachers make an initial effort and seek advice from a teacher consultant or teacher support team before making a referral to special education.

FORMAL PROCEDURES FOR IDENTIFYING HIGH-RISK STUDENTS

All state guidelines list formal procedures for identifying high-risk students (Chalfant, 1984). These procedures include screening examinations for health, general intelligence, academic skill levels, social and adaptive functioning, and language, and for children who are making transitions from elementary schools to middle schools and junior high schools or from those schools to senior high schools. In many states screening examinations are recommended for all students at specified intervals and for all new students.

A formal referral process requesting a comprehensive evaluation is another identification procedure. Such referrals may originate from school personnel, parents or guardians, agencies outside the school, or the students themselves. Referrals for evaluation usually occur when teachers have exhausted their strategies and the recommendations of others and the student is still having difficulty.

DECISION-MAKING PROCEDURES

The multidisciplinary team makes decisions about the nature of a student's problem and the kinds of services the student should receive. A wrong decision can result in a denial of services for a student who needs them or in the inappropriate provision of services to students who might need another kind of intervention. Multidisciplinary teams engage in decisions such as

1. Validating referrals for testing
2. Developing an assessment plan
3. Integrating and interpreting findings
4. Using diagnostic teaching to supplement traditional testing procedures.
5. Determining eligibility
6. Writing individualized education programs

There seem to be three approaches to selecting members for the multidisciplinary team. The first approach is to have a standing team consisting of a group of specialists who act on every case. This approach makes special education expertise available for every case. The disadvantage of this model is that cases may not require the expertise of all members of the team.

The second approach is to convene a multidisciplinary team for each student with those included determined by the kind of problem the student seems to present. This avoids involving the time of specialists whose area of expertise is not needed for a particular case.

The third approach is to have a core team of two or three persons who are typically involved in most cases (e.g., an administrator, a resource teacher, and a counselor). Additional team members are added as needed. This approach provides team continuity as well as helping manage staff time effectively.

Finally, the necessity of including parents as part of a multidisciplinary meeting cannot be overemphasized. Parents contribute valuable information about student behavior outside the school setting as well as background information. Team members who have relevance to the assessment of the student should be selected; the participation of professionals who are not directly involved in the assessment of those problems should be avoided.

Team meetings should be scheduled with an agenda and timeframes. These assist the team in staying on task and provide a method for monitoring a team's progress during a meeting. Many team leaders and team members need training to improve the efficiency and effectiveness of their meetings. Training in group dynamics and communication skills will enhance team efforts through positive, productive problem solving instead of confrontation and conflict over different points of view.

TRANSITIONING AND EXITING PROCEDURES

Most state guidelines devote many pages to the identification, evaluation, and placement of learning disabled students. Only a few paragraphs or pages are concerned with the transition of students into less intensive levels of services or how to dismiss students when services are no longer needed.

A wide array of alternative levels of services delivered, ranging from the regular classroom to full-time residential placement, is necessary to allow the appropriate transition of students to more intense or less intense levels of service. The criteria of many states for the transition of students from one level to another or for exiting special education are not clear or precise. Some state guidelines do not address these issues at all. More precise criteria are needed to guide multidisciplinary teams in deciding whether to transfer a student to a more or less intensive level of service, to discontinue service, or to leave a student in the present placement.

There are four recommendations for improving the decisions to maintain placement, transfer, or discontinue service. First, placement criteria should be written for entry to each level of service: (1) regular class placement with teacher consultation, (2) individual and small group supportive service 50 percent or less of the instructional day, (3) special education instruction programs 50 percent or more of the school day, (4) special day schools, or (5) residential schools.

Second, procedures should be established for program review and evaluation. P.L. 94-142 requires that one individual education program (IEP) meeting (annual review) be held each year to review and revise each student's program. Procedures and guidelines are needed to help multidisciplinary teams decide whether the student has benefitted or will continue to benefit from the present placement; the nature of the student's academic, social, emotional, or physical needs; and the environmental expectations for both the proposed placement and the present placement.

Third, guidelines are needed for four kinds of transitional placement alternatives: (1) continuation of placement, (2) alternative placement in another level of service or another special education program, (3) reassessment for further diagnostic or evaluative information, and (4) regular classroom placement and termination of special education services.

Guidelines for several states mention the difficulty in developing specific transition criteria for terminating, decreasing, maintaining, or increasing special education services because of the diversity of the students and the differences in teacher expectations for students within a particular service level. A recommendation for beginning the development of behavioral transition criteria for each level of service is to ask the following questions about each student being considered for transition. In time, these questions will help generate transition criteria for each level of service.

1. Is the student moving to a less intensive level of support service able to cope with the curriculum demands at that level?
2. Has an achievement battery been given to the student to check on normative standings?
3. Are improvements in the student's learning behavior observable within the special education program?
4. Is there a specified transition time for reentering (mainstreaming) the learning disabled student currently in a full-time special education program into the regular class?
5. What are the criteria for the graduation of a learning disabled student at the high school level?
6. Can the student succeed in the less intensive level with reduced special education support from the learning disabilities teacher?

Whenever a student can respond in accordance with the minimum behavioral and achievement standards of the regular classroom, evaluation of a student's readiness for full-time regular class placement should include

1. Assessment of the instructional program in the regular classroom. Can the existing instructional program accommodate the student without major changes?
2. Assessment of the student's skills and behavior. Can the student cope with the behavioral demands of the classroom, curriculum requirements, and group dynamics of his or her classmates?
3. Assessment of the progress reports from both the special education teacher and the classroom teacher. Do the reports reflect progress on IEP goals and objectives?

Several states strongly recommend that the student being considered for removal from the learning disabilities program be placed in the regular classroom gradually for longer periods of time. Placement on a part-time basis in a resource room is often recommended. During the time the student is being mainstreamed on a trial basis, school personnel should monitor the student's progress to determine efficacy of placement.

Specific exiting or dismissal criteria vary from state to state. The decision to terminate services is a team decision, with parents actively involved in the process. Consideration for dismissal usually originates from the accomplishment of the goals and objectives in the IEP or as the result of the 3-year evaluation. Although dismissal or exiting criteria are rather general in most state guidelines, there seems to be general agreement that discussion for dismissal focuses on many of the same variables that were considered in determining eligibility and placement. For example:

1. Is the student performing commensurate (100%) or nearly commensurate (80%) with his or her ability based on achievement test scores and classroom performance?
2. Is the student's performance in the regular classroom at the same level of performance as it is with the learning disabilities teacher?
3. Can the student succeed in a regular classroom without support from the learning disabilities teacher?
4. Is the receiving classroom teacher able to make any minor adjustments that may be necessary?
5. Is the staffing committee agreeable to issuing a recommendation for dismissal?
6. Have the parents been involved in or informed of their due process rights?
7. Has the special programs administrator or designee reviewed and approved the committee's recommendation for dismissal?

Trial placements are sometimes helpful in considering exiting or dismissal. For example, learning disabled students may be returned to the regular classroom full time with no support from the learning disabilities teacher. A predetermined limit is placed on a trial placement (e.g., 45 school days), and the student's performance is monitored during that time. After that trial period, the student can be reinstated in special education if the trial placement is unsuccessful.

Special consideration must be given to learning disabled students who have been enrolled in special education for a significant portion of their school careers; are in the eleventh and twelfth grades; and who are no longer classified as handicapped. All requirements for a standard diploma become effective when a student is dismissed from a special education setting and returned to the regular classroom. These students then face different credit requirements, have fewer options to obtain credit, and are more likely to receive a certificate of completion instead of a diploma. Dismissal means that the support system on which learning disabled students depend will be withdrawn. To succeed in the regular classroom, these students need to have mastered time-management skills, note taking, test taking, classroom behavior, and the use of textbooks. Personnel considering dismissal should evaluate these skills before making their decision. Exiting and dismissal criteria need to be presented in just as great detail as entering criteria if sound decisions about students are to be made.

STATEMENT OF STATUS AND NEEDS

Current diagnostic practices are being used for three purposes: to specify and verify the problems contributing to children's failure to learn, to classify children as learning disabled as required by law, and to provide data for making decisions about individual instruction and educational placement. A nationwide review of the current status of diagnostic procedures and criteria reveals certain areas of consensus within the field and certain areas of divergence. The needs within the field are clear and an action plan is needed to resolve them.

AREAS OF CONSENSUS

The greatest area of consensus among diagnostic procedures for the learning disabled, as represented in the guidelines of 50 states and 50 local educational agencies and the District of Columbia, is in the administrative sequence of steps used in the decision-making process (Chalfant, 1984). Most states have established guidelines for a delivery of service system that usually includes

1. The involvement of regular education in prereferral activities such as teacher consultants, team teaching, and building-based support teams
2. Special education procedures for identifying children from the general pupil population who need help such as formal screening programs, referral procedures, and coordination with community agencies
3. Guidelines for the decision-making process that include the selection of team members, structuring multidisciplinary conferences, determining eligibility, writing the individualized program, and placement practices

Although references to these practices can be found in most state guidelines and in the guidelines of local education agencies, the degree of specificity of these guidelines varies widely. The skeletal structure for administration is largely in place, but much needs to be done in implementing the functions of these administrative guidelines. The weakest areas of the administrative decision-making procedures are in the systematic program review and evaluation, the transition from one placement to another, and specific criteria for entry to and exit from special education programs.

AREAS OF DIVERGENCE

The greatest area of divergence found among state guidelines is the diagnostic procedures used to specify the nature of a student's problem and the criteria for classification as learning disabled. Although 48 states and the District of Columbia use the federal definition of learning disabilities or some modification thereof, the nation's schools are having difficulty implementing the criteria for identification drawn from the five component parts of the definition. The problems associated with each of the five criteria are outlined as follows:

1. The task failure criteria does not differentiate the learning disabled student from students who are failing for other reasons.
2. The criteria for discrepancy between academic achievement and intellectual potential do not differentiate learning disabled students from other underachievers.
3. The etiologic criteria sometimes can be helpful by identifying conditions that might contribute to a learning disability. This information, however, is of little use to the teacher in the classroom.
4. The exclusionary criteria will not identify the learning disabled student, but they will help identify students having difficulty learning primarily because of visual or hearing impairment; motor or health impairment; slow learning; social/emotional maladjustment; or cultural, environmental, or economic factors. The exclusionary criteria are helpful in identifying students who are not learning disabled.
5. For many, a severe dysfunction in one or more of the psychological processes is a "learning disability." It is unfortunate that the federal rules and regulations (*Federal Register*, 1977) did not include this most important consideration as part of the criteria. This omission has led states and local educational agencies away from the one consideration that could resolve our diagnostic dilemma.

The heterogeneity of the learning disabled population always has been a problem in defining the population in question. By excluding the psychological process as a criterion and by emphasizing the discrepancy between the student's level of academic achievement and intellectual potential, the waters have become even more muddied. Now thousands of underachieving children are being classified as learning disabled, and the enrollment in special services keeps soaring.

Diagnosticians have experienced difficulty in testing for processing disabilities for several reasons. No single theoretic base has been adopted by the field, and no great consensus exists as to which psychological processes or syndromes of processes should be considered in the diagnosis (Weller, 1987; Kavale, 1987). Furthermore, reliable and valid instruments for assessing or measuring process dysfunctions are lacking. Cognitive abilities cannot be observed directly, and they are not as obvious or as easily understood as academic behaviors. Only inferences about psychological abilities or disabilities can be made from observation.

Despite these concerns, all of which have some validity, it is possible for trained diagnosticians to make reliable inferences about psychological processes by observing children's behavior on intelligence tests, special abilities tests, or classroom tasks. Inferences about information processing can be made from a qualitative analysis of children's behavior performed on standardized tests or on classroom tasks. Inferences about information processing can be made by first selecting subtests or classroom tasks on which a child is having difficulty. Second, the behavioral and cognitive skills necessary to perform the task (task analysis) should be determined. Third, the point in the task at which the child was unsuccessful should be identified, and which psychological processes were involved at that point should be hypothesized. Fourth, the hypothesis should be validated by predicting and observing the child's success or failure on other tasks that require that same process. The results of standardized tests and informal task-process assessment should be compared to confirm diagnosis. Much work needs to be done to refine our diagnostic procedures in this area. Rather than throwing up our hands and walking away, attention (a psychological process?) should be given to this important criterion.

THE FUTURE

If support for learning disabled children is to be continued by federal, state, and local agencies, the field of learning disabilities must accomplish four tasks.

First, the field must clearly describe the learning disabled population as distinct and separate from children who are underachieving or failing in school. These children often manifest behaviors of central nervous system dysfunction and are characterized by intra-individual differences with an uneven pattern of development academically or intellectually (Gallagher, 1986; Adelman & Taylor, 1983; Hallahan & Kauffman, 1976). Their behavioral symptoms are diverse, so it may make sense to stop speaking of a general group and begin defining subgroups of learning disabilities that require special education intervention (Torgensen, 1982; Lyon, 1987; McKinney, 1984, 1987; Keogh, 1987).

Second, more valid and reliable diagnostic procedures need to be developed for identifying specific kinds of learning disabilities. These should consist of standardized tests as well as reliable clinical techniques.

Third, since one of the most important goals of diagnosis is to improve instruction, matches must be made between specific special education techniques and specific kinds of disabilities. Data and documentation must be gathered to demonstrate that these interventions make a difference in how children perform in the classroom.

Fourth, the field needs an action plan similar to the plan proposed by Gallagher (1986), which would assist in the search for the most effective policy to cope with the mild behavior and learning problems often called "learning disabilities" in our schools. Leaders from special education and regular education should engage in a joint planning effort to resolve the issues of the marginal child. Demonstration centers should be established to evaluate different service delivery models including preschool, elementary, and secondary programs; intense concentrations of service delivery; and mainstreaming models. Such a plan offers a logical and national approach to the problem.

Diagnostic procedures will play a central role in these documentation models. Diagnosis will be used to identify the children to be served in each model. Diagnosis will be used to match the most appropriate instructional procedures to the child. Diagnosis will be included in the procedures for evaluating the effectiveness of different models as different kinds of learning problems or disabilities. Educators' skills or lack of skills in diagnostic procedures will be a major factor in influencing future policy, future program designs, and the future support of services for learning disabled children.

REFERENCES

Adelman, H. S., & Taylor, L. (1983). *Learning disabilities in perspective.* Glenview, IL: Scott, Foresman.

Algozzine, B., Forgnone, C., Mercer, C., & Trifiletti, J. (1979). Toward defining discrepancies for specific learning disabilities: An analysis and alternatives. *Learning Disability Quarterly, 2*(4), 25–31.

Binet, A. (1911). L'education de l'intelligence. In *Les idees modernes sur les enfants.* Paris: Flammarion.

Bond, G. L., & Tinker, M. A. (1973). *Reading difficulties, their diagnosis and corrections* (3rd ed.). New York: Appleton-Century-Crofts.

Chalfant, J. C. (1984). *Identifying learning disabled students: Guidelines for decision making.* Northeast Regional Resource Center, Trinity College, Burlington, VT. Washington, DC: Special Education Programs, U.S. Department of Education.

Chalfant, J. C., & Pysh, M. V. (November 1981). Teacher assistance teams. A model for within-building problem solving. *Counterpoint.*

Chalfant, J. C., Pysh, M. V., & Moultrie, R. (1979, Summer). Teacher assistance teams: A model for within-building problem solving. *Learning Disability Quarterly, 2,* 85–96.

Chalfant, J. C., & Scheffelin, M. A. (1969). *Central processing dysfunctions in children: A review of research*. (NINDS Monograph No. 9.) Washington, DC: U.S. Department of Health, Education, and Welfare.

Clements, S. D. (1966, January). *Minimal brain dysfunction in children*. (Public Health Service publication No. 1415.) Washington, DC: U.S. Department of Health, Education, and Welfare.

Cone, T. E., & Wilson, L. R. (1981). Quantifying a severe discrepancy: A critical analysis. *Learning Disabilities Quarterly, 4*, 359–371.

Cruickshank, W. M. (Ed.). (1966). *The teacher of brain-injured children. A discussion of the bases for competency*. (Syracuse University Special Education and Rehabilitation Monograph Series 7.) Syracuse, NY: Syracuse University Press.

Danielson, L. C., & Bauer, J. N. (1978). A formula-based classification of learning disabled children: An examination of the issues. *Journal of Learning Disabilities, 11*, 163–176.

Education for all Handicapped Children Act: Public Law 94-142.

Erickson, M. T. (1975). The Z-score discrepancy method for identifying reading disabled children. *Journal of Learning Disabilities, 8*, 308–312.

Federal Register. (1977, December 29).

Gallagher, J. J. (1986). Learning disabilities and special education: A critique. *Journal of Learning Disabilities, 19*(10), 595–601.

Hallahan, D. P., & Kauffman, J. M. (1976). *Introduction to learning disabilities: A psychobehavioral approach*. Englewood Cliffs, NJ: Prentice-Hall.

Halstead, W. C. (1947). *Brain and intelligence*. Chicago: University of Chicago Press.

Harris, A. (1970). *How to increase reading ability: A guide to developmental and remedial methods* (5th ed.). New York: McKay.

Head, H. (1926). *Aphasia and kindred disorders of speech* (Vols. 1, 2). New York: Macmillan.

Hinshelwood, J. (1917). *Congenital word blindness*. London: Lewis.

Jackson, J. H. (1915). On the physiology of language. *Brain, 38*, 59–64.

Johnson, D. J. (1987). Assessment issues in learning disabilities. In S. Vaughn & C. S. Bos (Eds.), *Research in learning disabilities. Issues and future directions* (pp. 141–149). Boston: College-Hill.

Johnson, D. J., & Myklebust, H. S. (1967). *Learning disabilities: Educational principles and practices*. New York: Grune & Stratton.

Kaluger, G., & Kolson, C. (1969). *Reading and learning disabilities*. Columbus, OH: Merrill.

Kavale, K. A. (1987). Theoretical quandaries in learning disabilities. In S. Vaughn & C. S. Bos (Eds.), *Research in learning disabilities. Issues and future directions* (pp. 19–29). Boston: College-Hill.

Keogh, B. K. (1987). A shared attribute model of learning disabilities. In S. Vaughn & C. S. Bos (Eds.), *Research in learning disabilities. Issues and future directions* (pp. 3–12). Boston: College-Hill.

Kirk, S. A., & Chalfant, J. C. (1984). *Academic and developmental learning disabilities*. Denver: Love.

Lerner, J. W. (1984). *Learning Disabilities: Theories, diagnosis, and teaching strategies* (3rd ed.). Boston: Houghton Mifflin.

Luria, A. R. (1966). *Higher cortical functions of man* (B. Haigh, Trans.). New York: Basic.

Lyon, G. R. (1987). Learning disabilities research: False starts and broken promises. In S. Vaughn & C. S. Bos (Eds.), *Research in learning disabilities. Issues and future directions* (pp. 69–80). Boston: College-Hill.

McKinney, J. D. (1987). Research on the identification of learning-disabled children: Perspectives on changes in educational policy. In S. Vaughn & C. S. Bos (Eds.), *Research in learning disabilities. Issues and future directions* (pp. 215–233). Boston: College-Hill.

McKinney, J. D., & Feagans, L. (1984). Academic and behavioral characteristics: Longitudinal studies of learning disabled children and average achievers. *Learning Disability Quarterly, 7*(3), 251–265.

McLeod, J. (1979). Educational underachievement: Toward a defensible psychometric definition. *Journal of Learning Disabilities, 12,* 42–50.

Mellard, D., Cooley, S., Poggio, J., & Deshler, D. (1983). *A comprehensive analysis of four discrepancy methods* (Research Monograph No. 15). Lawrence: University of Kansas Institute for Research in Learning Disabilities.

Meyen, E. L. (1982). *Exceptional children and youth: An introduction* (2nd ed.). Denver: Love.

Minskoff, E. H., & Minskoff, J. G. (1975). A unified program of remedial and compensatory teaching for children with process learning disabilities. *Journal of Learning Disabilities, 9,* (4).

Orton, S. T. (1928). Specific reading disability-Strephosymbolia. *Journal of the American Medical Association, 90,* 1095–1099.

Penfield, W., & Roberts, L. (1959). *Speech and brain mechanisms.* Princeton, NJ: Princeton University Press.

Reitan, F. M., & Davidson, L. A. (1974). *Clinical neuropsychology: Current status and application.* Washington, DC: Winston.

Reynolds, C. R., Berk, R. A., Boodoo, G. M., Cox, J., Gutkin, T. B., Mann, L., Page, E. B., & Wilson, V. L. (1984). *Critical measurement issues in learning disabilities.* Washington, DC: United States Department of Education.

Spearman, C. (1927). *The nature of intelligence and the principles of cognition.* London: Macmillan.

Taylor, J. (Ed.). (1958). *Selected writings of John Hughlings Jackson.* New York: Basic.

Thurstone, L., & Thurstone, G. (1965). *Primary Mental Abilities Test (PMA).* Chicago: Science Research Associates.

Torgesen, J. K. (1982). The use of rationally defined subgroups in research on learning disabilities. In J. P. Das, R. F. Mulcahy, & A. E. Wall (Eds.), *Theory and research in learning disabilities.* New York: Plenum.

Vaughn, R. W., & Hodges, L. (1973). A statistical survey into a definition of learning disabilities: A search for acceptance. *Journal of Learning Disabilities, 6,* 658–669.

Wechsler, D. (1974). *Wechsler Intelligence Scale for Children-Revised.* New York: Psychological Corporation.

Weller, C. (1987). A multifaceted hierarchical theory of learning disabilities. In S. Vaughn & C. S. Bos (Eds.), *Research in learning disabilities. Issues and future directions* (pp. 35–46). Boston: College-Hill.

Wernicke, C. (1872). The symptom-complex of aphasia. In A. Church (Ed.), *Diseases of the nervous system.* New York: Appleton-Century-Crofts.

CHAPTER 2

Specific Learning Disabilities in Preschool Children

JEANNE McRAE McCARTHY

Chapter 2 is the first of three chapters that focus on the diagnosis of learning disabilities for a specific age group. Dr. McCarthy addresses the special problems with the preschool child. How does one classify a child as learning disabled before he or she has been challenged with the task of academic learning? Yet there are preschool children at risk, and it is critical to identify them before they face failure in school.

Dr. McCarthy reviews the recent events that have highlighted the need to work with the preschool child (aged 3–5) and with the infant and toddler (aged 0–2) who are at-risk, delayed, or handicapped. She provides an extensive review of the research and applied literature on marker variables, sample characteristics, assessment instruments, and interventions.

All of the problems, issues, and questions that have plagued the field of specific learning disabilities (SLDs) since its inception are magnified when considering the preschool population. Questions of definition and nomenclature become more critical, issues surrounding etiology seem more urgent, identification and assessment seem more difficult, and problems of efficacy of early intervention or prevention seem more pressing.

In a similar fashion, all of the questions, problems, and issues facing the field of early intervention with at-risk, delayed, or handicapped infants, toddlers, and preschoolers are magnified when considering young children with SLDs. Classification and labeling issues seem intensified, problems of diagnosis and assessment seem to be more critical, and delineation of a discrete group of SLD preschoolers seem impossible.

The subject of learning disabilities in preschool children is being treated in a variety of ways in the current literature. An amazing total of 7,198 documents were included in an Educational Research Information Center (ERIC) search for publications using the descriptors *preschool learning disabilities*. Some authors have addressed the topic in a detailed, definitive fashion, as in the case of Kirk and Chalfant in their book *Developmental and Academic Learning Disabilities* (1984), in which five chapters are devoted to learning disabilities in the preschool years. McCarthy (1987a, b) has examined the issues in depth in her discussion of definition, prevalence, characteristics, relevance of the SLD subtype literature, assessment, and marker variables. Lerner (1981) has detailed the possible at-risk signals useful in early identification of SLD children. Other authors present the topic in a general discussion of categories of handicapping conditions but are more tentative in their description of the appropriateness of the use of the SLD category in preschool children, as in the case of Peterson in her book *Early Intervention for Handicapped and At-Risk Children* (1987). Garwood (1983) includes learning disabled children in his eight groups of exceptional children and differentiates SLDs from general learning disabled or mildly retarded. He further addresses the learning disabled under the term *minimal brain dysfunction* in his chapter on physical bases of handicapping conditions. His chapter on intelligence and cognition adds clarity to concepts important in the 0 to 5 population. Other authors avoid the topic altogether, as in the case of Bricker's book *Early Education of At-Risk and Handicapped Infants, Toddlers and Preschool Children* (1986). Although her discussion of the target population to be served as at-risk or handicapped is extremely detailed, and the section on problems in identifying and labeling the target population is insightful, there is no mention of SLDs. Bricker comes close to the subject in the discussion of developmental delays but refers only to mental retardation and language-delayed or disordered children.

Historically, this apparent ambivalence about the existence of SLDs in preschool children is of fairly recent origin, dating from the 1960s, when an educational orientation began to dominate definitions that had previously emphasized perceptual problems of a neurologic origin (Hinshelwood, 1917; Orton, 1925; Strauss & Werner, 1942; Strauss & Lehtinen, 1947). The newer neuropsychological paradigms, as well as information-processing paradigms, share the notion that learning disabilities are intrinsic to the child and are neurologic or psychological in origin. Both of these major theoretic approaches to the field lend support to the concept of learning disabilities in preschool children, emphasizing the importance of brain-behavior relationships and the acquisition of cognitive and psycholinguistic processes in preschool development.

Recent federal policy, culminating in the passage of Public Law (P.L.) 99-457, has emphasized the need for a thoughtful resolution to some of the dilemmas facing the fields of early education of the handicapped and of SLDs. Preschool children with SLDs present a challenge to both areas of specialization. Preschool learning disabled children appear to represent a convergence of issues endemic to the fields of SLDs and the education of early childhood handicapped children.

In this chapter the importance of the problem is discussed in the context of recent events that focus on SLDs in preschool children (3–5 years and in at-risk, delayed, and handicapped infants and toddlers (0–2 years). Several themes will be examined, including the new definitions that continue to proliferate; etiology of SLDs; prevalence figures; characteristics; patterns in the subtype literature; marker variables useful in defining sample characteristics in preschool learning disability research; and assessment instruments and procedures, including several typical profiles of young children diagnosed as having an SLD. Curriculum and instruction are discussed briefly. On the basis of the data presented, tentative conclusions will be offered for thoughtful consideration by the reader.

RECENT EVENTS FOCUSING ON PRESCHOOL CHILDREN WITH SPECIFIC LEARNING DISABILITIES

Of the recent events that have called attention to this population of children, the most critical in terms of total impact has been the enactment of P.L. 99-457. As the Education of the Handicapped Act Amendments of 1986, P.L. 99-457 amends P.L. 99-372, P.L. 98-199, P.L. 95-561, P.L. 94-142, P.L. 93-380, and P.L. 91-230. Many of the components of these previous laws have been left intact, including the definition of the handicapped as spelled out in the rules and regulations of P.L. 94-142 (Section 121 a.5) in the *Federal Register* of August 23, 1977. Thus, young children with SLDs and their families are eligible for early intervention programs and services, as well as preschool services under the proposed rules and regulations in the *Federal Register* of November 18, 1987.

A recent publication of the Division for Early Childhood (DEC) of the Council for Exceptional Children (1987) includes position statements adopted by the National Executive Board of DEC to respond to policy issues raised by P.L. 99-457. The expansion of the eligibility criteria included in the statute (Section 672[1][A] and [B] and definitions of such terms as *developmental delays, diagnosed physical or mental condition which has a high probability of resulting in a developmental delay, and at risk of having substantial delays* may have a significant impact on the development of federal and state policies, regulations, and guidelines. The permissive "noncategorical" reporting provision of the statute is expected to have an effect on eligibility criteria in those states who choose not to submit federal counts of children served by diagnostic label. It will also change the ability of advocacy groups to track services to the handicapped categories composing their constituencies, such as the Association for Children and Adults with Learning Disabilities (ACLD).

A third recent event is the publication of the *Report to Congress* (1987) prepared by the Interagency Committee on Learning Disabilities after a year of conferences and study of learning disabilities programs in 13 federal agencies involved in research, service, and program development. This prestigious committee made the following recommendations in regard to "causes" to Congress: "A better understanding of the neurobiological bases of behavior is needed and an effort should be made to identify early biological and behavioral markers for learning disability" (p. 228). The report also addressed preschool learning disabilities under "prevention": "An ability for early diagnosis should provide a secondary prevention of learning disabilities, or at least averting and ameliorating disorders that might manifest later in life" (p. 232).

A fourth event sounded a more disconcerting note when the national Headstart office of the Department of Health and Human Services proposed a revision of the diagnostic criteria for Headstart programs that would have deleted the category of SLDs from the handicapping conditions to be served. Although the announcement of the proposed revision has not yet been published in the *Federal Register,* some regional and local Headstart programs have proceeded to eliminate SLDs as an eligible category. In gathering information about the proposed deletion by Headstart, part of the rationale centered on the numbers of children being diagnosed and served as learning disabled. However, the *Thirteenth Annual Report of the U.S. Department of Health and Human Services* (1986) includes this data: Of the 61,898 handicapped children professionally diagnosed and served in Headstart programs, speech impaired accounted for 61.9 percent; health impaired 11.1 percent; SLDs 6.2 percent; mentally retarded 5.3 percent; and orthopedically handicapped 5.4 percent. A 6.2 percentage of handicapped children being served is not an excessive number of children and seems an inadequate rationale for deletion of the category of learning disabilities. This is especially puzzling when looking at data on implementation of P.L. 94-142, finding that all 50 states provided services to learning disabled children ages 3 to 5, serving 20,219 children or 7.8 percent of all preschool children served as handicapped (N = 259,483). Congress was concerned about this proposed deletion and included in the Human Services Reauthorization Act of 1986 conference agreement a statement that the categories defined in P.L. 94-142 Section 602(a)(1.) will be served by Headstart and that "individuals who fall within this definition will continue to be served within the Headstart program" (p. 19).

A fifth series of events surrounds the apparently growing split between those professionals who view learning disabilities as a phenomenon of the school years and those who view learning disabilities as intrinsic to the child, reflecting his or her idiosyncratic information-processing system. Some who view learning disabilities as a phenomenon of the school years emphasize the academic components of the federal definition and criteria, placing little stress on the concepts of "one or more of the basic psychological processes involved in understanding or using language, spoken or written, which may manifest itself in an imperfect ability to listen, think, speak . . ." (P.L. 94-142, 1977).

In response to these events, the executive board of the Division for Learning Disabilities issued a position statement: "Learning Disabilities do exist in preschool children. It is important in the interest of prevention and early intervention that special education programs be provided to meet their needs."

The National Joint Committee on Learning Disabilities composed of eight national organizations involved in SLDs (American Speech, Language and Hearing Association, National Association of School Psychologists, Association for Children and Adults with Learning Disabilities, Division of Learning Disabilities, Orton Dyslexia Society, National Reading Association, the Council on Learning Disabilities, and the Division for Children with Communication Disorders) has issued a position paper entitled "Learning Disabilities and the Preschool Child" (1986), which discusses the issues in detail and which strongly supports the existence of SLDs in preschool children.

This commitment to the existence of learning disabilities in young children underlies the information presented in this chapter. Some approaches to resolution of these and other issues facing the field are offered in an attempt to serve young handicapped children and their families.

CRITICAL ISSUES

Five questions seem relevant to any discussion of preschool learning disabled children:

1. Who are they? (definition, characteristics, prevalence)
2. What caused it? (etiology)
3. How do we find them? When do we find them? (early identification, assessment, marker variables)
4. Do the subtypes of learning disabilities identified in school-age children also exist at the preschool level?
5. How do we teach them? (curriculum and instruction)

DEFINITIONS OF LEARNING DISABILITY

There are three concepts involved in SLDs that help to answer the question of who are the learning disabled children:

1. The learning disabled child is *intact* to the point that he or she is not eligible for services under any other category of the handicapped. The learning disabled child has adequate intelligence, sensory processes, emotional stability, and opportunities to learn.

2. The learning disabled child exhibits two kinds of *discrepancies:*
   a. Between capacity and achievement (of developmental milestones)
   b. Within the psychological processes that underlie learning, including attention, memory, perception, thinking, and language

3. The learning disabled child *deviates* so markedly from the norm of his or her peers as to require special education intervention. The SLD is due to a dysfunction within the child, not within the system.

This interpretation is consistent with the definition included in P.L. 94-142, which is embedded in most of the state definitions in current use. By substituting *pre*reading, *pre*writing and *pre*mathematics, the usefulness of this definition becomes even more apparent.

Two more recent definitions may help to answer some of the definitional issues, the first produced by ACLD and the second by the Interagency Committee on Learning Disabilities (ICLD).

The ACLD description of the term *specific learning disabilities* encompasses, endorses, and broadens the definition of SLDs as defined in the Education of the Handicapped Act of 1975:

Specific Learning Disabilities is a chronic condition of presumed neurological origin which selectively interferes with the development, integration, and/or demonstration of verbal and/or non-verbal abilities.
Specific Learning Disabilities exists as a distinct handicapping condition and varies in its manifestations and in degree of severity.
Throughout life, the condition can affect self-esteem, education, vocation, socialization, and/or daily living activities.

The concept of a lifelong condition places new emphasis on the importance of the early years for children with SLDs, and focuses on the intrinsic nature of SLDs.

The concern for early prevention, assessment, and intervention is also present in the proposed definition of ICLD:

> Learning disabilities is a generic term that refers to a heterogeneous group of disorders manifested by significant difficulties in the acquisition and use of listening, speaking, reading, writing, reasoning, or mathematical abilities. These disorders are intrinsic to the individual and presumed to be due to central nervous *system* dysfunction. Even though a learning disability may occur concomitantly with other handicapping conditions, (e.g., sensory impairment, mental retardation, social and emotional disturbance), with *socioenvironmental influences* (e.g., cultural differences, insufficient or inappropriate instruction, psychogenic factors) *and especially with attention deficit disorder, all of which may cause learning problems,* a learning disability is not the direct result of those conditions or influences.

The emphasis on the neuropsychological nature of SLDs and the importance of brain-behavior relationships are seen as supportive of the existence of SLDs in preschool children.

These definitions of SLDs can be fleshed out by looking at the characteristics of young children with SLDs as described in several sources in the literature: the subtype literature, Headstart data, and descriptions of parents.

IMPLICATIONS OF THE SUBTYPE LITERATURE FOR DEFINING THE CHARACTERISTICS OF CHILDREN WITH SLDs

Although a great deal of research has been done on subtypes of learning disabled youngsters of schoolage, studies of preschool learning disabled children are almost nonexistent. However, by looking at the subtypes described in school-age children, some important information can be derived on the characteristics of learning disabled children and the precursors of the deficit patterns of children at ages 6, 7, 8, and 9.

Eight subtype studies are presented in the appendix to this chapter, with a preliminary attempt to designate the psycholinguistic strengths and weaknesses reported in the data from each study. Because of the variability among the studies, it has been difficult to interpret them and to develop definitive conclusions based on the subtype literature For these reasons, an attempt has been made to designate the psycholinguistic functions sampled in each study and to delineate patterns of strengths and weaknesses across the studies. The attempt has been more or less successful, depending on the functions sampled in the original study, but is presented to encourage the reader to think about the cognitive styles of the subtypes and the implications for children in the preschool years.

A tentative conclusion from these studies supports the existence of three subtypes of learning disabilities:

1. A low verbal/high performance group (language disorder subtype)
2. A high verbal/low performance group (visual/perceptual disorder subtype)
3. Mixed perceptual/language deficits (discrepant verbal and performance)

Many of the studies analyzed also report a normal, asymptomatic, no-deficit group.

Figure 2-1 presents the group means on the Wechsler Intelligence Scale for Children (WISC) profiles of the four subgroups found in a sample of 57 learning disabled children placed in the South Carolina Child Service Demonstration Class and tested individually on the WISC (McCarthy & Elkins, 1974). As can be seen in group 1, means scores varied across both verbal and performance scales ranging from 7 to 11, with higher scores in

Fig. 2-1. Mean subtest scores on the Wechsler Intelligence Scale for Children for groups 1, 2, 3, and 4. (From J. McCarthy and J. Elkins. (1974). Psychometric characteristics of children enrolled in the child service demonstration centers. Tucson: Leadership Training in Learning Disabilities.)

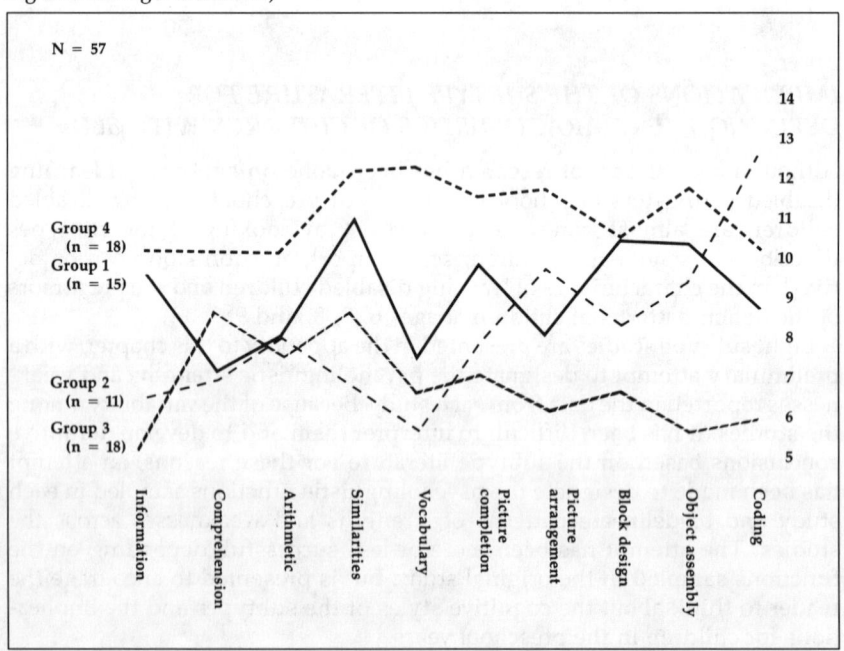

information, similarities, picture completion, block design, and object assembly. Lower scores were also found in both the verbal and performance scales, notably in comprehension, arithmetic, vocabulary, picture arrangement, and coding. Group 2 is typical of the low verbal/high performance subtype, with lowest scores in information and vocabulary and higher scores in picture arrangement and coding. Group 3 appears to be high verbal/low performance, except for the low score in information. Group 4 is a clear example of the asymptomatic subtype, with all scores at or above the mean of the test, although all of the children had been diagnosed as having SLDs. The most significant variable for groups 1, 2, and 3 was the lowered score on vocabulary.

Similar patterns can be detected on the Wechsler Preschool and Primary Scale of Intelligence (WPPSI) for preschool children or by some of the other measures available for this age group. These subtypes are undoubtedly present and findable in preschool children who exhibit developmental delays in body management, self-help, communication, cognitive, preacademic, and psychosocial skills. These subtypes are confirmed through an analysis of the children professionally diagnosed as specific learning disabled and served in Headstart, which indicates the following specific conditions or subtypes:

	PERCENT OF TOTAL
Motor handicap	30.7
Perceptual handicap	20.4
Sequencing and memory	16.9
Hyperkinetic behavior	12.7
Minimal brain dysfunction	6.7
Developmental aphasia	2.7
Dyslexia	.6
Other	9.3
	100.0

Thus, the subtype literature among school-age children may be useful in describing the kinds of abilities that identify a learning disabled child and that may help to diagnose the condition as early as possible.

In the Marker Variable Project, (Keogh & Glover, 1980) the most frequent characteristics of preschool children with SLDs lend additional clarity to the issue:

1. Short attention span/distractibility
2. Hyperactivity/constant motion/restlessness/impulsivity
3. Speech defect/delay
4. Visual/perceptual motor problems
5. Emotional lability problems

6. Poor social/school adjustment
7. Sleep disorders
8. Equivocal neurologic signs

The multidimensional characteristics of preschoolers with SLDs have been described by McCarthy and Smith (1988) in a brochure developed for ACLD, drawn from parents' descriptions of their children with SLDs, followed by the professional jargon used to describe each type of child.

"He knocks into the building blocks, bumps into the door, falls out of his chair, crashes into his playmates and catapults himself through space."

- Inability to plan for his body in space

- Poor estimates of space

- Poor coordination

- Lurches while walking

- Toe walking

- Sitting in double-jointed fashion

"She can talk about topiary trees but she can't pull up her zipper or draw a circle and hates putting toys and puzzles together."

- Inability to use hands to manipulate objects and toys

- Difficulties with hand-eye coordination

- Clumsiness in knocking over juice and milk

"He looks at everything but doesn't seem to see—in fact, his hands seem to see better than his eyes."

- Difficulties in focusing on pictures or objects

- Problems in seeing differences in shapes and colors

- Problems in remembering what he sees

- Cannot remember the order of things he sees

- Inability to make sense out of what he sees

"Her big eyes look up at me and she listens, but I don't seem to get through."

- Inability to understand what she hears

- Inability to remember what she hears
- Inability to remember a sequence of sounds
- Overreaction to noise
- Does not enjoy being read to

"He understands everything I say to him but he doesn't express himself well, not at all like his brother and sister."

- Delayed speech and language
- Sounds and words out of sequence (Where you are, aminals, pasghetti)
- Limited vocabulary
- Disorganized phrases
- Inappropriate use of words

"He never seems put together right and yet I dress him better than the others and tuck him in and fuss over him a lot."

- *Disorganized movement
- Disorganized language
- Disorganized appearance
- A disorganized self

"He's so smart yet he has the attention span of a flea—he jiggles all day long, flits from one thing to another and sometimes sounds like a broken record."

- *Distractibility
- Poor attention span
- Impulsivity
- Hyperactivity
- Perseveration

"She's four years old but acts much younger."

- Immature behavior
- Immature appearance
- Immature speech
- Immature movement
- Selection of younger playmates or solitary play
- Immature choice of and use of toys

"He overreacts or underreacts to everything—it's like his internal thermostat is not working."

- Indiscriminate reactions
- Losing emotional control inappropriately
- Laughing one moment and crying the next
- Very low or very high threshold for pain
- Dislike of being touched or cuddled
- No reaction or overreaction to being touched
- Catastrophic reactions

ETIOLOGY

Current knowledge of the etiology of learning disabilities is basic to the understanding of learning disabilities in preschool children. Those concerned with the study of the function of the central nervous system have suggested six possible causes of learning problems:

1. Genetic variations in the function of the central nervous system (e.g., anatomic abnormalities)
2. Chemical or physical trauma in utero, as in the case of rubella, blood incompatibilities, stroke, ingestion of drugs by the mother, and toxoplasmosis, resulting in prematurity, low birth weight, or other high-risk designations
3. Trauma during the birth process, anoxia, hypoxia
4. Damage to the central nervous system due to physical, chemical, or metabolic trauma or infection during childhood as in the case of encephalitis, meningitis, and galactosemia

5. Delayed maturation of the central nervous system
6. None of the above!

Bricker (1986) has noted that handicapping conditions can result from biological or environmental factors or both. Among the biological factors cited are as follows:

1. Genetic and chromosomal disorders
2. Neurologic and physical impairments
3. Infections prenatal and postnatal
4. Teratogens
5. Sensory impairments
6. Unknown or nonspecific

Bricker notes that "the more severely handicapped the child, the more probable the cause can be identified as biological as opposed to environmental. . . . The causes for 75 percent of the mentally retarded population are attributed to unknown or environmental factors" (p. 148).

In most cases, it is not scientifically sound to ascribe learning disabilities to any of these causes, since many children with similar or worse birth experiences seem to have survived with no apparent learning problems. A report of the President's Committee on Mental Retardation (Cobb, 1976) points out that

Modern medicine and biological science . . . have identified several hundred specific factors which may cause damage to, or maldevelopment of, the central nervous system. The causes for most such defects, however, remain unknown. In a great many instances, the immediate cause of damage is the end product of a chain of circumstances and events, the causes and conditions of which are obscure.

It has been estimated (Gardner, 1978, p. 195) that genetic transmission is the chief cause of congenital anomalies in about 20 percent of cases, with unknown environmental factors being mainly responsible in the rest of the cases.

All but one of these possible causes has happened before a child comes to school, which leads to the conclusion that the learning disability must be present throughout early childhood — affecting the precursors of academic achievement.

HOW TO FIND THEM: ASSESSMENT AND MARKER VARIABLES

The answer to the question of how we find them depends on the age at which concerns for the child's health and development surface and the causes of the concern.

1. *0 to 3 months.* Some children who end up with a diagnosis of SLDs surface very early, and many of them spend their early days in the neonatal intensive care nursery as small for gestational age (SGA) babies or premature infants or as suffering anoxia or other trauma pre- or perinatally.
2. *3 to 12 months.* The next group may surface when the parents' concern over delayed motor or physical development causes them to seek help.
3. *6 to 12 months.* This group includes the infants who seem to have problems in affective behavior (i.e., bonding does not seem to occur, the social smile does not develop, they may be difficult to cuddle, and they may have unusual response patterns).
4. *18 to 36 months.* The next group to surface may have unusual delays in the development of speech and language.
5. *60 to 72 months.* Some children with SLDs may not surface until entry into school when they fail on first exposure to a symbol system.

A reasonable approach to assessment of young children will depend on the age of the child and the description of the problem, since the characteristics of each child will guide the transdisciplinary assessment process.

The assessment question has been addressed by presenting basic information on selected tests that have been found useful in assessing young children and by using information generated by Keogh and Glover in the Marker Variable Project (1980). These assessment concepts will be presented briefly in the hope that the reader will be motivated to dig further into the literature for additional information.

The concepts of *intactness, discrepancy,* and *deviation* have been used in Table 2-1, which lists some of the commonly used assessment instruments, sorted by level of intensity of the diagnostic process.

The three components of the definition of SLDs can be used in selecting an appropriate assessment battery that meets the criteria for determining the existence of a specific learning disability stated in P.L. 94-142. Table 2-1 includes assessment instruments used with preschool children that can substantiate that the child is *intact* intellectually and sensorially. The three columns across the top indicate the degree of intensity of each diagnostic instrument, with *Least intensive* including screening instruments and observational/anecdotal data, *Less intensive* including second-level screening devices, and *Most intensive* including norm-referenced and criterion-referenced individual measures requiring more time or more highly trained professionals. The *Discrepancy component* includes measures of achievement of the developmental milestones of early childhood, as well as measures needed to establish a severe disorder in the basic psychological processes involved in understanding or in using language. The *Deviation component* can be used to

Table 2-1. ASSESSMENT OF PRESCHOOL CHILDREN

	Most intensive	Less intensive	Least intensive
INTACT COMPONENT			
Cognitive development	Bayley Brazelton Griffiths Miskey-Nebraska KABC McCarthy Merrill-Palmer Stanford Binet WPPSI	Columbia Leiter PTI Raven's	Alpern-Doll Minnesota CDI PPVT Slossen Intelligence Test
Hearing	Audiologic Otologic	Amplaid Beltone Audiometric Maico Puretone Audiometric Seiko	Whispered Voice Test
Vision	Complete ophthalmologic	Keystone Orthorater Telebinocular Titmus	Acuity, Binocular Massachusetts Snellen E Chart Strabismus
DISCREPANCY COMPONENT			
Capacity/achievement	ABACUS Battelle Brigance UPAS Woodcock-Johnson	ABACUS Pass II Comprehensive Identification Process Developmental Indicators in the Assessment of Learning	ABACUS Pass I Behavior Characteristics Progression Denver Developmental Screening Test
Psychological processes: (c.f. Cognitive measures for specific subtests)			
Attention	Animal House DAS: Visual Search		Observational data
Memory	K-ABC McCarthy		
Visual perception	Bender-Gestalt CAT ITPA	VMI	

(continued)

41

Table 2-1. (continued)

	Most intensive	Less intensive	Least intensive
Auditory perception	ITPA		
Thinking	ITPA	Boehm Test of Concept Formation	
Problem solving	Picture Arrangement, comprehension		
Concept formation	Bracken Basic Concept Scale		
Language	ITPA		
Comprehension	Carrow PPUT	ABACUS PLS SICD	
Production	Language Sample	ABACUS PLS SICO	
Integration	ITPA		
Phonology	Templin-Darley		
Morphology	Carrow ELI		
Syntax	Northwestern		
Semantics	Mecham WPPSI/Binet		
Pragmatics		ABACUS Goralnick (N = 54) CAT Michigan Pictures Drawings	
Social perception			Observation check lists
DEVIATION COMPONENT			
Socialization	AAMD Adaptive Behavior Scale Scales of Independent Behavior Vineland	Behavior checklists	Anecdotal records Directed observation

determine that the child has failed to profit from normal learning experiences in the area of greatest discrepancy.

MARKER VARIABLES APPROPRIATE IN THE DIAGNOSIS OF PRESCHOOL LEARNING DISABLED CHILDREN

The University of California, Los Angeles (UCLA) Marker Variable Project was funded by the Bureau of Education for the Handicapped (BEH) in 1977 to 1980 to develop a set of descriptors or markers useful in defining sample characteristics in learning disabilities research (Keogh & Glover, 1980). "Markers are broadly defined as variables useful in describing subjects or samples. Conceptually, markers reflect the constructs that define a field of study" (Keogh & Glover, 1980). The Marker Guide that was developed has been useful in designing appropriate data-gathering procedures on which to base the diagnosis of preschool children suspected of having a SLD and to document the characteristics of children with SLDs across samples. The guide contains four classes of markers:

1. Descriptive markers: designate general sample characteristics
2. Substantive markers: information relevant to learning disabled samples derived from the definition of learning disability
3. Topical markers: most complete subject information
4. Background markers: Context for interpretation of findings and identification of background against which the learning disabled child's data are to be interpreted

Since data from a computer search that yielded a total of 4,618 citations and 408 data-based studies were categorized according to the age of subjects, the markers cited for the 2 to 5-year range appear to be most appropriate in gathering data about preschool children, as a check list for areas to be assessed. Note that the topical markers are consistent with the psychological process deficits described by Kirk and Chalfant as common to children with developmental learning disabilities (Kirk & Chalfant, 1984) and by Kirk and Gallagher (1986, pp. 379–381).

Tables 2-2 and 2-3 include the substantive markers and the topical markers measured by nine commonly used norm-referenced measures appropriate for preschool children and seven criterion-referenced developmental inventories. The instruments, appropriate ages, and scores obtained are listed in the upper portion of the table. Down the left-hand column are listed the substantive markers and the topical markers developed by Keogh.

The marker measured by each subtest is designated in the batteries presented. In some cases, varying judgments may suggest that a subtest is inappropriately placed in Table 2-2. For example, cognitive matching on the

Table 2-2. USE OF MARKER VARIABLES IN THE DIAGNOSIS OF PRESCHOOL CHILDREN: NORM-REFERENCED CHILD MEASURES

	McCarthy Scales of Children's Abilities	Wechsler Pre-School Primary Scales of Intelligence	Kaufman Assessment Battery for Children	Woodcock-Johnson Psycho-Educational Battery	Illinois Test of Psycholinguistic Ability	Pictorial Test of Intelligence	Griffiths Scale of Infant Development	Binet	Bayley
SUBSTANTIVE MARKERS									
General intellectual ability									
Age range	2½–8½ yrs	4–6½ yrs	2½–12½ yrs	3 yrs–adult	2–7 yrs	3–8 yrs	0–8 yrs	2 yrs–adult	2 mos.–30 mos.
Scores obtained	Verbal, perceptual-performance, memory, motor, general cognitive, index	Verbal score, performance score, full scale score	Sequential processing scale, simultaneous processing scale, mental processing composite, achievement scale	Preschool scale Cluster score Percentile rank Functional level		Mental age Percentiles Deviation IQ	Mental age Developmental quotient	Subscale standard age scores Composite score Percentiles Profile analysis	Mental developmental index (MDI) Psychomotor development index Age equivalent Infant behavior record
Pre-reading achievement			Naming pictured objects	Visual-auditory learning, blending					Picture book
Pre-math achievement	Number questions Counting and sorting		Arithmetic	Quantitative concepts		Size and number		Quantitative number series*	

Behavioral and emotional adjustment						Personal-social Practical reasoning	Rating scale	Social orientation Cooperativeness Fearfulness, tension General emotional tone Social responses to person, mirror
TOPICAL MARKERS								
Attention			Direct observation				Rating scale	Object orientation Goal directedness Attention span Endurance
Activity level			Direct observation				Rating scale	Activity picture book Reactivity
Auditory perception				Auditory closure test, Sound blending test				Response to bell, rattle
Visual perception	Conceptual grouping	Similarities Picture completion Animal house	Magic window Gestalt closure Triangles	Spatial relations	Visual reception Visual association Visual closure	Form discrimination Similarities	Performance (?)	Pattern analysis Matrices*	Red ring, red light Spoons Discriminates objects

*Age = 5.0

(*continued*)

Table 2-2. (continued)

SUBSTANTIVE MARKERS

General intellectual ability	McCarthy Scales of Children's Abilities	Wechsler Pre-School Primary Scales of Intelligence	Kaufman Assessment Battery for Children	Woodcock-Johnson Psycho-Educational Battery	Illinois Test of Psycholinguistic Ability	Pictorial Test of Intelligence	Griffiths Scale of Infant Development	Binet	Bayley
Age range	2½–8½ yrs	4–6½ yrs	2½–12½ yrs	3 yrs–adult	2–7 yrs	3–8 yrs	0–8 yrs	2 yrs–adult	2 mos.–30 mos.
Memory	Pictorial memory Verbal memory I Verbal memory II Numerical Memory I Numerical Memory II Tapping sequence Imitative action Counting and sorting	Immediate recall	Hand movements Number recall Word order Face recognition	Memory for sentences	Auditory sequential memory, visual sequential memory			Bead memory Memory for sentences Memory for digit* Memory for objects*	
Gross motor coordination	Leg coordination Arm coordination						Locomotive		Activity Reactivity

Fine motor coordination	Block building Puzzle solving Draw-a-design Draw-a-child	Geometric design Block design Mazes			Eye-hand coordination	Copying	Manipulative behavior Visual and manual behaviors Cubes Red ring Crayon and paper Peg board Pellet, cup Ring and string Boxes Blue/pink board
Oral language Comprehension	Word knowledge Opposite Analogies	Vocabulary	Riddles	Picture vocabulary	Auditory reception Auditory association	Information and comprehension Picture vocabulary		Comprehension rating scale	Verbal comprehension Prepositions
Production	Verbal fluency		Expressive vocabulary Word order		Verbal expression (manual expression) Grammatic closure		Hearing and Speech	Rating scale Vocabulary absurdities	Vocalizations and words Naming objects Naming and pointing to picture, naming objects Names watch

*Age = 5.0

Table 2-3. DEVELOPMENTAL INVENTORIES

SUBSTANTIVE MARKERS	ABACUS	Battelle	Brigance	Minnesota Child Development Inventory	Learning Accomplishment Profile	Scales of Independent Behavior	Vineland Adaptive Behavior Scale
General intellectual ability	Thinking skills	Cognitive domain Conceptual development	General knowledge and comprehension	General development Comprehension/conceptual Situation comprehension			
Age range	2-5 yrs	Birth-8 yrs	Birth-7 yrs	1-6 yrs	6 mos-72 mos	Infant to mature adult + 40 yrs up	
Scores obtained		Age equivalent score Percentile ranks Standard scores	Age level	Profile of Developmental Ages for Each Scale		Age level	
Pre-reading achievement	Pre-reading	Cognitive Domain Reasoning and academic skills	Readiness Basic reading skills				
Pre-math achievement	Pre-math		Math		Cognitive counting	Money and value	
Behavioral and emotional adjustment	Self-care Socialization	Personal/social domain Adult interaction Expression of feelings/affection Self concept Peer interaction Coping Social role	Self-help skills	Personal/social scale Self-help scale	Self-help	Social interaction Self care Domestic skills Work skills Home and community orientation Problem behavior	Daily living skills Socialization

TOPICAL MARKERS							
Attention	Pre-reading Communication prerequisites	Adaptive domain					
Activity level							
Auditory perception	Communication prerequisites						
Visual perception		Cognitive domain Perceptual discrimination			Cognitive matching		
Memory		Cognitive domain Memory					
Gross motor coordination	Body management	Motor domain Muscle control Body coordination Locomotion	Pre-ambulatory motor skills and behaviors Gross motor skills and behavior	Gross motor scale	Gross motor Body movement Object movement	Motor skills Gross motor	Motor skills Gross
Fine motor coordination	Body management	Motor domain Fine muscle Perceptual motor	Fine motor skills and behavior Manuscript writing	Fine motor skills	Fine motor Manipulation Writing	Motor skills Fine motor	Motor skills Fine
Oral language		Communication domain			Language/cognitive	Social and communication skills	
Comprehension	Comprehension	Receptive communication			Cognitive Naming Comprehension	Language comprehension	Receptive
Production	Production	Expressive communication	Pre-speech Speech and language skills	Expressive language scale		Language production	Expressive

49

LAP may not be perceived as a visual/perceptual task by some, or magic window on the K-ABC may not be judged to measure visual perception. Each professional may want to double check Table 2-2 and individualize it to match his or her own view of perception and cognition. The major point of the exercise is to alert the diagnostician to the numbers of behaviors sampled as opposed to the numbers relevant to an adequate assessment. The need for supplementary assessment may become clearer as awareness of which functions are sampled on each test increases.

ASSESSMENT OF INFANTS AND TODDLERS

Table 2-4 has been developed for the 0 to 2 years population and reflects the requirements of the IFSP detailed in P.L. 99-457. The left-hand column lists the six areas required in P.L. 99-457 to be assessed: physical development, cognitive development, language and speech development, psychosocial development, self-help skills, and family strengths and needs. Examples of procedures in common use are then categorized as most intensive, less intensive, and least intensive. The reader is cautioned against viewing any listing as a recommendation for use. Table 2-3 includes what is being used across the country. It may also be useful in determining what an unknown test measures with some indication of the level of intensity of diagnostic effort expended.

The six areas specified in P.L. 99-457 have been expanded to include a breakdown of each area. For example, P.L. 99-457 specifies assessment of physical development but does not require a measure of general physical development, central nervous system functioning, gross or fine motor development, or hearing and vision testing. The subcategories are those found most useful in clinical practice.

TYPICAL PROFILES OF PRESCHOOLERS WITH SLDs

Four profiles are presented that typify those found in individual preschool children with SLDs as well as those found in groups of children diagnosed as having SLDs.

The mean scores of groups of children may be less discrepant than the individual scores of the children in the group. The higher scores of some children tend to raise the lower scores of others and vice versa. *Thus, the difference required for significance in group means is less than that required for individual scores.*

Figure 2-2 presents the typical profile of a child with a severe oral language handicap, based on a study of 237 aphasic children completed by Luick, Kirk, Agronowitz, and Busby (1982). The central processing deficit apparent

Table 2-4. SELECTED INSTRUMENTS USEFUL IN DEVELOPING AN INDIVIDUALIZED FAMILY SERVICE PLAN (PRESENT LEVELS OF DEVELOPMENT 0–2 AND 0–35 MONTHS)

	Most intensive	Less intensive	Least intensive
PHYSICAL DEVELOPMENT			
General physical development	Complete physical examination	Well-baby checkup	Caregiver history Family history
Nervous system			
Gross motor	Complete neurologic examination Electrophysiologic Imaging (CT scan, PET, MRI) Neurometrics (Quantified EEG and elicited potentials)	Brazleton Neonatal Behavior Inventory Milani-Comparetti Carolina Curriculum Bayley Motor Scale	Denver Developmental Screening Test (DDST) DIAL Minnesota Child Development Inventory Revised Developmental Screening Inventory
Fine motor		ABACUS Brigance (A, B, C) Battelle	SIB DDST
Sensory			
Hearing	Otologic examination Operant conditioning audiometry (6 mos +)	Audiometric screening Impedance audiometry Brainstem audiometry	Whispered-voice Test Informal behavioral observation
Vision	Complete ophthalmologic (retinoscope)	Simultaneous discrimination procedures Visual preference test (Parsons) Evoked visual response	Informal behavioral observation (acuity, strabismus, tracking)
COGNITIVE DEVELOPMENT			
General intellectual ability	Bayley Scales Griffiths Scales Stanford-Binet Cattel Merrill-Palmer Scales of Mental Development	Carolina Curriculum Brigance Battelle Hawaii Early Learning Profile	Slossen Alpern Boll Minnesota CDI DASI Callier Azusa Scale
Attention	Bayley Mental Scales	Assessment of Attentional Skills	Binet Rating Scale
Memory	Stanford-Binet Bayley		

(continued)

Table 2-4. (continued)

	Most intensive	Less intensive	Least intensive
Visual perception	Bayley Griffiths		
Auditory perception	Bayley Griffiths		
LANGUAGE AND SPEECH DEVELOPMENT			
Receptive language/comprehension		Bayley Brigance Battelle Environmental Prelanguage battery	DIAL PPVT
Integrative language	REEL SICD		
Expressive language/production	Preschool Language Scale		DIAL DDST
PSYCHOSOCIAL DEVELOPMENT	Bayley Infant Behavioral Record	Vineland Battelle Developmental Inventory Griffiths Developmental Scale ABACUS Maxfield-Buchholz Scale of Social Maturity for Preschool and Blind Children	Symbolic Play Scale Checklist Symbolic Play Levels DDST
SELF-HELP SKILLS		ABACUS Vineland Battelle Brigance Maxfield-Buchholz Scale of Social Maturity	Parent observation
FAMILY STRENGTHS/NEEDS	Parent Stress Index Impact on Family Scale	Questionnaire on Resources and Stress (Friedrich, Ed.)	FACES II Scale Family Satisfaction Scale
Child domain/characteristics			
Parent domain/problems			
Life stress scale/financial burden/person			
Family social support/cohesion/adaptability			

Key: CT = Computed tomography; PET = positron emission tomography; MRI = magnetic resonance imaging; EEG = electroencephalogram.

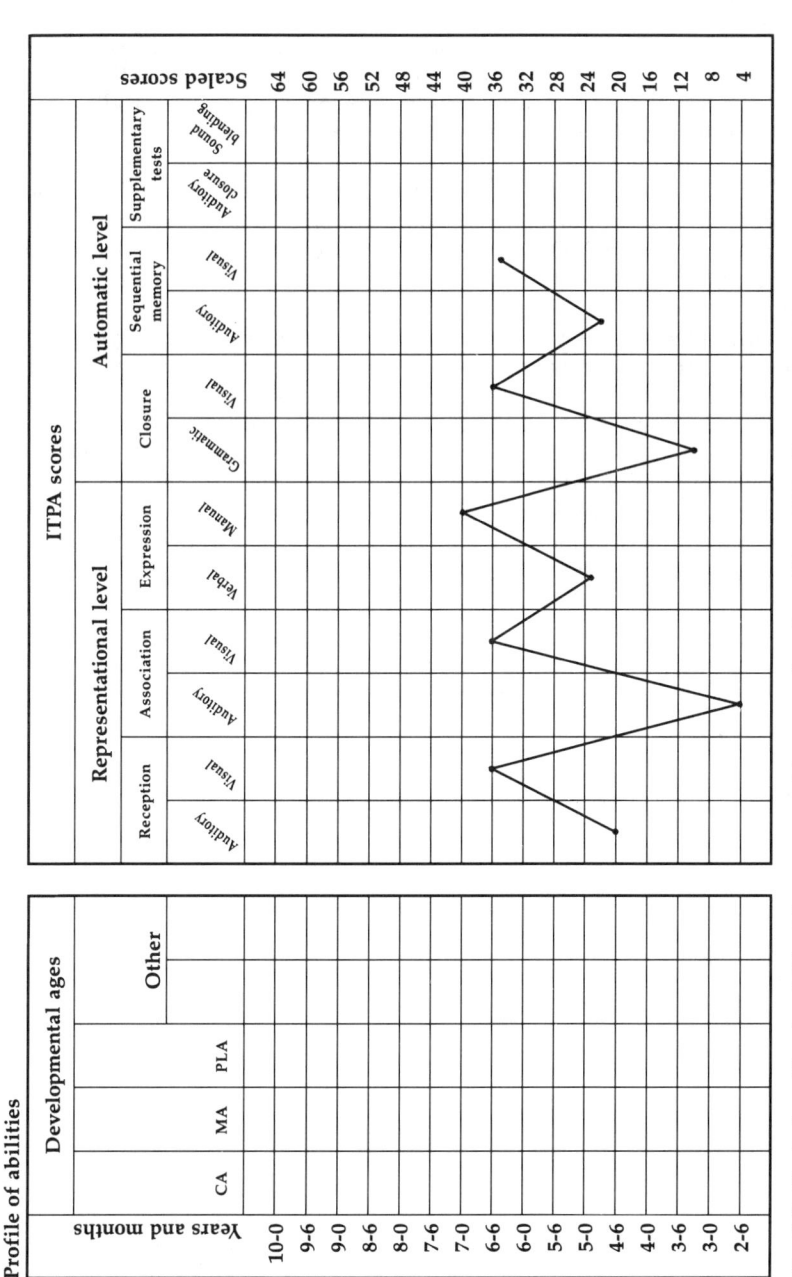

Fig. 2-2. Typical profile of a child with a severe oral language handicap (N = 237). (From A. Luick, S. A. Kirk, Agronowitz, and Busby (1982, February). Profiles of children with severe oral language disorders. *Journal of Speech and Hearing Disorders, 19*(47), 88–92.)

in the lower scores in auditory association at the representation level of the Illinois Test of Psycholinguistic Ability and Grammatical Closure at the Automatic Level, together with lowered auditory scores across the profiles, are typical of young children with severe oral language handicaps.

Figure 2-3 presents the WPPSI profile of 59 postkindergarten children selected for placement in a developmental first grade (McCarthy, 1971). Using the mean-scaled score of 10 for the standardization sample as a criterion, this group of children with SLDs shows lowered functioning on both the verbal scale (arithmetic) and the performance scale (block design). This pattern is typical of that found in children with little difference between verbal and performance scales but with significant discrepancies in subtest scores.

Figure 2-4 is the protocol of the Kaufman Assessment Battery for Children of a Hispanic Headstart girl diagnosed after a complete transdisciplinary evaluation as having an SLD. A 22-point difference in subtest scores between sequential and simultaneous processing and a 23-point difference between the achievement and simultaneous scales resulted. Her strengths in visual organization and cognitive flexibility were noted, as well as her weaknesses in motor and numerical memory and word order. Data from other instruments supported eligibility for services.

Fig. 2-3. The WPPSI profile of 59 postkindergarten children selected for placement in a developmental first grade. (From J. M. McCarthy (1971). How to find them in kindergarten. Final report to Bureau of Education for Handicapped. Tucson: Leadership Training Institute in Learning Disabilities.)

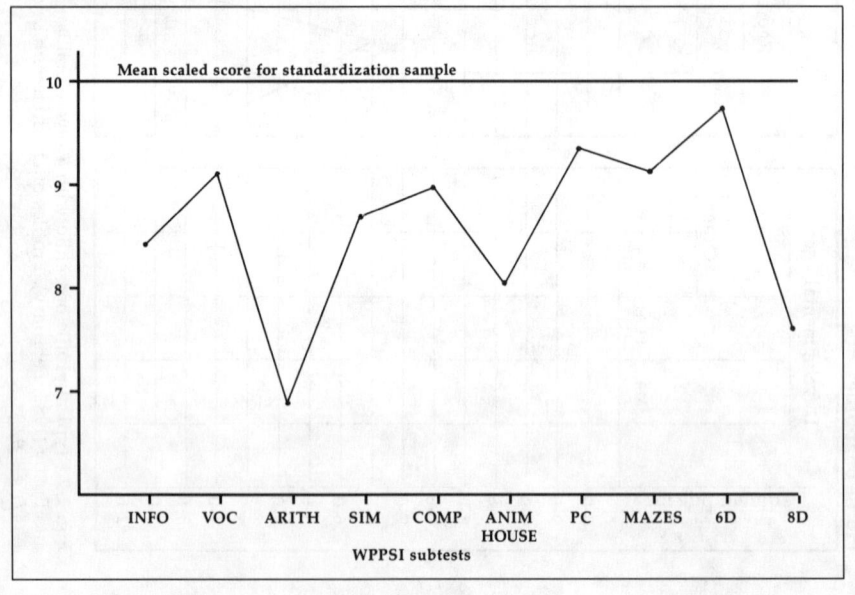

Specific Learning Disabilities in Preschool Children 55

The last profile, Fig. 2-5, is that of a Hispanic child (4 years, 5 months) with a general cognitive index of 78 on the McCarthy Scales of Children's Abilities. Her lower verbal score, especially on verbal fluency, memory, and opposite analogies, would make one question the impact of her limited English proficiency on her performance on the McCarthy Scales. Her relatively better functioning on perceptual-performance items might indicate a significant discrepancy. However, the decision of whether she does have a SLD could not be made on the basis of this test alone but would need much more data.

HOW TO TEACH THEM: CURRICULUM AND INSTRUCTION

Two documents emerged on the preschool scene that have focused the attention of the field on curriculum and instruction for young handicapped children: P.L. 99-457 and the *Position Statement on Developmentally Appropriate Practice in Early Childhood Programs Serving Children from Birth Through Age 8*, issued by the National Association for the Education of Young Children (Bredekamp, 1986).

The first, P.L. 99-457, has served as an extrinsic force in effectively delineating the content of the curriculum for the 0 to 2 year and the 3 to 5 year population of at-risk, delayed, and handicapped children to be funded under the new law. As discussed earlier, all of the components of P.L. 94-142 relating to "least restrictive environment" and the "continuum of services" (the "mainstreaming" and "normalization" emphasis) also apply to the infant, toddler, and preschool populations. Thus, P.L. 99-457 has the potential of focusing on the integration of handicapped preschoolers into programs for normally developing preschoolers. This focus places renewed emphasis on these questions: "What does the teacher of preschool handicapped children need to know in addition to what the teacher of normally developing preschoolers needs to know? What knowledge and skills are required to teach infants, toddlers, and preschoolers who are at-risk, delayed, or handicapped?

Some of the questions that have been raised and that are discussed in this section derive from assumptions implicit in the (NAEYC) Developmentally Appropriate Practice document (Bredekamp, 1986):

1. Are there universal, predictable sequences of growth and change that occur in handicapped children during the first 9 years of life?
2. In what way must a developmentally appropriate curriculum for young children be modified to meet the diversity among young handicapped children?
3. Do handicapped children learn "through self-directed play activ-

Fig. 2-4. Protocol of the Kaufman Assessment Battery for Children of a Hispanic Head-start girl diagnosed after a complete transdisciplinary evaluation as having an SLD. (© 1983, American Guidance Service, Inc., Circle Pines, Minnesota 55014.)

K-ABC Kaufman Assessment Battery for Children
INDIVIDUAL TEST RECORD

Name: MARIA   Sex: F
Parents' names: _____
Home address: _____
Home phone: _____
Grade: ___ School: _____
Examiner: _____
SOCIOCULTURAL INFORMATION (if pertinent)
Race: HISPANIC
Socioeconomic background: HEADSTART ELIG.

Test date: 86 / 10 / 1
Birth date: 82 / 10 / 3
Chronological age: 4 - 0

Achievement Subtests (X = 100; SD = 15)

Subtest	Standard score ± band of error 85% confidence	Nat'l %ile rank	Sociocultural %ile rank	S or W	Age Equiv.
11. Expressive Vocabulary	72 ± 8	3			<2-6
12. Faces & Places	83 ± 9	13			2-6
13. Arithmetic	<72 ±	(INT.)			<2-6
14. Riddles	<72 ±	(INT.)			<2-6
15. Reading/Decoding	±				
16. Reading/Understanding	±				

Sum of subtest scores: <75

Mental Processing Subtests (X = 10; SD = 3)

Subtest	Sequential	Simultaneous	Nonverbal	Nat'l %ile rank	S or W	Age Equiv.
1. Magic Window		6		9		2-9
2. Face Recognition		11		63		4-6
3. Hand Movements	6			9		2-9
4. Gestalt Closure		13		84		5-0
5. Number Recall	7			16		3-0
6. Triangles		9		37		3-9
7. Word Order	56					
8. Matrix Analogies						
9. Spatial Memory						
10. Photo Series						

Sum of subtest scores: 76 / 98 / 91

Global Scales (X = 100, SD = 15)

Scale	Sum of subtest scores	Standard score ± band of error 85% confidence	Nat'l %ile rank	Sociocultural %ile rank	Age Equiv.
Sequential Processing	76	76 ± 6	5		3-0
Simultaneous Processing	98	± 7	45		4-0
Mental Processing Composite	86	± 6	18		3-3
Achievement	<75	± (INTERPOLATED)			
Nonverbal	91	± 8	27		3-9

Global Scale Comparisons

	Indicate >, <, or =		Circle the significance level
Sequential ___	Simultaneous (Table 10)	NS .05 .01
Sequential ___	Achievement (Table 10)	NS .05 .01
Simultaneous ___	Achievement (Table 10)	NS .05 .01
MPC ___	Achievement (Table 10)	NS .05 .01

(22 pts. diff between Sequential and Simultaneous Scales [p<.01])
(23 pts. diff between Achievement and Simultaneous Scales)
Strengths in Visual Organization and Cognitive Flexibility

(continued)

Fig. 2-4 (continued)

Comments and Observations

_____
_____
_____
_____
_____
_____
_____
_____
_____
_____
_____
_____
_____
_____

Ceiling item = highest item administered
Errors = total number of items scored 0

See the *Administration and Scoring Manual* for exceptions to the stopping points and the method for calculating raw score.

1. Magic Window
Simultaneous Processing Scale
Ages 2-6 through 4-11

	Item	Response	Score
All ages ☞	Sample: tree		
2½-4 ☞	1. car	_____	___
	2. girl	_____	___
	3. snake	_____	___
	4. elephant	_____	___
	5. scissors	_____	___
	6. apple	_____	___
	7. boat	_____	___
	8. bell	_____	___
	9. hat	_____	___
	10. turtle	_____	___
	11. leaf	_____	___
	12. saw	_____	___
	13. spoon	_____	___
	14. watch	_____	___
	15. table	_____	___

2½-4 ✋

Ceiling Item ___
minus Errors ___
equals Raw Score ___

1. Magic Window Scaled Score ___
Table 1

2. Face Recognition
Simultaneous Processing Scale
Ages 2-6 through 4-11

	Item	Score
All ages ☞	Sample	
2½-4 ☞	1.	___
	2.	___
	3.	___
	4.	___
	5.	___
	6.	___
	7.	___
	8.	___
	9.	___
	10.	___
	11.	___
	12.	___

2½-3 ✋

	13.	___
	14.	___
	15.	___

4 ✋

Ceiling Item ___
minus Errors ___
equals Raw Score ___

2. Face Recognition Scaled Score ___
Table 1

Fig. 2-5. Profile of a Hispanic child with a general cognitive index of 78 on the McCarthy Scales of Children's abilities. (From the McCarthy Scales of Children's Abilities. Copyright © 1970, 1972 by the Psychological Corporation. Reproduced by permission. All rights reserved.)

McCARTHY SCALES OF CHILDREN'S ABILITIES

Record Form

NAME AMANDA AGE 4-5 SEX F

HOME ADDRESS

NAMES OF PARENTS OR GUARDIAN

SCHOOL GRADE

PLACE OF TESTING TESTED BY

REFERRED BY

MSCA PROFILE

Enter the 6 Scale Indexes on the appropriate lines below. Then circle the mark representing the Index for each Scale. Draw a line connecting the circles. Note that the values for GC are different from those for the other Scales.

SCALE INDEX	Verbal	Perceptual-Performance	Quantitative	General Cognitive	Memory	Motor
	32	44	35	78	41	35

	Year	Month	Day
Date Tested	1985	10	6
Date of Birth	1981	4	27
Age	4	5	9

COMPOSITE RAW SCORES AND SCALE INDEXES

Enter the composite raw scores from the back cover. *Obtain the composite raw score for GC by adding V+P+Q.* Determine the corresponding Scale Indexes from Table 16. (See page 151 of manual for detailed directions.)

Scale	Composite Raw Score	Scale Index
Verbal (V)	25	32
Perceptual-Performance (P)	28	44
Quantitative (Q)	11	35
General Cognitive: Add composite raw scores V+P+Q	64	78 GCI
Memory (Mem)	20	41
Motor (Mot)	19	35

LATERALITY

(Enter information from Laterality Summary on page 5.)

Hand

Eye

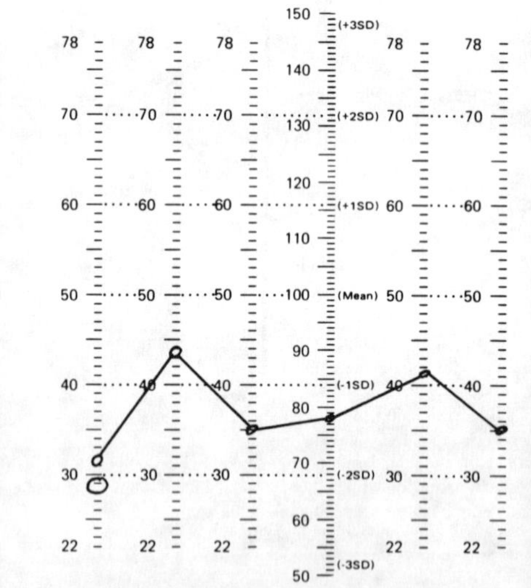

(continued)

Fig. 2-5 (continued)

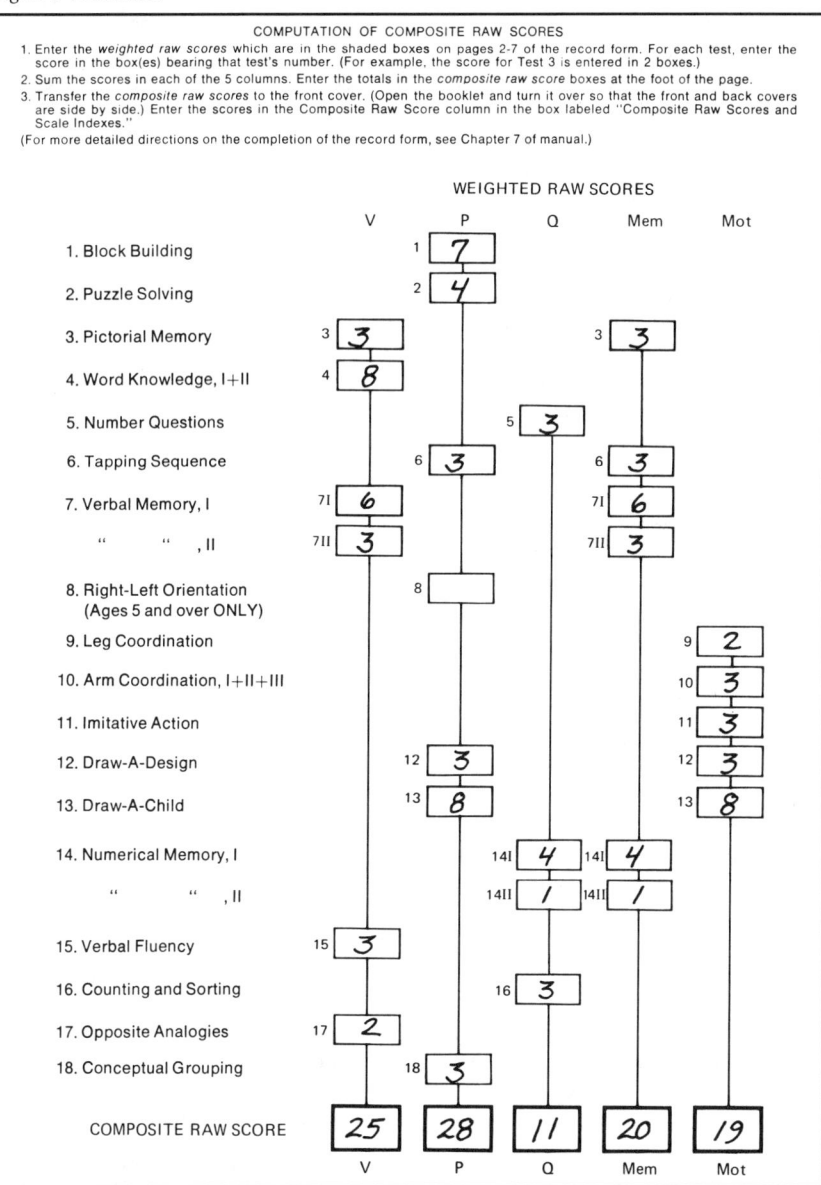

```
COMPUTATION OF COMPOSITE RAW SCORES
1. Enter the *weighted raw scores* which are in the shaded boxes on pages 2-7 of the record form. For each test, enter the
   score in the box(es) bearing that test's number. (For example, the score for Test 3 is entered in 2 boxes.)
2. Sum the scores in each of the 5 columns. Enter the totals in the *composite raw score* boxes at the foot of the page.
3. Transfer the *composite raw scores* to the front cover. (Open the booklet and turn it over so that the front and back covers
   are side by side.) Enter the scores in the Composite Raw Score column in the box labeled "Composite Raw Scores and
   Scale Indexes."
(For more detailed directions on the completion of the record form, see Chapter 7 of manual.)
```

WEIGHTED RAW SCORES

Test	V	P	Q	Mem	Mot
1. Block Building		1: 7			
2. Puzzle Solving		2: 4			
3. Pictorial Memory	3: 3			3: 3	
4. Word Knowledge, I+II	4: 8				
5. Number Questions			5: 3		
6. Tapping Sequence		6: 3		6: 3	
7. Verbal Memory, I	7I: 6			7I: 6	
" " , II	7II: 3			7II: 3	
8. Right-Left Orientation (Ages 5 and over ONLY)			8:		
9. Leg Coordination					9: 2
10. Arm Coordination, I+II+III					10: 3
11. Imitative Action					11: 3
12. Draw-A-Design		12: 3			12: 3
13. Draw-A-Child		13: 8			13: 8
14. Numerical Memory, I			14I: 4	14I: 4	
" " , II			14II: 1	14II: 1	
15. Verbal Fluency	15: 3				
16. Counting and Sorting			16: 3		
17. Opposite Analogies	17: 2				
18. Conceptual Grouping		18: 3			
COMPOSITE RAW SCORE	**25**	**28**	**11**	**20**	**19**
	V	P	Q	Mem	Mot

ities," "through active exploration and interaction," and "through creative activity and intensive involvement" as described for normally developing children?
4. Among handicapped infants and toddlers, can it be said that "the most appropriate teaching technique is to give ample opportunities for the children to use self-initiated repetition to practice newly acquired skills and to experience feelings of autonomy and success?" (p. 8).

Other questions have been raised by Jeannette Walker and Margaret Hallau (1981) in their discussion of the ways in which handicapped children violate many assumptions about how children learn:

1. Do handicapped children have an inner motivation to seek out learning experiences?
2. Do handicapped children attempt to satisfy their curiosity by actively exploring the environment?
3. Do handicapped children selectively attend to those elements of the environment that provide the experiences they need to progress?
4. Does learning occur in "clusters" as they accommodate their thinking to new experiences and form new rules for assimilating information? Do handicapped children engage in incidental learning as do normally developing children?
5. Does learning occur in fairly predictable sequences?
6. Do handicapped children generalize from what is known to what is unknown, as normal children do?

Other questions raised and answered by Dennis Embry (1980) include

1. In teaching concepts, do children learn better if given only examples of the concept, nonexamples, or some combination?
2. What language style of the teacher is most effective?
3. Do young children prefer color to form or form to color?
4. Does a motor response (e.g., pointing, tracing) enhance attention to stimuli and lead to superior learning?
5. Is it better to teach discriminations sequentially or simultaneously? Should you put match-to-sample tasks on the same page or on the flip side of the page?
6. Should you teach concepts sequentially or concurrently?

Before discussing specific responses to these questions, several basic assumptions implicit in thinking about curricular decisions and instructional programming for young handicapped children will be presented.

The first assumption involves the heterogeneity of the population including within-group variance and between-group variance.

The emphasis on categorical labels in the field of special education has led to the erroneous assumption that "a rose is a rose is a rose," that is, all members of the designated group share characteristics common to the category of handicapping condition.

Thus, some approaches to the education of learning disabled youngsters may assume a homogeneity within the population that denies the range of impairment from mild to moderate to severe; the multiplicity of cognitive, linguistic, or neuropsychological deficits in some of the members; and the diversity attributable to the etiology of the condition, the age of emergence of symptoms, and epigenetic influences. This within-group variance is also present within subgroups of the SLDs category. A prime example is that of children with SLDs who exhibit delays in language that may vary from problems in comprehension to problems of production to problems of association, memory, concept formation, or use. The important conclusion to be drawn is that *what* to teach and *how* to teach each child depends on the unique characteristics of that child and the factors present in the environment that can be used to reinforce his or her growth and development, not on the categorical label.

HETEROGENEITY OF THE POPULATION: BETWEEN-GROUP VARIANCE

In spite of the uniqueness of each child and the differences between members of subpopulations, educators need to be aware of the similar needs among children with specific handicaps and the way they may vary in their instructional needs from children with other handicapping conditions. Thus, children with SLDs should not be taught like children with other handicaps, unless their present level of performance is similar and learning potential is carefully monitored. Small groups or individualized instruction are mandatory for preschool children.

The general principle of instruction to be drawn from this assumption is to be aware of the uniqueness of each child and each family regardless of the handicap, but to be aware of the similar needs of the children and parents of a particular group.

HETEROGENEITY/HOMOGENEITY DUE TO AGE-RELATED EFFECTS

In relating to infants, toddlers, preschool, and primary-age children, the homogeneity of each age group is striking. Young infants, with a limited repertoire of skills, may seem to be functioning totally at the sensory motor/

vegetative level, with major energies invested in developing visual skills, auditory skills, and motor skills in the primary vegetative functions (eating, drinking, spitting up). The needs of the early infant period are probably more homogeneous than at any other period of the child's life. For many handicapped children, the infancy period is extended months beyond that of normally developing youngsters. This delayed emergence of motor milestones, of the social smile, and of receptive language may trigger an awareness of the ways in which handicapped children may differ from normally developing toddlers. The age-related characteristics of normally developing youngsters may be present in handicapped children, or each developmental period may see the child further behind his or her peers in some or all of the developmental areas. Motor development, cognitive development, self-help skills, and socialization may be age related and language development delayed. Motor development may be delayed but socialization, language, and cognition may be at norms for age. Across many developmental variables, children with SLDs are more like their normally developing peers than they are like each other in such things as seeing, hearing, touching, walking, and feelings. A learning disabled 4-year-old is probably more like normally developing 4-year-olds than he is different. Educators need to keep the similarities at the level of conscious awareness, as well as the differences.

Now, some specific answers to the questions raised in exploring the topic of how to teach children with SLDs are examined.

The four assumptions implicit in the Developmentally Appropriate Practice document of NAEYC are closely related to many of the basic assumptions examined by Walker and Hallau (1981). These authors have concluded that "a handicapped child may thus violate many assumptions about how children learn. . . . Young handicapped children cannot be assumed to be inner directed, incidental learners. . . ." They may lack the motivation, curiosity, tools, and opportunities to explore their environments. "Sensory, motor, and cognitive deficits all negatively affect the use of such tools" (p. 63). Selective attention may be impaired to the point that they are unable to focus on relevant stimuli. Children with SLDs may lack "cluster learning" and be unable to formulate cognitive rules and strategies. They may be unable to learn sequentially and need to be taught piece by piece and then taught how to integrate. Children with SLDs "often exhibit both uneven growth across development areas and the learning of splinter skills within areas" (p. 63). Prerequisite skills may be missing. Preschoolers with SLDs may have difficulty "generalizing from what is known to what is unknown." If generalization is to be learned, it must be built into the teaching process. The same can be said of maintenance of new learning. Many youngsters with SLDs are "leaky buckets." The teacher may pour in new knowledge one day and it has all leaked out the next. The authors conclude that "every component of an educational program for young handicapped children is potentially affected by their possible difference from normal children."

The implications of these differences for preschool programs that integrate handicapped with nonhandicapped children are extremely important. Competent teachers of normally developing preschoolers may be interested in adding some principles of teaching handicapped children to their established repertoires. Teachers prepared to teach school-age children with SLDs may be interested in some specific techniques useful with younger children. The following suggestions have been drawn from the research literature and are offered to whet the appetite of the reader to explore further the fascinating topics of curriculum and instruction for young handicapped children.

PRINCIPLES OF LEARNING FOR PRESCHOOL CHILDREN WITH SLDs

1. Error-free learning, especially in the initial trials of a new instructional task, will reduce errors on later trials. By providing full or partial aids, prompts, or props, the teacher can ensure success on the initial steps of the task.
2. Use the principle of minimal change, building it into each lesson. Start with what the child is doing successfully and introduce only one change at a time.
3. Progress from easy to hard, based on a detailed analysis of the task. Be sure the child has the prerequisite skills for the next step in the sequence (e.g., pincers grasp before stringing beads).
4. Individualize instruction to control attention and maximize progress. This can be managed with individual one-to-one instruction for brief periods each day, or in small groups in which each child is permitted to work at his or her own level (e.g., puzzles and formboards).
5. Use first person pronouns (I, we) to facilitate imitation of storybook narratives.
6. Recognize the learners who need simultaneous presentations in match-to-sample tasks, and present the match and the sample concurrently on the same page rather than on another page or another flash card. Sequential learning may present unusual difficulty for children with SLDs.
7. To reduce overgeneralization when teaching concepts, keep the ratio of positive to negative examples high (e.g., three or four examples of the concept to one nonexample). The procedure used in Distar is an example of this principle: "This is a truck, this is a truck, this is a truck, this is *not* a truck."

8. Encourage children to observe other children making active responses and receiving appropriate reinforcement.
9. Use brightly colored pictures with little detail, shading, or depth cues.
10. Be aware of young children's preference for color to form, especially in color-form discrimination tasks or in puzzles where color is an irrelevant cue.
11. Use color photos rather than line drawings to facilitate recall of pictures.
12. Encourage children to respond by finger tracing to enforce attention to salient stimuli.
13. Accentuate the positives in each child, recognizing that the behaviors the teacher reinforces are the behaviors that will continue.

To summarize, the content of instruction for young handicapped infants and toddlers (0 to 2 years) will need to address the areas specified in P.L. 99-457:

- Physical development

- Cognitive development

- Language and speech development

- Self-help skills

- Psychosocial development

In addition, for preschoolers (3 to 5 years) prereading, prewriting, and premath will need to be emphasized. Curricular decisions may also need to be based on the requirement of each state. For example in Texas the Early Childhood Essential Elements document (1983) has had a significant impact on what is being taught in programs for young handicapped children.

Figure 2-6 presents an analysis of curricula for young at-risk, delayed, and handicapped infants, toddlers, and preschool children. The curricula are listed alphabetically across the top of the table, with four Headstart curricula in Spanish listed last. The left-hand column lists the areas delineated in P.L. 99-457, with the expansions suggested by the author. Sixteen of the curricula were then analyzed to determine how closely the content matched the requirements of the new statute. Eleven of the curricula were not available for analysis. Completion of the data would constitute a challenging task for the reader and lead to a keen appreciation of the materials available for use with young children.

The methods of instruction to be used are much less specifically defined. The "art of teaching" may yet become a "science of teaching" as concerned educators dedicate themselves to maximizing the learning of each child in their classrooms.

These comments on the existence of SLDs in preschool children lead to the following conclusions:

1. SLDs exist in preschool children and are not merely a phenomenon of the school years.
2. SLDs can and should be diagnosed in young children to prevent the development of more serious handicaps.
3. Assessment devices have been developed that are appropriate for the preschool child. Many professionals serving school-age children may need specialized training to appropriately serve the preschool population.
4. Those assessment devices that lead to appropriate curriculum programs for infants and young children offer greatest promise for maximizing the potential of our most important natural resource — our young handicapped children.
5. Curriculum and instruction for preschoolers with SLDs must be responsive to the needs of each youngster and reflect the statutory requirements of state and federal rules and regulations.

Fig. 2-6. An analysis of curricula for young at-risk, delayed, and handicapped infants, toddlers, and preschool children.

	ABACUS	Beginning Milestones	Carolina Curriculum	Carolina Developmental	Down's Syndrome (DSPI)	Goal/PEECH	HELP	High Scope Curriculum	Learning Accomplishment Profile	NWM Program	Niños pequeños en Accion
Developmental areas/ Age range (yr)	2–5	1½–5	0–2	3–5	0–9	0–3 3–6	0–3 3–6	3–5			3–5
PHYSICAL DEVELOPMENT	X					X	X				
General health											
Vision											
Hearing											
Neurologic motivations											
Activity level											
Gross motor	X	X	X	X	X	X	X				
Fine motor	X	X	X	X	X	X	X				
COGNITIVE DEVELOPMENT	X	X	X	X	X	X	X	X			X
Crystallized intelligence	X	X	X		X	X		X			X
Vocabulary	X	X			X	X		X			X
Knowledge	X	X			X	X		X			X
Comprehension	X	X			X			X			
Fluid intelligence	X		X	X	X	X		X			X
Reasoning	X	X	X	X	X	X	X	X			X
Concept formation	X	X			X		X	X			X
Problem solving	X	X			X	X		X			X
Auditory processing	X	X	X	X	X	X	X				
Visual processing	X	X	X	X	X	X	X		Not analyzed	Not analyzed	
Memory	X			X							
Short-term	X			X		X					
Digits, words	X										
Long-term	X			X		X					
Attention/involvement level	X										
LANGUAGE AND SPEECH DEVELOPMENT	X	X		X	X	X	X	X			X
Prerequisites	X	X	X		X	X	X	X			
Comprehension (receptive)	X	X	X	X	X	X	X	X			
Production (expressive)	X	X	X	X	X	X	X	X			
Use	X										
SELF-HELP SKILLS	X				X	X	X				
Dressing	X		X		X	X	X				
Toileting	X	X			X	X	X				
Grooming	X	X	X		X	X	X				
Eating	X	X	X		X	X	X				
Mechanical know-how	X				X						
Safety	X	X			X						
PSYCHOSOCIAL DEVELOPMENT	X	X	X	X	X	X	X				X
Awareness of self and others	X	X			X	X	X				
Awareness of feelings	X	X			X	X	X				X
Social information	X	X			X	X	X				
Play behavior	X	X			X	X	X				
Interactive behavior	X	X			X	X	X				
Self-regulation	X	X	X		X	X	X				
PRE-ACADEMICS	X			X		X					
Pre-reading	X	X			X			X			
Pre-math	X	X			X	X		X			
Pre-writing	X				X	X		X			
Others: fine arts		X			X			X			

	Optimal Learning Environment	PEEK	PLDK	Portage Guide to Early Education	Project MEMPHIS	RADEA	Rutland Developmental Therapy	SKI-HI Curriculum	Small Wonder	Teaching Research	Unistape Curriculum	UPAS Uniform Performance	Amonocar	Fronteres del Aprendi zajo	Un Marco Abierto	Alerts
	0–3	2½–4		0–5	0–5		2–14			0–5	0–3 3–6					
				X	X											
	Not analyzed	X X	Not analyzed	X X	X X	Not analyzed		Not analyzed	Not analyzed	X X	Not analyzed	Not analyzed	Not analyzed	Not analyzed	Not analyzed	Not analyzed
		X		X	X					X						
		X X X			X X X X											
		X X X X X			X X X X											
		X		X X	X X											
				X	X		X			X						
		X X		X X X X		X X X		X X							
				X						X						
				X X												
				X												
		X		X	X											
		X		X	X											
		X X X		X X X			X X									
				X					X							
							X X X		X X							
	X			X												

APPENDIX
ANALYSIS OF SUBTYPE STUDIES

PSYCHOLINGUISTIC FACTORS

Study	Aud. rec.	Vis. rec.	Tactile rec.	Aud.-voc. assoc.	Vis. mot. assoc.	Tactile assoc.	Verbal exp.	Manual exp.	Aud. percep.-recep.	Vis. percep.-recep.	Vis. spatial ability	Tactile percep. ability (finger localization)	Fine motor	Aud. closure	Vis. closure	Grammatic closure	Aud. seq. mem.	Vis. seq. mem.	Long-term aud. & vis. mem.	Sound blending	Percept. speed	Obj. assembly/puzzles	Verbal IQ	Performance IQ	Full-scale IQ
WILSON & RISUCCI (1983)																									
Receptive subgroup	−	−		−			−										−	−	−						
Global subgroup	−	−		−	−												−		−						
Auditory memory and retrieval subgroup	+	+		+	+												−		−						
Expressive subgroup		−		+	−		−									+		−							
No deficits							+		+								−	+							
DENCKLA (1972)																									
Specific language disability (dyslexia)											−					−									
Specific visuospatial disability (Gerstmann)										−	−	−	−												
Dyscontrol syndrome	−								−	−			−				+								
BODER (1973) SUBTYPES																									
Dysphonetic group		+												−			+								
Dyseidetic group		−													−			−		+					
Mixed dysphonetic-dyseidetic		−		−																+	−				
McCARTHY & ELKINS (1974) CLUSTERS																							+	+	+
Asymptomatic (high) group																							−	+	
Low verbal/high performance group																							+	−	+
High verbal/low performance group																							+	+	+
Discrepant verbal and performance																							−	−	−
Asymptomatic (low)																							−	−	
MATTIS, FRENCH, & RAPIN (1975) SUBTYPES																									
Language disorder				−			−							−		−	−								
Articulatory and dyscoordination							−													−					

Appendix (continued)

Study	Aud. rec.	Vis. rec.	Tactile rec.	Aud.-voc. assoc.	Vis. mot. assoc.	Tactile assoc.	Verbal exp.	Manual exp.	Aud. percep.-recep.	Vis. percep.-recep.	Vis. spatial ability	Tactile percep. ability (finger localization)	Fine motor	Aud. closure	Vis. closure	Grammatic closure	Aud. seq. mem.	Vis. seq. mem.	Long-term aud. & vis. mem.	Sound blending	Percept. speed	Obj. assembly/puzzles	Verbal IQ	Performance IQ	Full-scale IQ
Visual/perceptual disorder										−												−			
SATZ & MORRIS (1981) LD SUBTYPES																									
Global language	−			−			−																−		−
Specific language fluency							−																		
Global language and perceptual		−					−			−	−														
Visual-perceptual motor		−			−					−															
Unexpected (no impairment)																									
LYON & WATSON (1981) SUBTYPES																									
Auditory-visual deficits									−								−								
Linguistic/visual motor deficits										−															
Phonetic deficits																− −				−					
Visual perception deficits										−															
Auditory sequencing deficits																									
Normal profile																									
McKINNEY, SHORT, & FEAGANS (1985) CLUSTERS																									
Normal																									
Mixed perceptual–Severe language deficits (mild)	−									− −							+	+				−			
Linguistic comprehension deficit (severe)							−																		
Linguistic production deficit (mild)																						−			
Flat (low coding)							+																+	−	+
Mixed perceptual (mild) language deficits										−															
Normal (high coding)																							+	−	+

REFERENCES

Bredekamp, S. (Ed.). (1986). *Developmentally appropriate practice in early childhood programs serving children from birth through age 8*. Washington, DC: National Association for the Education of Young Children.

Bricker, D. D. (1986). *Early education of at-risk and handicapped infants, toddlers, and preschool children*. Glenview, IL: Scott, Foresman.

Chamberlin, R. W. (1987). Developmental assessment and early intervention programs for young children. *Pediatrics in Review, 8*(8).

Cobb, G. (1976). *President's Committee on Mental Retardation*. DHEW Publication No. (OHD) 76-21008, Washington, DC: Department of Health, Education, and Welfare.

Education Service Center, Region VI. (1983). *Early childhood essential elements*. Huntsville, TX: Stewart.

Gardner, J. (1978). *Morale*. New York: Norton.

Garwood, G. (Ed.). (1983). *Educating young handicapped children: A development approach*. Rockville, MD: Aspen.

Head, H. (1926). *Aphasia and kindred disorders of speech*. Cambridge, England: Cambridge University Press.

Hinshelwood, J. (1917). *Congenital word blindness*. London: Lewis.

Keogh, B. K. & Glover, A. T. (1980). Research needs in the study of early identification of children with learning disabilities. In *Thalamus*. Ann Arbor: Academy for Research in Learning Disabilities.

Kirk, S. A., & Chalfant, J. C. (1984). *Developmental and academic learning disabilities*. Denver: Love.

Kirk, S., & Gallagher, J. (1986). *Educating exceptional children*. Boston: Houghton Mifflin (pp. 379–381).

Lerner, J. (1981). *Learning disabilities: Theories, diagnosis and teaching strategies*. Boston: Houghton Mifflin.

Luick, A., Kirk, S. A. Agronowitz, & Busby. (1982, February). Profiles of children with severe oral language disorders. *Journal of Speech and Hearing Disorders, 19*(47), 88–92.

McCarthy, J. M. (1971). *How to find them in kindergarten. Final report to Bureau of Education for Handicapped*. Tuscon: Leadership Training Institute in Learning Disabilities.

McCarthy, J. M. (1986). The preschool learning disabled child: Does he or does he not exist? In *Proceedings of the South Carolina Learning Disabilities Symposium*. Columbia, SC.

McCarthy, J. M. (1987). *Curriculum and instruction for preschool handicapped children*. Presented at Networking 1987 Conference. Arizona Department of Education, Phoenix, AZ.

McCarthy, J., & Elkins, J. (1974). Psychometric characteristics of children enrolled in the child service demonstration centers. Tuscon: Leadership Training Institute in Learning Disabilities.

McCarthy, J., & Smith, S. (1988). *Early warning signs of learning disabilities*. Pittsburgh: Association for Children and Adults with Learning Disabilities.

National Joint Committee on Learning Disabilities. (1986). *Learning disabilities and the preschool child*. (Unpublished manuscript)

Orton, S. T. (1925). "Word blindness" in school children. *Archives of Neurology and Psychiatry*, XIV, 581–615.

Peterson, N. L. (1987). *Early intervention for handicapped and at-risk children*. Denver: Love.

Strauss, A., & Werner, H. (1942). Disorders of conceptual thinking in the brain-injured child. *Journal of Nervous and Mental Disorders* 96, 153–172.

U.S. Department of Education. (1987). *Ninth Annual Report to Congress on the Implementation of the Education of the Handicapped Act*. Washington, DC: U.S. Department of Education.

U.S. Department of Health and Human Services. (1986). *Thirteenth Annual Report to Congress*. Washington, DC: U.S. Department of Health and Human Services.

Walker, J. A., & Hallau, M. G. (1981). Why the 'H' in ECEH? Considerations in training teachers of young handicapped children. Reston, VA: *Journal of Division for Early Childhood. 2*, 61–66.

CHAPTER 3

Assessment of School-Age Children

JOANNE F. CARLISLE
DORIS J. JOHNSON

This second of three chapters focusing on a specific age group addresses the special problems involved in assessing and diagnosing the school-age child with learning disabilities. Using the primary focus of the assessment process, Doctors Carlisle and Johnson discuss each school-age population—early childhood, middle childhood, and adolescence.

For each group, they discuss models for assessing social, motor, perceptual, cognitive, and language development. They then address the specific assessment of reading, writing, and mathematics skills.

The assessment procedures used to identify and determine appropriate educational programs for learning disabled students have come under serious attack in recent years. Common complaints are that the performance on standardized tests of students identified as learning disabled does not differ from that of students described as low achieving (Ysseldyke, Algozzine, Shinn, & McGue, 1982), that the definition by which learning disabled students are identified is vague and imprecise (Algozzine & Ysseldyke, 1986; Kavale & Forness, 1985), and that designation of students as learning disabled is made on the basis of subjective judgments (Ysseldyke, Algozzine, Richey, & Graden, 1982). In addition, dissatisfaction with standardized tests and the growing numbers of learning disabled students in various states have led to arguments over more precise ways to quantify learning disabilities. The use of discrepancy formulae has been one popular solution (Valus, 1986); the use of a test battery with supposedly better technical characteristics has been another (Breen, 1986; Inglis & Lawson, 1986). However, neither of these modifications appears to have solved the problem.

Although learning disabled children typically perform below expectancy in one or more areas of achievement, not all underachievers are learning disabled. One of the reasons for the current high incidence of classification as learning disabled is that children are often classified as learning disabled if they are underachieving in relation to others in the classroom. Such individuals may not have a discrepancy between their mental ability and achievement and may be performing as well as they can. In other instances, children may be classified as learning disabled simply if they have severe discrepancies between potential and achievement. This practice may yield a heterogeneous group of underachievers, not a group of specifically learning disabled students, unless one includes a thorough evaluation of the history and type of instruction and a more detailed analysis of learning and achievement. For example, in a large study of third- and fourth-grade children, Myklebust and Boshes (1969) found that approximately 15 percent of the population was underachieving when given a battery of standardized tests and a pupil rating scale. This number was reduced by half, however, after the children were seen for intensive diagnostic studies that included more extensive analyses of vision, physical status, cognitive ability, language, and academic performance. Many achievement tests are screening instruments at best, and educators should be aware that screening is not synonymous with diagnosis. No tests "diagnose" learning disabilities. Rather, the diagnosis is made on the basis of total child study together with a comprehensive home and school history.

While the struggle to standardize and legitimize the identification of learning disabled students continues, practitioners must do their best to determine which students are learning disabled and which are not, and they must help design effective educational programs for those who are learning disabled. Concern for accurate distinctions and diagnoses should be the province of both researchers and practitioners (Keogh, 1986). Educators should attempt to prevent the kind of situation encountered in some states where the evaluation procedures specified by federal and state regulations have not been followed consistently, resulting in a sizable proportion of the students who have been serviced as learning disabled but who may in fact not have been learning disabled at all (Shepard & Smith, 1983). To accomplish this end educators must approach the assessment of students within the framework of a theory of learning disabilities that shapes the process of assessment. One useful model has been proposed by Adelman and Taylor (1986), who recommend examining learning disabilities on the basis of four interacting dimensions: cause, severity of problem manifestations, pervasiveness of problem manifestations, and chronicity. These dimensions suggest several important principles for designing and carrying out an effective and theoretically meaningful assessment of learning disabilities.

A plan of assessment must be thorough. It should have sufficient depth and breadth to ensure an adequate understanding of the child's learning and performance over time and in various contexts. An assessment with depth and breadth will show the child's development in relation to expectations, both general developmental expectations and the specific expectations of the classroom. Many forces play a role in the development of the child as an effective learner. A child's performance in school is not just a matter of achievement on various tests; it also depends on the ability to grasp concepts that are the teachers' tools for explaining new lessons (cognitive and linguistic development) and on the types of motivation and experiences the child brings from home.

This general philosophy suggests that various kinds of information must be collected to help understand the child's development. A study of learning over time and in various contexts is essential. Performance on a test battery resembles a "snap shot" when something comparable to a slow-motion video tape is needed to investigate chronicity, pervasiveness, and severity of problems. For the purposes of identification of a learning disability, information must be gathered about the child's life history, including prenatal and perinatal events that affect the growth and integrity of functioning, achievement of developmental milestones, and educational history. Information regarding rate of learning is useful in differentiating generalized developmental delays from specific disabilities; information about the achievement of siblings and parents may provide insights into possible familial learning disabilities. Information must also be sought to help address the "exclusionary criteria" that continue to be integral to identification of specific learning disabilities, including sensory, intellectual, and social/emotional functioning.

In selecting standardized tests to measure intellectual and academic functioning, we should be guided not only by the reliability of the tests but also by their content and construct validity. Educators must consider whether the test will yield meaningful information. For example, a test may be called a test of reading and yet provide no measure of the development of particularly important skills of reading, such as word recognition. In addition, educators must consider how various disabilities might mask potential or performance. This is particularly important when selecting intelligence tests. Schools or states that require the use of full-scale I.Q. tests rather than either verbal or performance may penalize certain learning disabled children, just as they penalize the hearing impaired or physically handicapped.

To obtain a comprehensive picture of the child's overall performance, the diagnostic team should be prepared to examine various aspects of cognitive development, oral language, reading, written language, mathematics, and social skills. They should also note whether certain output problems (e.g., perceptual motor deficits or speech disorders) prevent children from demonstrating what they know. While emphasis should be given to the presenting problems, the team should be aware that certain symptoms tend to co-occur, and that a disability in one area might impede performance in another. For example, students with visual/spatial problems frequently have difficulty in handwriting, arithmetic, and self-help skills (Johnson, 1987). Similarly, listening comprehension problems typically affect reading comprehension, mathematical reasoning, and perhaps the development of some social skills. By examining patterns of problems across areas of achievement, a more integrated view of the child's strengths and weaknesses can be obtained. As a result, educators might be able to help classroom teachers understand how they can modify assignments and prevent fragmentation of services.

Depth of assessment is a somewhat different but equally important issue. To obtain a complete picture of a given child and to design an appropriate educational program, a comprehensive evaluation must go beyond the use of standardized, norm-referenced tests. Information needs to be collected about the child not just in relation to developmental expectations but also in relation to the expectations that form the contexts in which learning is meant to occur (i.e., classroom, playground). After all, learning does not take place in a vacuum. A child described as disabled in learning has been attempting to learn in some specific environment. Therefore, detailed descriptions of the content of the curriculum and some indication about the quality of instruction are needed. The latter issue was highlighted in the study of Jansky and deHirsch (1972), who found that high-risk children who were taught by teachers rated above average by their supervisors performed better than those who were taught by teachers who were rated average or below.

The diagnostic study can be strengthened by observing the child in several contexts. Such observations contribute several kinds of insights. First, visits to the classrooms offer an opportunity to see how the child responds to different types of instruction. For instance, some children have particular difficulty with implicit learning. Hence, they fail to acquire certain social rules, language, or spelling principles that are not made explicit. Second, observations of learning and behavior across contexts provide information about pervasiveness of problems and self-esteem. Students with specific reading disabilities may be leaders in sports, graphic design, or social situations, whereas those with more global disorders often have difficulty in both academic and social contexts. Third, observing children in classrooms with varying degrees of structure can highlight possible attention disorders or difficulty with independent learning.

The ability levels of other children in the group should be considered as well. Although the severity of a child's academic difficulty should be determined by the degree of discrepancy between potential and achievement, in many schools severity is judged by comparing a child's performance with other students in the class. Thus, a bright child with a moderate disability might appear less disabled in a group of average learners than in a group with superior ability. When making decisions about placement, it is helpful to examine the levels of achievement and rate of instruction in various classrooms. Even youngsters with mild problems can fall behind quickly if they fail to understand directions or learn at the expected rate. Furthermore, the types of responses and feedback they receive from their classmates may influence their self-esteem and motivation.

In addition to these observations, a thorough diagnostic study includes nonstandard or non–test-based methods of assessment to supplement the information gathered by the norm-referenced tests, a practice recommended by many experts (Oka & School, 1985; Salvia & Ysseldyke, 1988; Taylor, 1984; Zigmond, Vallecorsa, & Silverman, 1983; Wallace & Larsen, 1978). In both educational and clinical settings, evaluation with standardized tests can be followed up with diagnostic teaching or "informal" assessment. Methods of non–test-based assessment might include the use of interviews, rating scales, and other sociometric methods. Detailed error analyses of language, reading, and spelling patterns also can be used in diagnosis and in planning remediation. These methods require expertise on the part of the examiner and may require assessment by professionals trained in specific fields. The use of such methods emphasizes the fact that assessment of learning disabled children is a problem-solving activity (Johnson, 1987; Weaver, 1984). No simple formulaic approach that is known will yield diagnostically valid results.

Over the last few decades the conception of the influences on children's learning has broadened. As a result, the issues that evaluators must grapple with have become more comprehensive. Researchers from many different domains have contributed significantly to the understanding of normal development, which in turn has created a framework for understanding learning disabled children at different stages in their school careers. Often practitioners are made to reach beyond the scope of their original professional training to understand new perspectives. Because these new perspectives enrich the understanding of learning disabled students, expectations that arise from this understanding of normal child development and that constitute the context for learning in the classroom are discussed and certain aspects of school or instruction that might interact with certain types of learning disabilities are suggested. In addition, salient issues in areas that should, as a rule, be part of a thorough assessment are described. Because of the importance of developmental considerations, this discussion divides the school-age population into three stages—early childhood, middle childhood, and late childhood or adolescence—and highlights critical issues that need to be considered at each stage.

EARLY CHILDHOOD

A diagnosis of specific learning disabilities during the early childhood years is difficult to make because of the variability in rate of development and background experience. One needs only to observe kindergarteners entering school for the first time to see how they vary in size, social competence, independence, language development, risk-taking behavior, and desire to learn. In addition, exposure to various types of media may influence language and cognitive development (Greenfield, 1984). Some can read words and simple stories (Durkin, 1966), whereas others are reluctant to go to school because they cannot read. Along with observable differences in their skills and rates of adjustment to school, children have had a range of different experiences. Some come from homes in which they have listened to bedtime stories for years, yet others may never have had a book read to them. Some have attended preschools, and others have not. The nature of early school experiences is also quite varied. Nursery schools or day-care centers range from loosely structured centers with emphasis on socialization to those that demand quiet control and academic learning.

Because of these and other factors, many diagnosticians are reluctant to classify children as handicapped without having ample opportunity to observe them over time. Nonetheless, some youngsters enter school having been diagnosed as learning disabled because they have a discrepancy between potential and achievement—most often in language, but occasionally because of severe nonverbal or perceptual motor problems.

Whether the child is identified as learning disabled before or after entry in school, it is important for the diagnostician to remember that the nature and severity of the problems may vary over time and with the demands of the environment. For example, children may enter school with primary receptive language disorders, but with remediation, may later have only expressive problems. Similarly, those with early reading problems may, with early intervention, need subsequent help only in written language.

Individual school systems vary with regard to early labeling of children and provision of services. Some schools have developmental kindergartens or first grades for children who are not deemed ready for the standard curriculum. These programs are often helpful in differentiating children with generalized delays from those with specific disabilities. Often a "wait and see" approach is used in hopes that children will gradually "catch up." While there may be merit in waiting, the school should have a systematic plan for monitoring progress lest the anticipated developmental growth does not occur and the presenting problems are deemed to be more severe. Jansky (1975) emphasizes the need for helping the "marginally ready child" to prevent more serious learning and emotional problems from developing. In other school systems, students are bussed to other communities to obtain special services. While these services are essential, the children are expected to adjust to several different teachers and learning environments. Those who already have difficulty making friends may be even more troubled by moving from school to school.

All of these factors suggest that a comprehensive evaluation should include a thorough study of the child as well as the environment. Most theories of early childhood development now emphasize the need for interaction analysis (Sameroff, 1979). Focus must be on the amount and quality of instruction as well as on children's learning and behavior. Since schools vary considerably in the amount of time they devote to reading readiness and written language, an attempt must be made to determine how well the child is learning what is being taught.

SOCIAL DEVELOPMENT

The social skills of young children vary, as do their levels of independence. On entering a kindergarten one sees the clinger, the fighter, the fearful, the withdrawn, the happy, and the outgoing child. The initial days in any school year often require gradual adjustments on the part of both teacher and children.

High-risk and learning disabled children often have difficulty adjusting and learning how to respond and interact in school. Those with problems of social perception and attention are particularly vulnerable since the expectancies and rules are not always explicitly defined. Youngsters with histories of learning and behavior problems often have been protected at home and may be unable to cope (Lewis, Strauss, & Lehtinen, 1960). Their inability to focus or maintain attention creates secondary emotional problems because of negative feedback and reprimands. Occasionally aberrant behavior is reinforced, and the children become class clowns.

Play, at least during kindergarten, is nearly as important as academic learning. McCune-Nicolich and Carroll (1981), Garvey (1977), and Bruner (1976) all emphasize the importance of play for both cognitive and social/

emotional development. By this age children should engage in extended periods of pretend play, construction, and exploration, yet many language learning disabled children have been found to be deficient in these skills (Blalock, 1977; Cable, 1981; Cicci, 1978). Because of the many cognitive, linguistic,and perceptual motor skills required for play, McCune-Nicolich and Carroll (1981) state that play can provide both context and material for assessment and intervention. Children's ability to abstract criterial attributes, draw conclusions on the basis of observation, test and check hypotheses, and perceive another point of view can be observed.

By age 7, children should learn to play games with rules (Piaget, 1962), many of which may be difficult because of memory for sequence, motor skills, rule generalization, and problem solving. Table and board games require perceptual, quantitative, and reading skills. Failure to play well may result in isolation, teasing, and other negative feedback. It is important to observe children during these complex activities since structured laboratory tests may not reveal the severity of the problems.

MOTOR DEVELOPMENT

Most screening programs for young high-risk children include an evaluation of both gross and fine motor development (Denhoff et al, 1971; Frankenburg & Dodds, 1968; Gesell & Lehtinen, 1947). Although motor problems may not interfere with the acquisition of knowledge, they sometimes interfere with overall sensory motor performance and with the children's ability to demonstrate what they know. At times, the problems may interfere with exploration and subsequent cognitive development. Careful observations of certain types of play (e.g., blocks) may differentiate children with spatial orientation problems from those who have difficulty with motor control. Problems with balance and organization are often evident on the playground and may be indicative of developmental delay or central nervous system dysfunctions.

In the classroom, problems of manual dexterity create numerous problems, particularly when children are unable to cut with scissors or hold a pencil properly. Minor visual motor disorders also prevent children from writing legibly. Hence, spelling skills may need to be evaluated by other means, such as spelling aloud.

Early graphic representation may be limited if children cannot cut, paint, or draw, and their failure creates more frustration when teachers display art work and crafts on bulletin boards. The faulty performance of children with perceptual motor deficits is often a permanent reminder of their weaknesses.

PERCEPTUAL DEVELOPMENT

The years between 5 and 7 often produce dramatic increases in perception and perceptual motor development. Hence, one must be somewhat cautious in making early diagnoses of perceptual disorders. Sheldon White (1970) says that children also acquire better test-taking skills during this period. Thus children who have had limited school experiences may not perform well on tests.

During the period from 5 to 7 years, children develop better ability to deal with part-whole and figure-ground relationships (Ausubell & Sullivan, 1970) and become more adept at identifying and discriminating shapes, sounds in words, and other percepts. Until the age of 7 we expect to see occasional reversals, transpositions, misarticulations, and misperceptions.

During the early childhood years, Piaget (1962) and Zaporozhets and Elkonin (1971) report that children's patterns of haptic and visual exploration also change. They engage in different types of exploratory behavior when given familiar and unfamiliar material and become more aware of distinctive features. They learn *how* to look, to feel, and to listen.

According to White (1970), Birch and Belmont (1965), and others, children also develop better intersensory integration and can make hypotheses about information between sensory systems. That is, they can identify visual representations of objects that they feel and can associate rhythmic patterns with visual/spatial configurations.

While there has been considerable controversy over the evidence and prevalence of perceptual disorders among learning disabled children, part of the problem in the field has arisen because of the definition of *perception*. Whereas Strauss and Lehtinen (1947) defined perception very broadly, others have used it to denote simple discrimination skills. Although many researchers have found new perceptual deficits among poor readers (Liberman, Shankweiler, Fischer, & Carter, 1974; Vellutino, 1979), one cannot ignore the children who continue to exhibit problems in discriminating letters, words, or phonemes, particularly in the early childhood years. Furthermore, recent auditory investigations suggest that current clinical procedures may not be precise enough to detect subtle disorders of perception. Elliott and Hammer (1987) tested two large groups of normal and language learning disabled children on measures of fine-grained auditory discrimination and found significant problems among the latter group. These difficulties are probably not simply maturational delays since Elliott and Busse (1987) found the performance of many adults with learning disabilities to be as poor, or even poorer, than that of 6-year-old children on their fine-grained auditory discrimination task. Defects of auditory perception have also been reported in several studies of Tallal and Piercy (1978).

COGNITIVE DEVELOPMENT

Many components of cognitive development are included on standardized tests of mental ability such as the Wechsler Intelligence Scale for Children

(1986). However, it should be noted that the nonverbal scale for young children includes a high proportion of tasks that require perception, memory, and visual motor functions rather than conceptualization. Therefore, it is helpful to include tests such as the Woodcock-Johnson Psycho-Educational Battery of Cognitive Abilities Test (1977) to examine more aspects of concept formation, analysis, and synthesis. Diagnosticians also might include piagetian tasks such as seriation and conservation. Kamii (1971) provides several excellent guidelines for the evaluation of cognitive ability. These tasks often highlight deficits in cognition and language. For example, some children with language disorders may classify objects but be unable to label attributes. Many also have difficulty with syntax and oral formulation so they cannot explain a phenomenon (Blalock, 1977). For example, James (1972) found that learning disabled children understood the concept of measurement but could not explain it. Lavatelli (1970) lists several syntactic patterns that are needed for explanations (e.g., use of comparative and superlative forms, relational words).

In general, studies of thinking skills should be assessed both with and without language to determine the possible bases for learning problems.

LANGUAGE DEVELOPMENT

Most children enter kindergarten with relatively good language development so they can convey their needs and share experiences with others. Studies of pragmatics indicate they also can adjust their language for various listeners and can convey their needs to others. Speech is generally intelligible although some children may continue to have difficulty with certain phonemes (e.g., r, l, s, and th). Despite these competencies, Loban (1976) and others report that many aspects of language continue to develop, including breadth and depth of vocabulary, complex syntax, and discourse (Halladay & Hasan, 1976).

Studies of young language learning disabled children indicate that all facets of receptive and expressive language should be examined carefully (Menyuk, 1978; Snyder, 1983). In addition, relationships between language and various aspects of cognition, reading, writing, and mathematics should be investigated (Johnson & Blalock, 1982; Rice, 1983). For example, certain children have particular difficulty with the language for spatial and temporal relationships, perhaps because of nonverbal disorders. Others have problems with homonyms, multiple word meanings, and the detection of ambiguity (Groshong, 1980). Many have difficulty with superordinate vocabulary, such as tools, utensils, fruits, and vegetables. However, the bases for these problems may be cognitive rather than verbal (Friedman, 1984). In our experience, most vocabulary tests are insufficient to measure accuracy, breadth, and depth of word meaning. Therefore, more informal tests are needed.

Tape-recorded language samples are invaluable for error analyses and can be used as supplemental data from standardized tests. The child's conversation and story-telling abilities might be examined. Language learning disabled children have been found to have difficulties with discourse and conversational skills (Craig & Chapman, 1987; Woolf, 1983). During early childhood, youngsters gradually learn to tell stories that include a central core or theme (Applebee, 1978). However, studies of young learning disabled children indicate that they grasp the general structure of stories but have a spare, rather nonspecific vocabulary (Podhajski, 1980).

Special attention should be given to the language of instruction and vocabulary used primarily in school. Although children have been given directions at home for years, they typically have contextual clues to aid them. In contrast, many instructions in school are decontextualized and require more precision; this is particularly true of paper and pencil tasks.

Downing (1979) found that young children do not understand the language related to reading and school readiness. He found that 5-year-olds understood the word *sound* as it related to the tick of a clock or a horn but not to phonemes. Since traditional readiness tests do not assess this type of vocabulary, examiners may need to construct informal tasks, perhaps with the assistance of the child's classroom teachers.

The child with a learning disability rarely has a global language disorder; rather, the problems may be quite specific to one or more rule systems. The evaluation should include a careful analysis of vocabulary, syntax, morphology, prosody, articulation, and pragmatics. Special attention should be given to their rate of learning and their ability to abstract word meanings and rules from both natural and verbal contexts. Diagnosticians should also observe the child's ability to remember and generalize from one situation to another. Careful studies of language should be included in research on high-risk children since problems of word retrieval, sentence repetition, and other linguistic skills are often related to reading disabilities (Jansky & deHirsch, 1972).

READING

Perhaps no subject in school is of greater concern than reading. Every parent, teacher, and child hopes (either consciously or unconsciously) that reading skills will be acquired easily since literacy is the basis for success in schooling (Ferreiro & Teberosky, 1979). Whereas some children enter school knowing how to read familiar words and simple stories, others have little understanding of the process (Gillam & Johnston, 1985). They may not yet differentiate letters from words and are unaware of the recurring patterns in print. On the other hand, most know that we read from left to right in this culture, and they have some notion of the purpose of reading.

During the kindergarten years most children are in Chall's stage 0 or 1, or both (1983). This is a period when they use their background knowledge and context to make hypotheses about labels on cartons or signs and use their language and memory to "read" familiar books. During first grade, they begin to learn the code in order to generalize from known to unknown words. Generally they read words they already understand, and, because they have relatively well-developed syntax, they can make predictions about some unfamiliar words. Typically they read for confirmation rather than for new information (Chall, 1983).

Reading assessment during the 5- to 7-year level takes many forms. Most school systems give standardized readiness tests during kindergarten or early first grade to identify and place children according to ability levels. Tests usually include measures of word meaning, listening comprehension, auditory discrimination, letter name recognition, copying, and word matching. Some also included reading of logos and simple signs (Reid, Hresko, & Hammill, 1981). Because most tests yield a global score, a detailed item analysis is needed to look for patterns of errors. The results should be compared with content of the curriculum and classroom instruction.

Although group tests are useful for screening, diagnosticians should be aware of their limitations and the multiple reasons for failure. For instance, children with attention deficits may be unable to cope with multiple stimuli in test booklets; those with auditory language disorders may be confused by lengthy group instructions; and those with picture interpretation or nonverbal deficits may have difficulty with certain reading comprehension tests (Johnson, 1987). Others may perform better on group tests because they do not have to respond aloud. Studies of high-risk children indicate that picture naming, letter naming, and sentence repetition were among the best predictors of later reading failure (Jansky & deHirsch, 1972). Since these skills are not generally included on group readiness tests, success on such tests does not rule out the possibility of learning problems.

In addition, many standardized tests do not include measures of segmenting, a skill that often differentiates good from poor readers (Liberman, Shankweiler, Fischer, & Carter, 1974). By age 5 most children should be able to segment the stream of language into words, segment words into syllables by age 6, and segment by phoneme by age 7. Performance on tasks of this type indicates the children's growing metalinguistic awareness and ability to manipulate the sounds of language. Linguistic awareness is also demonstrated by their ability to rhyme, to categorize sounds, and to apply rules in novel situations (Bradley & Bryant, 1985). Numerous studies have found poor readers to be less proficient in these skills (Fox & Routh, 1980; Savin, 1972; Williams, 1984).

Since reading requires the use of multiple strategies, even in the early grades diagnosticians should note the child's ability to use context (both pictorial and linguistic), phonics, and morphologic cues and to remember sight words. Some poor readers are not aware of the need for multiple strategies and try to "sound out" every word; others try to memorize every new word. Often, one can gain insight into a child's understanding of the reading process by discussing his or her overall approach.

It is important to evaluate students' reading performance in both highly structured and naturalistic contexts. In addition, the diagnostician should seek to determine whether children retain what has been taught and whether they can generalize their learning to new reading lessons.

GRAPHIC REPRESENTATION AND EARLY WRITING

When children enroll in school, they typically have some notions about the functions of writing from observing adults write messages, lists, and letters. By age 5 they have acquired many perceptual motor skills for drawing geometric designs, including circles, squares, and triangles (Thomassen & Teulings, 1983). In favorable environments they have learned to color pictures, draw simple figures, and copy numerals, letters, and their names. However, they may have difficulty with complex figures, alignment, and spatial orientation. Early writing may not follow traditional English orthography, but research on early literacy indicates that these early "invented" spelling patterns do reveal patterns of development (Read, 1983, 1986; Temple, Nathan, & Burris, 1982). Many children begin by writing letter strings or the first letter of a word; later they use letter names to represent syllables (e.g., MT for empty). Gradually they attempt to represent all of the sounds in words, but the spellings may still not be correct (e.g., boe for boy; mak for make). With additional experiences and instruction they learn the correct orthography. This process requires the acquisition and use of multiple rule systems as well as memory (Hanna, Hodges, & Hanna, 1971; Frith, 1980).

Diagnosticians should be aware of these developmental patterns lest they make premature judgments about mistakes during the early grades. For instance, "Dade kam hom" may be considered a good representation for "daddy came home," since the child has indicated an awareness of the correct number of phonemes in each word. The diagnostic study should also include an analysis of a child's ability to remember words that are taught, both for weekly tests and for long-term memory. It is not unusual, however, to see even normal children obtaining perfect scores on spelling tests while still using some "invented" spelling in their spontaneous writing.

The evaluation should include copying ability to determine whether the vehicle for writing is intact. If children have severe visual motor problems, it may be necessary to assess spelling by asking them to spell aloud or write on a primary typewriter.

Visual access or revisualization also should be assessed. Some learning disabled children can read and copy figures that remain present, but they may not be able to write the alphabet or words spontaneously. A child may exhibit no reversals in reading or copying but might make numerous errors in written discourse. During the early grades it is important to determine whether children can read and write the same words and whether they can read their own writing. Bryant and Bradley (1980) suggest that children tend to use visual clustering strategies when reading and more analytical skills when writing.

During the early grades children show an increasing awareness of the relationships between spoken and written language (Frederiksen & Dominic, 1981; Larson, 1975; Litowitz, 1981). By age 7 they should be able to segment words by phoneme and should be trying to write as they speak. In addition, they should show a rudimentary awareness of strategies they can use to remember words (e.g., rehearsal and copying). In general, their written language at this age will resemble their speech. They write simple descriptions of pictures, messages, and letters. They may, with the help of a teacher, also write about previous experiences. Learning disabled children, in contrast, use fewer words and sentences, make more spelling and punctuation errors, and are more concrete (Myklebust, 1965).

MATHEMATICS

Most children acquire rudimentary number skills long before they enter school. The learn about one-to-one correspondence while listening to parents sing number songs and count fingers and toes. They learn about seriation as they stack pots and pans. They acquire concepts of quantity such as "all gone" and "no more" when eating and playing, as well as concepts of distance and measurement when directed not to go "too far" or "too fast." By kindergarten they should have a relatively basic understanding of cardinal and ordinal numbers, should recognize some numerals, and be able to solve simple oral story problems (Ginsburg & Baroody, 1983). During first grade they add to their knowledge and begin to solve written problems. They acquire new vocabulary but also learn that words have new meanings in mathematics (e.g., set, times).

Learning disabled children require careful assessment in mathematics because of their uneven patterns of strengths and weaknesses. Some may be able to count dot patterns but cannot recognize numerals. Some may count in rote fashion but have no idea about one-to-one correspondence. Others memorize mathematics facts without understanding. Careful attention should be given to forms of representation, types of input, and expected modes of response. A child with auditory memory problems may not be able to handle oral arithmetic problems but may be perfectly capable of understanding concepts. Those with visual/spatial problems may understand the concepts of money but fail to recognize coins in pictures. Strategies for problem solving (e.g., counting on fingers) should also be noted since they provide some insights into possible cognitive deficits (Garnett & Fleischner, 1987).

Thus, the difficulty for the learning disabled child is usually not mathematics in general but a specific facet of the symbol system. The diagnostic battery should be sufficiently comprehensive to determine whether the student has difficulty with numbers concepts or with some form of representation. Even in the first grade, students with specific reading disabilities begin to have difficulty with mathematics if they cannot read the signs or words in their mathematics books. Assessment in this case, as with other symbol systems, should include observations and diagnostic teaching as well as standardized tests.

MIDDLE CHILDHOOD

The middle school years constitute a period of dramatic growth and change. The students are expected to master the basic academic skills of reading, writing, and mathematics. They are also becoming proficient at the business of going to school. Therefore, assessment of learning disabled students must be concerned with students' adjustment to school and their social skills as well as their reading and writing.

SOCIAL DEVELOPMENT AND BEHAVIORAL ADJUSTMENT

There are several reasons to pay particular attention to learning disabled students' social and behavioral characteristics. First, once students have spent several years in schools, they ordinarily have internalized rituals of behavior and expectations. Students who do not conform or for whom clear expectations do not prompt appropriate behavior may have deficits in social perception or social learning. Evaluation of these students' social skills might help us understand important aspects of their learning disabilities. Research studies indicate that learning disabled students' deficits may be evident in such areas as listening to others, sharing equipment or toys, recognizing the moods of others, or accepting responsibility (Gresham & Reschly, 1986). One important aspect of an evaluation would be to determine whether appropriate social skills have not been learned or simply are not used (Schumaker & Hazel, 1984).

Second, students normally become more social, and in the process, the relative importance of the people in their world changes. Parents and other adults become less godlike; peers and their judgments become more important (Erikson, 1968). Students often judge themselves in relation to perceived standards embraced by others they admire. Learning disabled students become more aware of ways in which they differ from their peers (Cohen, 1986). Difficulties fulfilling academic and social roles in the classroom may affect the development of self-concept and the manner of interacting with others. Learning-disabled children risk loss of self-esteem that may lead to loss of ambition and motivation. Excessive dependence on others, sometimes called "learned helplessness," may be the result for some children (Bryan, 1986); increasingly rebellious behavior and lack of compliance may be the result for other children (Epstein, Cullinan, & Lloyd, 1986). These have their seeds in the children's first experiences with success and failure in the elementary years and emerge with some force as the children cope with their changing world in the middle years.

A preschool child thought to be at risk for learning disabilities may be described as immature or disorganized (deHirsch, 1984), but school-age children are more apt to be described as having social/emotional problems belonging to discrete diagnostic categories—attention deficit with or without hyperactivity, for example. Furthermore, studies have shown that behavioral or emotional problems first noted in elementary school are rated by parents and teacher as more severe at the junior and senior high levels (Epstein, Cullinan, & Lloyd, 1986; Pihl & McLarnon, 1984). To prevent the onset of more serious and pervasive behavior problems, educators need to help children learn to cope with their learning problems. For this reason, evaluation of social skills, peer relationships, and school adjustment seems to be a necessary component of a complete assessment of middle school learning disabled students.

The most effective methods of evaluation of classroom adjustment and behavior for middle school–age students include behavior-rating scales and observations (Gresham, 1985). Ideally, rating scales are completed by the student as well as by the teacher and a parent. Observations of the student's functioning should be gathered by visits to classes on a number of occasions by a person trained in methods of observation. Care should be taken to observe the student in different settings at different times of the day and during different kinds of lessons. It is also extremely important to observe one or more students who have not been referred for evaluation in order to determine the extent to which the child's behavior differs from that of others in the same setting. If particular problems with self-esteem or rejection by peers are described by the parents or teachers, a "peer nomination" technique for assessing peer approval and acceptance might provide insights into the student's acceptance by the other students. (For more details see Oka & Scholl, 1985; Schumaker & Hazel, 1984; Taylor, 1984.)

COGNITIVE DEVELOPMENT

It was commented earlier that the administration of an individual intelligence test provides information about learning disabled students' intellectual capabilities and pattern of verbal and nonverbal strengths and weaknesses, but it is generally wise to assess cognitive skills more widely. Cognitive development in the middle school years includes mastery of certain aspects of logical reasoning. To consider whether learning disabled students' cognitive development is keeping pace with that of their peers, it might be helpful to look at their judgments about relationships (such as part-whole or causal), their concept formation, and their problem-solving strategies. Deliberate selection of effective strategies to aid recall or solve problems is not usually noted in children under 7 years but becomes increasingly evident in middle school children. Learning disabled students have been found to be deficient in their selection and use of basic strategies for remembering or learning in a number of academic areas (see Gerber, 1986, and Wong, 1987 for examples), and so this may be an important component of cognitive development to assess in middle school learning disabled students.

The level of students' cognitive development may affect the development of their mathematic reasoning. Although ordinarily children have mastered one-to-one correspondence, most types of conservation (including volume and weight), and transitive reasoning before age 10 (Piaget, 1962), researchers suggest that the ability to solve problems using these logical operations may depend on vocabulary or language development, memory capacity, and attentional strategies (Gelman, 1972; Rose & Blank, 1974). Because learning disabled children often have deficits in these areas, it is not surprising that they sometimes have trouble using reasoning to execute tasks in a manner that is age appropriate (Derr, 1985; Gallagher & Reid, 1981). For this reason, when deficiencies in verbal problem solving are evident, the examiner should consider whether there are differences in the learning disabled students' verbal and nonverbal reasoning abilities.

LANGUAGE DEVELOPMENT

As noted earlier, by about age 7 students have generally mastered the basic structure of the language. Overall they understand normal adult speech with its varied complexities, although fine tuning in comprehension and the use of complex grammatical structures in their speech develop more slowly (Athey, 1977). Through the middle school years they are still learning word forms (aspects of inflectional and derivational morphology), appropriate uses of language (pragmatics), and the complexities of word relationships (semantics). One fascinating and little understood aspect of growth in oral language skills is the effect of learning to read and write. It is believed that literacy helps a student analyze the internal structure of words (phonology and morphology) and sentences (Ehri, 1984; Johnson, 1985). One inevitable consequence of difficulties in learning to read and write, then, is potentially less growth in spoken language abilities as well (Stanovich, 1986).

Another important factor in this period is the dramatic increase in the size of students' vocabulary. Estimates vary widely, but a conservative estimate is that a student's vocabulary doubles between third and seventh grades

(Anderson & Freebody, 1985). How this happens is not clear. Possible explanations include incidental learning from encountering different words over time in different reading materials and morphologic generation. The latter refers to building a gradual understanding of the system by which base words and affixes to make many word forms (e.g., lovely, lovable, loveliness). Morphologic knowledge has been found to be acquired more slowly by some learning disabled students than their normal peers (Carlisle, 1987; Wiig, Semel, & Crouse, 1973). Learning disabled students' vocabulary might be expected to develop more slowly then. Since the size of students' vocabularies also bears a close relation to their reading achievement (Rosenshine, 1980), educators should worry about language learning disabled children. As time goes on, limitation in their vocabulary acquisition is apt to affect the comprehension of their reading adversely.

Assessment of language skills in the middle school years, then, should include the evaluation of breadth and depth of vocabulary, the comprehension and use of grammatically complex sentences, the understanding of morphologic relationships, and the appropriateness of a student's spoken language in different contexts. Standardized tests are available, but observation and analysis of the student's understanding and use of language in classroom settings are also important.

Problems of articulation and sound discrimination are most often detected before children reach the middle school level. Remediation may extend well into the middle school years, however. Certainly the student's mastery of the sound system of the language (the phonology) should not be ignored in determining the appropriate components of an evaluation: Auditory discrimination, auditory analysis of spoken words and sentences, and metalinguistic abilities such as judgments of rhyme may reveal subtle but pervasive language-related difficulties that can affect the development of reading and writing skills.

DEVELOPMENT OF READING SKILLS

The first few years in school are generally thought of as the period in which students learn to read. That is, they become able to recognize a number of words and, it is hoped, work out the pronunciation of new words they have not memorized. Learning the code is the crucial component in the first stage of learning to read (Chall, 1983). In the second stage (roughly second and third grade), the students become more proficient in word recognition. They generalize the principles they have learned to more and more words, and they become more fluent and adept at reading tasks. They gradually learn how to use reading for different purposes and how to do the tasks associated with school-related reading assignments. They begin to pick up reading strategies to help them do what they are asked. Since many learning disabled students have difficulty learning the code and learning to be fluent readers, the strategies that they devise may or may not be effective in the long run.

In fourth through eighth grade, the students read to learn (Chall, 1983). They are offered more and more challenging texts in their content courses. They must learn study skills and the beginnings of what are called "critical" reading skills (Darch & Kameenui, 1987). Thus, reasoning and problem solving become more important components of the process of acquiring meaning from texts. In these years, it may be important to determine whether the poor reader is making an effort to acquire meaning from the texts of if he or she is essentially unengaged in the process (Carlisle, 1983).

Methods for teaching reading and the effectiveness of reading teachers vary from school to school and from region to region. Although experts remind us that most children learn to read successfully, regardless of the method of instruction or the expertise of the teacher, children with learning disabilities may experience difficulties learning because they are not receiving the kinds of instruction they need to address their specific problems. They may not be able to meet the expectations of their teachers and their curriculum. In addition, it should be remembered that learning to read is an interactive, social experience (Wigfield & Asher, 1984). Difficulties performing successfully in reading groups in the first years of school may make learning disabled students reticent to participate in reading activities. A negative attitude formed early on may adversely affect students' acquisition of reading skills for their entire school careers. The instructional and social/motivational factors are important enough to take into account in an assessment of learning disabled students' reading skills.

Evaluation of a students' reading skills between second and eighth grade must be multifaceted, taking into consideration not only word recognition skills and oral reading abilities, but also comprehension skills (see Calfee, Spector, & Piontkowski, 1979, for one model). Problems with accurate and fluent word recognition are particularly prevalent among middle school learning disabled students and have an adverse effect on comprehension skills. Where a breakdown in decoding skills is observed, further assessment should include knowledge of phoneme-grapheme correspondence rules and recognition of irregular words. If initial screening shows deficits in comprehension, evaluation should include a comparison of language abilities in spoken and written language. It is important to determine if difficulties in reading comprehension stem from difficulties in listening comprehension (Sticht & James, 1984). Some areas not traditionally included in an assessment of comprehension might also be considered. In particular, the students' background knowledge and problem-solving strategies might be explored through informal assessment or diagnostic teaching, perhaps using the students' textbooks.

ASSESSING SKILLS OF WRITTEN EXPRESSION

Experts in writing quite consistently believe that children want to write and will do so if given the proper environment and encouragement (Burrows,

Jackson, & Saunders, 1984; Graves, 1983; Temple, Nathan, & Burris, 1982). However, a large proportion of children assessed for learning problems have particular difficulties acquiring writing skills and commonly resist or state their dislike for writing tasks. Young children, even learning disabled children, draw and write without being self-conscious about the final product (Clay, 1975), but by the middle school years learning disabled children are more aware of their problems and are embarrassed about revealing their shortcomings through writing (Morocco & Neuman, 1986).

One of the reasons so many learning disabled students have difficulties with writing skills is that the act of writing involves the coordination of many subskills: a conceptual component where the student conceives of an idea; the formulation component where the student thinks about how to put the idea in words; and then the act of writing down the idea, which involves handwriting, spelling, and knowledge of the conventions of written expression. Students may experience difficulties with any or all of these components. An evaluation of writing skills should therefore delineate the students' strengths and weaknesses in each of these areas.

A number of different approaches to teaching writing skills are found at the middle school levels. Some teachers devote their primary efforts to teaching the mechanics and conventions of composition. They tend to teach and correct grammar, capitalization, punctuation, and spelling. Other teachers believe that classroom time should be devoted to encouraging students' self-expression in writing (Burrows et al, 1984; Graves, 1983), on the assumption that mechanics can be learned as children become more proficient. Because instructional approaches and the amount of time devoted to writing are so varied, evaluation of learning disabled students' writing skills really must be carried out with some understanding of the particular classroom practices they have been exposed to.

Standardized tests of writing skills are limited in their abilities to provide insights into the full range of the learning disabled students' writing abilities. Other approaches to assessment must be used to ensure an understanding of the sources of difficulty. One approach is to regard writing as a process. With this orientation, students' writing abilities are analyzed within the stages of the process where breakdown might occur (Moulton & Bader, 1985). A different approach is to analyze the products of writing. Students' writing samples might be analyzed for various types of errors. One model classifies errors as to whether or not they disrupt meaning (Giordano, 1984). Whether examining the process or the product of writing, several writing samples should be collected to provide a fair representation of the students' productivity and skill. The classroom teachers from different content areas may be able to contribute samples of the students' writing on different types of assignments.

Finally, difficulties with acquisition of writing skills must be considered in relation to the development of skills in other areas. For instance, reading and writing are truly collaborative processes, so that facility in one will often engender facility in the other (Dobson, 1985). Students' ability to read words might be profitably compared with their ability to write the same words (Boder, 1971). Similarly, breakdowns in the formulation of ideas in writing should be compared to the students' formulation of ideas to spoken language. For example, the students' ability to tell a story aloud could be compared to their ability to write the same story.

In summary, evaluation of a student's skill in writing must examine content, structure, and accuracy of presentation. The last of these areas includes the fluency and accuracy of the student's handwriting and the accuracy of spelling of age-appropriate words, grammatical accuracy, and the use of common conventions such as margins. Spelling should be examined in light of developmental stages and strategies (Gentry, 1982; Moats, 1983). A separate task might involve assessment of the rules of grammar, capitalization, and punctuation that have been taught in class. Comparisons can then be made of the students' knowledge of the rules taught in class and their ability to use these rules spontaneously in their writing.

Finally, the student's attitude toward writing should be considered. Such information is usually elicited by a conversation or an informal interview with the student (Giordano, 1984). A look at the student's school history and a discussion with the family may indicate whether pencil-and-paper activities have always been distasteful or whether they have developed in relation to academic expectations.

MATHEMATICAL KNOWLEDGE

Learning mathematics involves not one but a cluster of academic activities, each of which places different cognitive and social demands on the student. It is not enough to give students a test of arithmetic computation and feel satisfied that their mastery of mathematical learning is understood. Mastery of number concepts and problem solving needs to be assessed as well as learning about their reasoning, manner of learning (e.g., abstract or concrete), and ability to use knowledge about numbers in various real-life contexts.

Along with assessment of students' mastery of number concepts and mathematical reasoning, mastery of the forms of calculation or number manipulation they have been taught in school need to be evaluated. Assessment of calculation is ordinarily carried out with pencil-and-paper tests, but for learning disabled children with written language difficulties (e.g., reading or handwriting) assessment should also include oral presentations and responses or problems based on pictures or objects (Cawley, 1985). Care must be taken to determine whether students understand the purpose or meaning of the calculations they are performing. Some learning disabled students learn mathematical operations by mastery of steps in a procedure with a fixed order; errors appear when the problem is presented in a different format or when the test is made up of a variety of problem types. Error analysis might be undertaken, but the examiner is cautioned to make sure there are enough problems of each type to allow for such analysis. Error analysis must be based on observation of a *pattern* of difficulties (i.e., repetition of the error on a number of similar problems) (Ashlock, 1982). For the purpose of understanding why students make specific types of errors, criterion-referenced tests, informal inventories, or diagnostic teaching could be used (Reisman, 1978; Underhill, Uprichard, & Heddens, 1980; Zigmond & Miller, 1986).

An additional concern is the automaticity with which the student carries out mathematical calculations. Both speed and accuracy play a role in eventual success in mathematics. Some learning disabled students are as competent as their nondisabled peers at mathematical reasoning but cannot translate this superiority into successful performance in calculating and applying mathematical principles (Steeves, 1983). These may include the students who cannot remember their multiplication tables even after years of drill and the students whose handwriting leads to errors in graphic representation and alignment of rows and columns. Lack of automaticity may result in particularly poor performance on standardized tests where time is a factor the student must contend with. Rapid recall of number facts and automaticity of basic whole-number operations can be assessed informally with timed drills or even oral recitations.

The examiners' work is not done when they have assessed what students know or do not know about mathematics. Examiners also need to determine *how* students learn mathematical concepts. Researchers interested in mathematical learning feel that difficulties learning mathematics may be aggravated by a mismatch of the teacher's method of presentation and the child's developmental ability to learn (Bruner, 1966; Cawley, 1985; Underhill, 1981). Thus, abstract, symbolic, oral explanations would be inappropriate for a student who needs to handle objects or see pictorial representations in order to learn mathematical concepts. For this reason the mode of presentation and response by which students learn mathematics successfully should be determined. Published tests are not adequate to determine how the student learns mathematics; diagnostic teaching or informal testing is required. The examiner might also gather useful information by observing him or her in mathematics class and by interviewing the teacher.

SUMMARY

Middle school–age students move from being newcomers to the world of education to being adept at using basic skills. They must learn two symbol systems (the alphabet and mathematic notation). Ordinarily students become fluent users of numbers and letters for the purposes of reading, writing, calculating, and solving problems of all sorts. Automaticity is a key to continued progress beyond the first few years of school: Rapid and accurate word recognition, spelling, and calculation facilitate the development of mathematic problem solving, comprehension in reading, and written expression. Areas in which the learning disabled student has not achieved fluency must be explored fully.

Middle school–age children ordinarily become experts in the business of going to school. The rituals and routines of the school day and the close relationships with peers and adults provide a structure for their learning. When learning disabled students have trouble mastering routines and learning social interactions, the reasons for the difficulties should be investigated. The source of the problem may be learning of social skills, but it may also involve other nonverbal areas. For example, adjustment problems result from poorly developed concepts of time and space or difficulties following oral directions. An interview can elicit some of this information. In addition, the examiner should observe the student's left-right orientation, ability to find his or her way around the school, and ability to follow routine oral instructions. Because school adjustment is important, the evaluation of the learning disabled student's social and cognitive development may offer insight into attitudes and motivation, as well as daily performance in academic areas.

ADOLESCENCE

In the adolescent years, questions of chronic learning problems, the severity of academic deficits, and the pervasiveness of the learning problems are particularly important to address but are also decidedly difficult to answer. One reason is that learning disabled adolescents' school experiences are usually quite fragmented. Typically, they study some subjects in regular classes and receive remediation or supportive instruction for other subjects in special education classes. Their teachers may see them for only an hour a day and during this time may or may not be involved in adjusting the materials or method of learning for them. The learning disabled students and those who set out to assess them have equal difficulty in coping with the fragmentation.

Despite the complexities of assessing present skills, an effort must be made to determine how learning disabled students have progressed from their earlier years in elementary and middle school. Examiners need to know not only what they have learned but how they have compensated for their difficulties. The variability of individual students' responses to their disabilities is extreme. One student with a severe disability in spelling, diagnosed in perhaps the third grade, may have developed an extreme dislike for writing. Another student with a comparable disability in spelling may have learned to use a word processor with a "spell check" program, may have been encouraged to write despite spelling errors, and so may have a more positive attitude toward writing assignments.

Examiners must also be aware that the manifestation of a learning disability may change over the years. A student diagnosed as having a deficit in word-recognition skills in the second grade may be diagnosed as having a reading comprehension problem in the seventh grade. A student described as hyperactive in second grade may be described as socially maladjusted as an adolescent (Epstein, Cullinan, & Lloyd, 1980). In most cases where assessment for potential learning disability is requested in high school, scrutiny of the student's record will yield indications of previous difficulties and probably some sort of educational effort to correct them. Often chronicity is an important factor in the diagnosis. Rarely is a learning disability manifested only during adolescence or adulthood. Where a student apparently has no history of difficulties of any kind, the examiner would be wise to take a careful look at environmental factors, including the difficulty of the courses and the stability of the family life. The student's physical and psychological well-being should also be checked.

Students with a long history of remediation for learning disabilities may in adolescence wish to be free of the burden of a special program. It is also common at the high school level to find school personnel recommending regular education classes at a low level of proficiency or within a vocational program for students who had previously received special educational services. Several factors might be considered where these issues are part of the referral problem. First, some learning disabled students are more able to cope with education in the mainstream than others (Zigmond, Levin, & Laurie, 1985). Evaluation of personality and of behavioral adjustment provides a way to predict the success of placement in the mainstream. Second, it is important to consider whether remedial instruction in the past has equipped them with skills that will allow them to do their work successfully in mainstream classes. Such a decision must involve a careful comparison of what the student knows and what the curriculum demands. Third, as is discussed in other parts of this section, the vocational and educational goals of learning disabled students and their families must be considered. Too often the purpose or outcome of educational training is not dealt with, and the transition from school to work is a rough one (Okolo & Sitlington, 1986).

SOCIAL AND COGNITIVE DEVELOPMENT

The assessment of 15-year-olds differs from that of 10-year-olds, not just because of the nature of their academic difficulties but also because of vast differences in social and cognitive growth. The assessment of learning disabled adolescents should take into consideration their view of themselves, their relationships with their peers and adults, their interests, ambitions, and plans for the future, and their levels of cognitive development. In addition, we might benefit from looking at adolescents' choice of and performance in extracurricular activities. Where learning disabled adolescents' self-esteem is strong and healthy, they may rely on their ability to excel in nonacademic areas (such as sports or the arts) for self-recognition (Winne, Woodlands, & Wong, 1982).

Adolescents' performance, motivation, and attitudes are colored by their experiences in and out of school. They not only have gathered personal experience dealing with the world at large but also have increasingly become able to understand people, events, and experiences never encountered firsthand. They compare themselves to peers on a more abstract plane than middle school–age students, who tend to reflect on physical traits and observable activities. Adolescents' view of the world has a different time frame as well. They may look toward the future with more anticipation and anxiety and with less idealism than middle-school students. They are beginning to think about supporting themselves financially and choosing a career that reflects not just vague ambitions and dreams but a view of their actual capabilities and opportunities.

In both physical and psychological terms, adolescents typically want to be independent and to assert their individuality (Erikson, 1968). They may no longer take their parents' advice about how and when to study or even what courses to take. Furthermore, the search for identity and autonomy may affect attitudes toward course selection. For example, adolescent girls are less apt to choose to study math and science. Because learning disabled adolescents need to understand themselves in order to make decisions about their own lives, the assessment process can be used to help them learn about themselves. Soliciting their help and sharing test results may make the assessment a personally valuable experience.

Because social and personal problems are so prevalent in adolescence, it is particularly important to determine the extent to which academic difficulties are related to adjustment and behavior problems and the degree to which students' problems have changed over the year (Pihl & McLarnon, 1984). Learning disabled adolescents may be more dependent on adults than their peers and less sure of themselves when asked to work independently. They may also refuse to study or complete assignments because of frustration with their own lack of success or because of a desire to be accepted by their peers. At the high school level it is sometimes quite difficult to tell which is the primary underlying cause of failure in school—behavior problems or learning problems. In some cases, difficulties seem to stem from deficits in social perception or nonverbal reasoning (Bryan, 1986); in other cases, inappropriate behavior in school settings may be indicative of a conduct disorder (Gresham, 1985).

Particularly useful methods of assessment are interviews with parents and teachers and with the adolescent. In addition, behavior rating scales and check lists that reveal attitudes and motivations may give insight into social and personal factors. The older the student, the more difficult it may be to carry out valid observations in the classroom, but where possible, observations may provide insight into the validity of the interviews and questionnaires or behavioral check lists (Schumaker & Hazel, 1984). Because of the complexities of adolescent relationships, an evaluation by a social worker, guidance counselor, or clinical psychologist might be needed in order to understand certain types of school-related problems.

As in the social domain, the cognitive development of learning disabled adolescents needs to be examined thoughtfully. Successful academic work in high school may depend on the level of cognitive development. Students need to be able to plan their time, to use effective strategies given different sorts of learning tasks, and to monitor and evaluate how their own work affects their academic performance. The kind of work they are asked to do becomes more diverse. Course content contains highly abstract information and is presented almost exclusively in an expository manner through lecture or reading. Evaluators need to consider the extent to which adolescents' cognitive development is such that they can cope with high school learning requirements successfully.

Adolescents' ability to reason about abstract issues or events outside of their experience is considered the hallmark of the stage of formal operations in piagetian terms. Researchers have demonstrated that many adolescents and a large number of adults do not attain formal operations, at least as measured by classic piagetian tasks (Gardner, 1982; Stone, 1980). Educational background makes a difference. Students whose schooling has included encounters with scientific reasoning and procedures perform such tasks (and so demonstrate formal operations) more successfully than students whose school experiences do not include training in science. Since both adolescents and adults reason best in areas in which they have had previous experience, assessment of cognitive development should be accomplished not only with standardized tests, whose content may be unfamiliar, but also with tasks and information that are clearly part of the student's experience.

Researchers have isolated certain characteristics of adolescents' reasoning as distinct from that of younger children. These include a cluster of metacognitive abilities, the most important of which are the ability to plan and reason systematically, to manipulate and control for multiple variables in a problem, to select effective methods of problem solving, and to understand abstract ideas. Learning disabled adolescents may have difficulty learning to monitor their own reasoning (Wong, 1987). In part, their difficulties may be attributable to the level of their language development (Stone, 1980). For example, understanding of conditional reasoning (e.g., "if—then") and of delimiters of times and space (e.g., "usually" or "seldom") is often necessary to grasp the nature of the problem or explain the solution.

Collectively, research on adolescent cognitive development and on problems experienced by learning disabled adolescents suggests that strategies of reasoning, planning abilities, and problem attack should be assessed. No standardized tests can effectively measure such components of cognitive development. Observations of the student while taking standardized tests provide some insight into cognitive growth. In addition, tasks such as the "bending rods" (Stone, 1980) or "twenty questions" (Siegler, 1977) might be used to measure problem-solving strategies as directly as possible.

LANGUAGE DEVELOPMENT

Ordinarily, difficulties with language development have been diagnosed and remediated long before adolescence. However, students' progress in mastering language skills should be monitored. Language learning disabled adolescents have been found to have poorer immediate recall of semantically and syntactically varied sentences than their peers (Wiig & Semel, 1975a). Similarly, their language production differs significantly from that of their peers in some important aspects, including word-finding abilities, length of phrases, and the grammatical forms of their expressions (Wiig & Semel, 1975b).

Research has suggested another perspective on adolescent language development: The mastery of higher levels of language may reflect the learning of strategies more than the learning of basic skills (Wiig, 1984). Deficiencies are in keeping with the view of learning disabled students as inactive and inefficient in their use of strategies (Torgesen & Licht, 1983). Inefficient language-processing strategies affect learning disabled adolescents' appreciation of metaphor, the understanding of multiple meanings of words or ambiguous sentences, and the use of socially acceptable expressions (Wiig, Semel, & Abele, 1981).

A different issue that affects a large segment of the adolescent population is whether their language skills are sufficiently developed so that they can be successful studying a second language. While standardized tests are available to provide guidance in making this decision (Gajar, 1987), an informal inventory of language and study skills is advisable. Learning disabled students' ability to devise effective learning strategies may make a difference in learning vocabulary and verb forms, for example. Their ability to understand abstract grammatical terminology and the flexibility with which they can manipulate the ideas and grammatical structures in sentences will affect their mastery of the structure of the language. Whether or not they have a good "ear" for language should help students decide which language to study. Latin places fewer demands on the students' mastery of phonology than French, for example.

READING SKILLS

Screening of adolescents' reading skills is apt to focus on their understanding of grade-level texts and to ignore other components of reading skills, such as accuracy and speed of word recognition and fluency of reading. This approach appears to be related to the belief that secondary school is too late for remediation of basic skills (e.g., "If they haven't learned phonics by now, they won't ever learn it"). This attitude is based on invalid and unproductive assumptions (Lewkowicz, 1987). A full evaluation of the components of reading skill should be carried out for any student who has been referred for difficulties in reading, much as it would be for a younger student. Theories of acquisition of reading skills and empirical research indicate that basic processes must be able to proceed with some degree of automaticity to facilitate comprehension of the text (Stanovich, 1986). Thus, if word recognition skills are poorly developed, no amount of training on comprehension (e.g., making inferences or finding main ideas) will make the student a successful reader (Perfetti & Roth, 1981). As for the "it's too late" attitude, the student's educational history should be investigated to determine what types of training worked or did not work to date.

Two areas of assessment of reading skills are specifically important for students who have reasonably well developed basic reading skills but who have difficulty doing their course reading. One is assessment of reading in different types of text structures in different content areas (Englert & Thomas, 1987; Richgels, McGee, Lomax, & Sheard, 1987). Several factors should be examined: vocabulary development, appropriateness of background information, and understanding of text structures. Students understand their texts more readily and fully if they have prior knowledge about the topic and about the text structures or forms of exposition used in that content area (Spiro, 1980). Assessment of reading in content areas can be carried out by informal tests made from the students' textbooks (Darch & Carnine, 1986). Another approach is the development of curriculum-based assessment instruments (Blankenship, 1985). Certainly standardized tests cannot be used to evaluate a student's ability to understand the material read for specific courses.

The second area is students' reading strategies, now often called "metacognitive strategies" (Baker & Brown, 1984). Poor readers are characterized as nonstrategic readers or as users of ineffective and immature reading strategies. They tend to read at the same speed, regardless of the purpose of reading; they make little use of visual aids on the page; and they have few methods for coping with breakdowns in their own comprehension processes. For these reasons, it is important to determine not only what strategies adolescents *can* use but also what they *do* use when left to their own devices.

Because learning from reading (as opposed to learning to read) is such an important part of junior and senior high school course work, many instructional programs focus on providing strategies or study skills that can be used in different content areas (Darch & Kameenui, 1987). Unfortunately, such methods do not always bring about lasting improvements in students' comprehension (Zirkelbach, 1985). One reason may be that students do not use the techniques on their own (Baker & Brown, 1984). Another reason may be that even well-learned study techniques cannot compensate adequately for deficiencies in word recognition and word knowledge. Although evaluation of the students' metacognitive strategies or study skills in reading is difficult to carry out, one method is to observe students as they tackle different reading tasks set up for the purpose of the evaluation. A second method is to use a "talk-aloud" procedure, asking students to talk their way through a reading assignment, telling what they are thinking and how they are coping with difficulties with the text.

In assessing adolescents whose reading skills are at a very low level, the pressing concerns are whether they are functionally literate and how best to equip them with the kinds of reading skills they will need to lead as safe and independent adult lives as possible. Where a severe reading disability suggests a relatively poor prognosis for acquiring normal adult reading proficiency, a careful survey must be made of the situations in which reading skills will be required of the individual. These might include reading of road signs, directions, recipes, bus and train schedules, and packaging labels. One approach is to compile a list that reflects the student's environment and goals for later life. Informal tests can be devised on the basis of this list; the student's performance can be used to determine instructional objectives.

SKILLS OF WRITTEN EXPRESSION

By high school, adolescents have become accustomed to completing regular writing assignments for their courses. Their writing is often at least as coherent and sophisticated in vocabulary and structure as their speech. For many learning disabled adolescents, however, writing assignments are the most stressful of all their academic requirements, and skill in written expression is acquired slowly (Bain, 1976). The first step of a diagnostic assessment should be to determine the extent to which difficulties in writing are related to difficulties in oral language usage. It is important to know whether the adolescents speak and write at approximately the same level of proficiency. Where the students' spoken language is significantly better than their written language, further exploration should specify the areas of deficit. Fluency and legibility of handwriting are important to observe. Sometimes awkwardness of handwriting, poor spelling, and embarrassment keep the student's productivity in writing very low. A sentence or two is all that many will put on paper. On the sentence level, components that should be considered are formulation and mechanics. On the text level, the full writing sample should be examined on the basis of productivity and articulateness. Learning disabled adolescents may have difficulties with the organization and expansion of their ideas, and since they are not good at evaluating their own writing, they do not notice incompletely explained ideas or ambiguities (Ganschow, 1984).

Diagnostic teaching might help determine ways of compensating for writing difficulties. One possible measure would be exploring the effectiveness of using a word processor for writing (Morocco & Neuman, 1986). Another approach would be to have students dictate a composition or test essay to the examiner. If the product is superior to their previous compositions, this approach could be used to facilitate academic work, at least on a temporary basis. It may be important to help students learn that limitations in writing need not hold them back from acquiring knowledge in content areas or demonstrating mastery of such knowledge.

Where learning disabled students' written expression is seriously deficient, care should be taken to assess their ability to carry out writing tasks that will be necessary for an independent adult life. These might include writing checks, writing letters, and filling out forms that require personal information. As with reading, a list of situations in which adults are required to write should be used to develop an informal test, which in turn can be used to determine the educational objectives appropriate for each student.

MATHEMATICAL SKILLS AND KNOWLEDGE

As in writing, learning disabled adolescents may present uneven profiles in their acquisition of mathematical skills and knowledge. The complexities of the psychological factors that cause disabilities in mathematical learning suggest the need for a complete psychoeducational assessment to determine the underlying causes of the disability (Kosc, 1981; Sharma, 1985b). The language factors so prevalent in learning mathematics may have an adverse effect on some students' acquisition of mathematical concepts and problem-solving abilities (Aiken, 1972; Ansara, 1973). Others may have relatively little difficulty with mathematical language and reasoning but extreme difficulty remembering sequential steps (as in long division) or number facts. Still others may have deficits in visual or spatial processing.

Attitudes toward mathematical learning are apt to become increasingly negative with prolonged failure, and frustration leads to an unwillingness to try. Perhaps because most mathematical problems are designed to yield only one right answer, actual or self-perceived failure can result in an unwillingness to complete homework assignments or take tests or a dislike for all courses in mathematics (McEntire, 1981).

In addition, understanding of the underlying deficits in mathematical learning is important for selecting effective and appropriate methods of instruction and courses (Shaw, 1985). For example, a student with spatial processing deficits but intact language skills may do better in algebra than in geometry. Students whose mastery of basic number concepts is seriously deficient should be assessed using an informal inventory of math survival skills (Sharma, 1985a). In addition, their educational records should be checked to determine what they have been taught and how much they have learned over the past few years. Mathematics skills that should be checked cover a wide range of skills including the use of a calculator, the ability to make change, the ability to check a bill or receipt, and the ability to read a map or a bank statement. Some effort should be made to survey the individual's personal needs and vocational goals in order to design an appropriate educational plan.

SUMMARY

One particular theme runs through our discussion of learning disabled adolescents: the tremendous variability in the range of skill deficits, both within one learning disabled adolescent and among adolescents. At the secondary school level, referral questions commonly range from how to adapt a college-preparatory curriculum for learning disabled students (Greenwood, 1983) to whether progress has been made in learning basic word-decoding skills. Certainly, when deficits are substantial, the focus must be on the practical outcome of education for the individual. Assessment can provide information that is helpful in making educational and vocational decisions. The problems that cause most learning disabilities in school ordinarily do not disappear just because students have completed their formal education.

A second part of this recurring theme is the variability within each learning disabled adolescent. Discrete strengths and weaknesses in learning may be particularly noticeable at this level. Students may be adequate storytellers but poor spellers, adequate at work recognition but deficient in reading strategies, and so on. An effort should be made to help the students appreciate their strengths, as well as to understand their deficits in learning. As was discussed earlier, adolescents are trying to figure out who they are and how they can function effectively in life. In most situations, the results of the full assessment should be shared with them so that they can participate in making decisions that affect their passage into adulthood.

CONCLUSION

The description of the learning disabled student at the three broad stages of his or her academic career reveals the complex factors in determining the manifestations of a disability, the pervasiveness of a disability, and the prognosis for successful remediation in academic and personal areas. As said at the outset, learning is certainly an interactive process; in the case of learning disabled individuals, the intrinsic factors, attributed to underlying psychological processes, evidence themselves in certain ways, depending on the environment in which the children grow up and are educated. Likewise, it has been stressed that as children grow and change, so might the manifestations of their disabilities change.

In general, the more pervasive the problem and the more severe the symptoms when the children are very young, the more likely it is that the individuals will experience significant learning problems throughout their lives. It is not true that every learning disability can be cured, using the medical terminology. However, at the other end of the continuum, particularly bright individuals with specific deficits (e.g., the specifically disabled speller) can often be given adequate remediation or be taught effective methods of compensation so that the impact of the disability on their educational achievement and life-style is relatively mild.

Distinguishing different types of learning disabilities may, in fact, be as challenging as distinguishing the learning disabled from the slow learner. Both types of distinctions require a thorough assessment that takes into consideration intelligence, social and cognitive growth, physical and health-related factors, sensory integrities, and academic abilities. Standardized tests must of course be used but should be amply supplemented with methods of assessment that are designed to determine how well children are functioning in their classrooms, given the level of development of their peers, the expectations of their teachers, and the difficulties of the learning materials and lessons they are asked to master. Where necessary, experts from other disciplines should be used to provide insight into children's learning difficulties. As asserted early in this chapter, assessment of learning disabled students is a problem-solving process that calls on the examiners to use sensitivity to the individual and a full understanding of the problems that constitute learning disabilities.

REFERENCES

Adelman, H. S., & Taylor, L. (1986). The problems of definition and differentiation and the need for a classification schema. *Journal of Learning Disabilities, 19*(9), 514–520.
Aiken, L. R. (1972). Language factors in learning mathematics. *Review of Educational Research, 42,* 359–385.
Algozzine, B. & Ysseldyke, J. E. (1986). The future of the LD field: Screening and diagnosis. *Journal of Learning Disabilities, 19*(7), 394–398.
Anderson, R. C., & Freebody, P. (1985). Vocabulary knowledge. In H. Singer & R. B. Ruddell (Eds.), *Theoretical models and processes of reading* (3rd ed.). Newark, DE: International Reading Association.
Ansara, A. (1973). The language therapist as a basic mathematics tutor for adolescents. *Bulletin of the Orton Society, 23,* 119–139.
Applebee, A. (1978). *The child's concept of story.* Chicago: University of Chicago Press.

Ashlock, R. (1982). *Error patterns in computation* (3rd ed.). Columbus, OH: Merrill.
Athey, I. (1977). Syntax, semantics, and reading. In J. T. Guthrie (Ed.), *Cognition, curriculum, and comprehension.* Newark, DE: International Reading Association.
Ausubel, D., & Sullivan, E. (1970). *Theory and problems of child development* (2nd ed.). New York: Grune & Stratton.
Bain, A. M. (1976). Written expression: The last skill acquired. *Bulletin of the Orton Society, 22,* 79–95.
Baker, L., & Brown, A. L. (1984). Metacognitive skills and reading. In P. D. Pearson (Ed.). *Handbook of reading research.* NY: Longman.
Birch, H., & Belmont, L. (1965). Auditory-visual integration, intelligence and reading ability in school children. *Perceptual and Motor Skills, 20,* 295–305.
Blalock, J. W. (1977). *A study of conceptualization and related abilities in learning disabled and normal preschool children.* Unpublished doctoral dissertation, Northwestern University.
Blankenship, C. S. (1985). Using curriculum-based assessment data to make instructional decisions. *Exceptional Children, 52*(3), 233–238.
Boder, E. (1971). Developmental dyslexia: Prevailing diagnostic concepts and a new diagnostic approach. In H. R. Myklebust (Ed.), *Progress in learning disabilities* (Vol 2). New York: Grune & Stratton.
Bradley, L., & Bryant, P. (1985). Rhyme and reason in reading and spelling. *International Academy for Research in Learning Disabilities. Monograph Series. No. 1.* Ann Arbor: The University of Michigan Press.
Breen, J. J. (1986). Cognitive patterns of learning disability subtypes as measured by the Woodcock-Johnson Psychoeducational Battery. *Journal of Learning Disabilities, 19*(2), 86–90.
Bruner, J. S. (1966). *Toward a theory of instruction.* New York: Norton.
Bryan, T. (1986). Personality and situational factors in learning disabilities. In G. T. Pavlidis and D. F. Fisher (Eds.). *Dyslexia: Its neuropsychology and treatment.* New York: Wiley.
Bryant, P., & Bradley, M. (1980). Why children sometimes write words which they do not read. In U. Frith (Ed.), *Cognitive processes in spelling.* New York: Academic.
Burrows, A. T., Jackson, D. C., & Saunders, D. O. (1984). *They all want to write* (4th ed.). Hamden, CT: Library Professional.
Cable, B. A. (1981). *A study of play behavior in learning disabled and normal preschool boys.* Unpublished doctoral dissertation, Northwestern University.
Calfee, R., Spector, J., & Piontkowski, D. (1979). Assessing reading and language skills: An interactive system. *Bulletin of the Orton Society, 29,* 129–156.
Carlisle, J. F. (1983). Components of training in reading comprehension for middle school students. *Annals of Dyslexia, 33,* 187–202.
Carlisle, J. F. (1987). The use of morphological knowledge in spelling derived forms by learning disabled and normal students. *Annals of Dyslexia, 37,* 90–108.
Cawley, J. F. (Ed.) (1985). Learning disability and mathematics appraisal. In J. F. Cawley (Ed.), *Practical mathematics appraisal of the learning disabled.* Rockville, MD: Aspen.
Chall, J. S. (1983). *Stages of reading development.* New York: McGraw-Hill.
Cicci, R. L. (1978). *A study of pretended use of objects and graphic-pictorial representation in language impaired and normal preschool children.* Unpublished doctoral dissertation, Northwestern University.
Clay, M. (1975). *What did I write? Beginning reading behavior.* Portsmouth, NH: Heinemann.
Cohen, J. (1986). Learning disabilities and psychological development in childhood and adolescence. *Annals of Dyslexia, 36,* 287–300.
Crais, E. R., & Chapman, R. S. (1987). Story recall and inferencing skills in language/learning-disabled and nondisabled children. *Journal of Speech and Hearing Disorders, 52,* 50–55.
Darch, C., & Carnine, D. (1986). Teaching content area material to learning disabled students. *Exceptional Children, 53*(2), 240–246.

Darch, C., & Kameenui, E. J. (1987). Teaching LD students critical reading skills: A systematic replication. *Learning Disability Quarterly, 10*(2), 82–92.
deHirsch, K. (1984). *Language and the developing child.* Baltimore: Orton Dyslexia Society.
Denhoff, E., Hainsworth, P., & Hainsworth, M. (1971). Learning disabilities and early childhood education: An information processing approach. In H. Myklebust (Ed.). *Progress in learning disabilities (Vol. 2).* New York: Grune & Stratton.
Derr, A. M. (1985). Conservation and mathematics achievement in the LD child. *Journal of Learning Disabilities, 18*(6), 333–336.
Dobson, L. N. (1985). Learn to read by writing: A practical program for reluctant readers. *Teaching Exceptional Children, 18*(1), 30–37.
Downing, J. (1979). *Reading and reasoning.* New York: Springer-Verlag.
Durkin, D. (1966). *Children who read early.* New York: Teachers College Press.
Ehri, L. (1984). How orthography alters spoken language competencies in children learning to read and spell. In J. Downing & R. Valtin (Eds.), *Language awareness and learning to read.* New York: Springer-Verlag.
Elliott, L. L., & Busse, L. A. (1987). Auditory processing by learning disabled young adults. In D. J. Johnson and J. W. Blalock (Eds.). *Adults with learning disabilities: Clinical studies.* New York: Grune & Stratton.
Elliott, L. L., & Hammer, M. A. (1987). *Fine-grained auditory discrimination in normal children and children with language-learning problems.* Unpublished paper, Northwestern University.
Englert, C. S., & Thomas, C. C. (1987). Sensitivity to test structure in reading and writing: A comparison between learning disabled and non-learning disabled students. *Learning Disability Quarterly, 10*(2), 106–111.
Epstein, M. H. Cullinan, D., & Lloyd, J. W. (1986). Behavior-problem patterns among the learning disabled: III—Replication across age and sex. *Learning Disability Quarterly, 9,* 43–54.
Erikson, E. H. (1968). *Identity: Youth and crisis.* New York: Norton.
Ferreiro, E., & Teberosky, A. (1979). *Literacy before schooling.* Portsmouth, NH: Heinemann.
Fox, B., & Routh, D. K. (1980). Phonemic analysis and severe reading disability in children. *Journal of Psycholinguistic Research, 9,* 115–119.
Frankenburg, W., & Dodds, J. (1968). *Denver Developmental Screening Test.* Denver: Ladoca Project and Publishing Foundation.
Frederiksen, C. H., & Dominic, J. F. (Eds.) (1981). *Writing: The nature, development, and teaching of written communication.* Hillsdale, NJ: Erlbaum.
Friedman, J. (1984). *Classification skills in normally hearing/achieving, oral deaf, and language impaired preschoolers: A study in language and conceptual thought.* Unpublished doctoral dissertation, Northwestern University.
Frith, U. (1980). *Cognitive processes in spelling.* New York: Academic.
Gajar, A. H. (1987). Foreign language learning disabilities: The identification of predictive and diagnostic variables. *Journal of Learning Disabilities, 20*(6), 327–330.
Gallagher, J. McC., & Reid, D. K. (1981). *The learning theory of Piaget and Inhelder.* Austin, TX: Pro-Ed.
Ganschow, L. (1984). Analysis of written language of a language learning disabled (dyslexic) college student and instructional implications. *Annals of Dyslexia, 34,* 271–284.
Gardner, H. (1982). *Developmental psychology* (2nd ed.). Boston: Little, Brown.
Garnett, K., & Fleischner, J. (1987). Mathematics disabilities. *Pediatric Annals, 16,* 159–176.
Garvey, C. (1977). *Play.* Cambridge, MA: Harvard University Press.
Gelman, R. (1972). Logical capacity of very young children: Number invariance rules. *Child Development, 43,* 75–90.
Gentry, J. R. (1982). An analysis of developmental spelling in GNYS at WRK. *The Reading Teacher, 36*(2), 192–200.
Gerber, M. M. (1986). Generalization of spelling strategies by LD students as a result of

contingent imitation/modeling and mastery criteria. *Journal of Learning Disabilities, 19*(9), 530–537.
Gesell, A., & Lehtinen, L. (1947). *Psychopathology of the brain-injured child*. New York: Grune & Stratton.
Gillam, R. B., & Johnston, J. R. (1985). Development of print awareness in language-disordered preschoolers. *Journal of Speech and Hearing Research, 28*, 521–526.
Ginsburg, H., & Baroody, A. (1983). *The test of early mathematics ability*. Austin, TX: Pro-Ed.
Giordano, G. (1984). Analyzing and remediating writing disabilities. *Journal of Learning Disabilities, 17*(2), 78–83.
Graves, D. H. (1983). *Writing: Teachers and children at work*. Portsmouth, NH: Heinemann.
Greenfield, P. (1984). *Mind and media*. Cambridge, MA: Harvard University Press.
Greenwood, J. A. (1983). Adapting a college preparatory curriculum for dyslexic adolescents: The rationale. *Annals of Dyslexia, 33*, 235–242.
Gresham, F. (1985). Behavior disorder assessment: Conceptual, definitional, and practical considerations. *School Psychology Review, 14*(4), 495–509.
Gresham, F. M., & Reschly, D. J. (1986). Social skills deficits and low peer acceptance of mainstreamed learning disabled children. *Learning Disability Quarterly, 9*, 23–32.
Groshong, C. (1980). *Ambiguity detection and the use of verbal context for disambiguation of language disabled and normal learning children*. Unpublished doctoral dissertation, Northwestern University.
Halliday, M., & Hassan, R. (1976). *Cohesion in English*. London: Longman.
Hanna, P. R., Hodges, R. E., & Hanna, J. S. (1971). *Spelling: Structure and strategies*. Boston: Houghton Mifflin.
Inglis, J., & Lawson, J. S. (1986). A principal components analysis of the Kaufman Battery for Children (K-ABC): Implications for the test results of children with learning disabilities. *Journal of Learning Disabilities, 19*(2), 80–85.
James, K. (1972). *A study of the conceptual structure of measurement of length in normal and learning disabled children*. Unpublished doctoral dissertation, Northwestern University.
Jansky, J. (1975). The marginally ready child. *Bulletin of the Orton Society, 25*, 69–85.
Jansky, J., & deHirsch, K. (1972). *Preventing reading failure*. New York: Harper & Row.
Johnson, D. (1987). Nonverbal learning disabilities. *Pediatric Annals, 16*, 133–144.
Johnson, D. J. (1987). Principles of assessment and diagnosis. In D. J. Johnson & J. W. Blalock (Eds.), *Adults with learning disabilities: Clinical studies*. New York: Grune & Stratton.
Johnson, D. J. (1985). Using reading and writing to improve oral language skills. *Topics in Language Disorders, 5*, 55–69.
Johnson, D. J., & Blalock, J. W. (1982). Problems of mathematics in children with language disorders. In N. J. Lass, L. V. McReynolds, J. L. Northern, & D. E. Yoder (Eds.), *Speech, language, and hearing* (Vol. 2). Philadelphia: Saunders.
Kamii, C. (1971). Evaluation of learning in preschool education: Socioemotional, perceptual-motor, cognitive development. In B. Bloom, J. Hastings, & G. Madaus (Eds.), *Handbook on formative and summative evaluation of student learning*. New York: McGraw-Hill.
Kavale, K. H., & Forness, S. R. (1985). Learning disability and the history of science: Paradigm or paradox. *Remedial and Special Education, 6*, 12–23.
Keogh, B. K. (1986). Future of the LD field: Research and practice. *Journal of Learning Disabilities, 19*(8), 455–460.
Kosc, L. (1981). Neuropsychological implications of diagnosis and treatment of mathematical learning disabilities. *Topics in Learning and Learning Disabilities, 1*, 19–29.
Larson, R. (1975). *Children and writing in the elementary school*. New York: Oxford University Press.
Lavatelli, C. (1970). *Piaget's theory applied to an early childhood curriculum*. Boston: Center for Media Development.

Lewis, R., Strauss, A., & Lehtinen, L. (1960). *The other child*. New York: Grune & Stratton.
Lewkowicz, N. K. (1987). On the question of teaching decoding skills to older students. *Journal of Reading, 31*(1), 50–57.
Liberman, I. Y., Shankweiler, D., Fischer, F. W., & Carter, B. (1974). Explicit syllable and phoneme segmentation in the young child. *Journal of Experimental Child Psychology, 18,* 201–212.
Litowitz, B. (1981). Developmental issues in written language. *Topics in Language Disorders, 1,* 73–89.
Loban, W. (1976). *Language development: Kindergarten through grade twelve* (pp. 81–84). Urbana, IL: National Council of Teachers of English.
McCune-Nicolich, L., & Carroll, S. (1981). Development of symbolic play: Implications for the language specialist. *Topics in Language Disorders, 2,* 1–15.
McEntire, E. (1981). Learning disabilities and mathematics. *Topics in Learning and Learning Disabilities, 3,* 1–18.
Menyuk, P. (1978). Linguistic problems in children with developmental dysphasia. In M. Wyke (Ed.), *Developmental dysphasia*. New York: Academic.
Moats, L. C. (1983). A comparison of spelling errors of older dyslexic and second-grade normal children. *Annals of Dyslexia, 33,* 121–140.
Morocco, C. C., & Neuman, S. B. (1986). Word processors and the acquisition of writing strategies. *Journal of Learning Disabilities, 19*(4), 243–247.
Moulton, J. R., & Bader, M. S. (1985). The writing process: A powerful approach for the language-disabled students. *Annals of Dyslexia, 35,* 161–173.
Myklebust, H. (1965). *Development and disorders of written language* (Vol. 1). New York: Grune & Stratton.
Myklebust, H. R., & Boshes, B. (1969). *Minimal brain damage in children*. Final Report. Bethesda, MD: Department of Health, Education, and Welfare.
Oka, E., & Scholl, G. T. (1985). Non-test-based approaches to assessment. In G. T. Scholl (Ed.), *The school psychologist and the exceptional child*. Reston, VA: Council for Exceptional Children.
Okolo, C. M., & Sitlington, P. (1986). The role of special education in LD adolescents' transition from school to work. *Learning Disability Quarterly, 9*(2), 141–155.
Perfetti, C. A., & Roth, S. (1981). Some of the interactive processes in reading and their role in reading skill. In A. M. Lesgold & C. A. Perfetti, (Eds.), *Interactive processes in reading*. Hillsdale, NJ: Erlbaum.
Piaget, J. (1962). *Play, dreams and imitation*. New York: Norton.
Pihl, R. O., & McLarnon, L. D. (1984). Learning disabled children as adolescents. *Journal of Learning Disabilities, 17*(2), 96–100.
Podhajski, B. (1980). *Picture arrangement and selected narrative language skills in learning disabled and normal seven year old children*. Unpublished doctoral dissertation, Northwestern University.
Read, C. (1986). *Children's creative spelling*. London: Routledge & Kegan Paul.
Read, C. (1983). Orthography. In M. Martlew (Ed.), *The psychology of written language* (pp. 143–162). Chichester, England: Wiley.
Reid, D., Hresko, W., & Hammill, D. (1981). *The test of early reading ability*. Austin, TX: Pro-Ed.
Reisman, F. K. (1978). *A guide to the diagnostic teaching of arithmetic* (2nd ed.). Columbus, OH: Merrill.
Rice, M. L. (1983). Contemporary accounts of the cognition/language relationship: Implications for speech-language clinicians. *Journal of Speech and Hearing Disorders, 48,* 347–359.
Richgels, D. J., McGee, L., Lomax, R. G., & Sheard, C. (1987). Awareness of four text structures: Effects on recall of expository text. *Reading Research Quarterly, 22*(2), 177–196.
Rose, S. A., & Blank, M. (1974). The potency of context in children's cognition: An illustration through conservation. *Child Development, 45,* 499–502.

Rosenshine, B. V. (1980). Skill hierarchies in reading comprehension. In R. J. Spiro, B. L. Bruce, & W. F. Brewer (Eds.), *Theoretical issues in reading comprehension*. Hillsdale, NJ: Erlbaum.

Salvia, J., & Ysseldyke, J. (1988). *Assessment in special and remedial education* (4th ed.). Boston: Houghton Mifflin.

Sameroff, A. (1979). The etiology of cognitive competence: A systems perspective. In R. B. Kearsley & I. E. Sigel (Eds.), *Infants at risk: Assessment of cognitive functioning*. Hillsdale, NJ: Erlbaum.

Savin, H. B. (1972). What the child knows about speed when he starts to learn to read. In J. F. Kavanagh & I. G. Mattingly (Eds.), *Language by ear and by eye*. Cambridge, MA: MIT Press.

Schumaker, J. B., & Hazel, J. S. (1984). Social skills assessment and training for the learning disabled: Who's on first and what's on second? Part I. *Journal of Learning Disabilities, 17*(7), 422–431.

Sharma, M. C. (1985a). Assessment of mathematics in the real world. In J. F. Cawley (Ed.), *Practical mathematics appraisal of the learning disabled*. Rockville, MD: Aspen.

Sharma, M. C. (1985b). Interdisciplinary assessment of mathematical learning disability: Diagnosis in a clinical setting. In J. F. Cawley (Ed.), *Practical mathematics appraisal of the learning disabled*. Rockville, MD: Aspen.

Shaw, R. A. (1985). Assessment techniques and practices in grades 5–12. In J. F. Cawley (Ed.), *Practical mathematics appraisal of the learning disabled*. Rockville, MD: Aspen.

Shepard, L. A., & Smith, M. L. (1983). An evaluation of the identification of learning disabled students in Colorado. *Learning Disability Quarterly, 6,* 115–127.

Siegler, R. S. (1977). The twenty questions game as a form of problem solving. *Child Development, 48,* 395–403.

Snyder, L. (1983). From assessment to intervention: Problems and solution. In J. Miller, D. Yoder, & R. Schiefelbusch (Eds.), *Contemporary issues in language intervention*. Rockland, MD: The American Speech-Language-Hearing Association.

Spiro, R. J. (1980). Constructive processes in prose comprehension and recall. In R. J. Spiro, C. B. Bertram, & W. F. Brewer (Eds.), *Theoretical issues in reading comprehension*. Hillsdale, NJ: Erlbaum.

Stanovich, K. E. (1986). Matthew effects in reading: Some consequences of individual differences in the acquisition of literacy. *Reading Research Quarterly, 21*(4), 360–407.

Steeves, K. J. (1983). Memory as a factor in the computational efficiency of dyslexic children with high abstract reasoning ability. *Annals of Dyslexia, 33,* 141–152.

Sticht, T. G., & James, H. J. (1984). Listening and reading. In P. D. Pearson (Ed.), *Handbook of reading research*. New York: Longman.

Stone, C. A. (1980). Adolescent cognitive development: Implications for learning disabilities. *Bulletin of the Orton Society, 30,* 79–93.

Strauss, A., & Lehtinen, L. (1947). *Psychopathology of the brain-injured child*. New York: Grune & Stratton.

Tallal, P., & Piercy, M. (1978). Defects of auditory perception in children with developmental dysphasia. In M. Wyke (Ed.), *Developmental dysphasia*. New York: Academic.

Taylor, R. L. (1984). *Assessment of exceptional students: Educational and psychological procedures*. Englewood Cliffs, NJ: Prentice-Hall.

Temple, C. A., Nathan, R. B., & Burris, N. A. (1982). *The beginnings of writing*. Boston: Allyn & Bacon.

Thomassen, A., & Teulings, L. H. (1983). The development of handwriting. In M. Martlew (Ed.), *The psychology of written language* (pp. 179–213). Chichester, England: Wiley.

Torgesen, J. K., & Licht, B. G. (1983). The learning disabled child as an inactive learner: Retrospect and prospects. In J. D. McKinney & L. Feagens (Eds.), *Current topics in learning disabilities*. Norwood, NJ: Ablex.

Underhill, B. (1981). *Teaching elementary school mathematics* (3rd ed.). Columbus, OH: Merrill.

Underhill, R. B., Uprichard, A. E., & Heddens, J. W. (1980). *Diagnosing mathematical difficulties*. Columbus, OH: Merrill.
Valus, A. (1986). Achievement potential discrepancy status of students in LD programs. *Learning Disability Quarterly, 9*(3), 200–205.
Vellutino, F. R. (1979). *Dyslexia: Theory and research*. Cambridge, MA: MIT Press.
Wallace, G., & Larsen, S. C. (1978). *Educational assessment of learning problems: Testing for teaching*. Boston: Allyn & Bacon.
Weaver, S. J. (Ed.). (1984). *Testing children: A reference guide for effective clinical and psychoeducational assessments*. Kansas City: Test Corporation of America.
Wechsler, D. (1986). *Wechsler Intelligence Scale for Children-Revised*. New York: Psychological Corporation.
White, S. H. (1970). Some general outlines of the matrix of developmental changes between five and seven years. *Bulletin of the Orton Society, 20*, 41–57.
Wigfield, A., & Asher, S. R. (1984). Social and motivational influences on reading. In P. D. Pearson (Ed.), *Handbook of reading research*. New York: Longman.
Wiig, E. H. (1984). Language disabilities in adolescents: A question of cognitive strategies. *Topics in Language Disorders, 4*, 41–58.
Wiig, E., & Semel, E. (1975a). Immediate recall of semantically varied "sentences" by learning disabled adolescents. *Perceptual and Motor Skills, 40*, 119–125.
Wiig, E., & Semel, E. (1975b). Productive language abilities in learning disabled adolescents. *Journal of Learning Disabilities, 8*(9), 578–586.
Wiig, E. H., Semel, E. M., & Abele, E. (1981). Perception and interpretation of ambiguous sentences by learning disabled twelve-year-olds. *Learning Disability Quarterly, 4*, 3–12.
Wiig, E. H., Semel, E. M., & Crouse, M. A. B. (1973). The use of English morphology by high-risk and learning-disabled children. *Journal of Learning Disabilities, 7*, 59–67.
Williams, J. P. (1984). Phonemic analysis and how it relates to reading. *Journal of Learning Disabilities, 17*(4), 240–245.
Winne, P. H., Woodlands, M. J., & Wong, B. Y. L. (1982). Comparability of self-concept among learning disabled, normal and gifted students. *Journal of Learning Disabilities, 15*(8), 470–45.
Wong, B. Y. L. (1987). How do the results of metacognitive research impact on the learning disabled individual? *Learning Disability Quarterly, 10*, 189–195.
Woodcock, R. W., & Johnson, M. B. (1977). *Woodcock-Johnson Psycho-Educational Battery*. Boston: Teaching Resources Corporation.
Woolf, C. (1983). *Responses to requests for clarification in normal and language disordered children*. Unpublished doctoral dissertation, Northwestern University.
Ysseldyke, J. E., Algozzine, B., Richey, L., & Graden, J. (1982). Declaring students eligible for learning disability services: Why bother with the data? *Learning Disability Quarterly, 5*, 37–44.
Ysseldyke, J. E., Algozzine, B., Shinn, M., & McGue, M. (1982). Similarities and differences among low achievers and students labeled learning disabled. *Journal of Special Education, 16*, 73–85.
Zaporozhets, A., & Elkonin, D. (1971). *The psychology of preschool children*. Cambridge, MA: MIT Press.
Zigmond, N., & Miller, S. E. (1986). Assessment for instructional planning. *Exceptional Children, 52*(6), 501–509.
Zigmond, N., Levin, E., & Laurie, T. E. (1985). Managing the mainstream: An analysis of teacher attitudes and student performance in mainstream high school programs. *Journal of Learning Disabilities, 18*(9), 535–541.
Zigmond, N., Vallecorsa, A., & Silverman, R. (1983). *Assessment for instructional planning in special education*. Englewood Cliffs, NJ: Prentice-Hall.
Zirkelbach, T. (1985). SQ3R: Sometimes it works; Sometimes it doesn't. *Reading Improvement, 22*, 178–181.

CHAPTER 4

Special Considerations in the Development of Models for Diagnosis of Adults with Learning Disabilities

SUSAN A. VOGEL

> Dr. Vogel writes on the third special age population, the adult. After discussing the models for defining an adult as learning disabled, she presents models for diagnosis. Because of the unique issues involved with adults, the issue of eligibility for services takes on special meaning. The criteria for acceptance and for providing services that are used by colleges, other postsecondary programs, and vocational rehabilitation programs differ and must be understood by professionals and other individuals who refer. Each setting is discussed in detail.

There is a growing awareness among learning disabled (LD) individuals, their parents, learning disabilities specialists, and other professionals that the manifestations of learning disabilities, though they may change, persist into adulthood, even among those who have above-average intelligence and who have completed advanced degrees (Blalock, 1981, 1982; Cox, 1977; Critchley, 1973; Dinklage, 1971; Frauenheim, 1978; Johnson & Blalock, 1987; Rawson, 1968; Rogan & Hartman, 1976; Silver, 1969; Silver & Hagin, 1964; Simpson, 1979; Vogel, 1985). This increased awareness is at least in part the result of improvements in elementary and secondary school identification and intervention. Increasingly larger numbers of school-age LD children have been identified through the public schools as a result of the implementation of the "search and serve" mandated by Public Law (P.L.) 94-142 (U.S. Department of Education, 1987). These individuals, having been identified, perhaps even at an early age, have benefitted sufficiently from intervention and have expectations for continuing their education in a postsecondary setting.

Another factor that has played a significant role in the growing numbers of LD adolescents and adults who have applied to and were accepted at a variety of colleges and universities is the passage and implementation of Section 504 of the Rehabilitation Act of 1973, which ensures the right of all qualified handicapped persons to equal postsecondary educational opportunities. According to the Higher Education Research Institute (as reported by HEATH, May 1986), the number of self-identified learning disabled college freshmen has increased in the last 4 years, constituting 14.3 percent of all handicapped freshmen. This percentage, in fact, is a minimal estimate of the incidence of LD college freshmen since students were excluded from this study if they were part-time or transfer students (thus excluding many LD persons). These LD students have benefited from the accommodations developed for handicapped students with visual and hearing impairments (e.g., taped texts; extended time for exams; use of notetakers, tape recorders, calculators, and word processors). Other institutions responded to Section 504 by developing comprehensive model programs for the LD (Mangrum & Strichart, 1984; Scheiber & Talpers, 1987; Vogel, 1982, 1987b). Demand for these comprehensive special programs increased rapidly in the early 1980s, so much that these institutions expanded their programs and other colleges followed suit.

A dramatic change has occurred over the last 5 years. The response to Section 504 and pressure from students with learning disabilities, their parents, and professionals have resulted in a rapid increase in awareness and support services for the LD across the country. This growth can be seen by comparing a number of directories written for LD students exploring postsecondary options, from the first ground-breaking efforts in the early 1980s of Ridenour and Johnston (1981) and Hopkins and Sullivan (1982), to the more recent college guides for LD students (Brill, 1987; Cowen, 1986a;

Cowen, 1986b; Liscio, 1986; Mangrum & Strichart, 1985; Moss & Fielding, 1984; Sclafani & Lynch, 1987; Skyer & Skyer, 1982, 1986).

Another major contributing factor to the increase in awareness of the persistence and pervasiveness of the effects of learning disabilities in nonacademic as well as academic endeavors was the policy change of the Rehabilitation Services Administration (RSA), U.S. Department of Education, the federal agency responsible for the state/federal program of vocational rehabilitation (VR). This policy change removed a key barrier to the consideration of the eligibility of a person with specific learning disabilities (SLDs) for VR services. In spite of protest from LD adults, parents, professionals, policy makers, and advocates, before 1980 LD adults were not eligible for VR services unless they also had a physical or mental disability as defined in the *Federal Register*, November 29, 1979 (Gerber, 1981; Martin, 1987; Newill, Goyette, & Fogarty, 1984). In May of 1980, in response to these pressure groups, the RSA composed a task force to develop an action plan to expand and improve the nature and scope of VR services to persons with learning disabilities by identifying the initiatives RSA could undertake on its own and also with other agencies to enhance the quality and quantity of services to persons with learning disabilities. Since a learning disability was recognized as a discrete medical disability (American Psychiatric Association, 1980; U.S. Department of Health and Human Services, 1980), adults with SLDs became eligible for VR services (RSA-PI-81-22, July 1981) providing they also met the other VR eligibility criteria (i.e., the disability results in a substantial handicap to employment and there is a reasonable expectation the person will benefit from VR services in terms of employability).

Since 1981, between 3 and 10 percent of the total client population served by VR are categorized under the SLDs diagnosis (McCue, 1987). Training for vocational counselors, special conferences for VR personnel on assessment, and services for adults with SLDs, as well as manuals and handbooks (Vocational Rehabilitation Center of Allegheny County, 1983; Zwerlein, Smith, & Diffley, 1984) devoted to the subject have contributed to this increased awareness (McCue, 1987; Sanchez, 1984).

DEFINITION OF LEARNING DISABILITY IN ADULTS

The early and most widely accepted definition of learning disabilities incorporated into P.L. 94-142, The Education for All Handicapped Children Act, refers to children (*Federal Register*, August 23, 1977], as did the initial concerns of the major pressure group behind the inclusion of the LD into that law as reflected in the organization's original name (The Association for Children with Learning Disabilities [ACLD]). Awareness of the persistence of learning disabilities into adulthood has been reflected in revised definitions, as well as the change in name of ACLD in March 1980 to the Association for Children and Adults with Learning Disabilities.

NATIONAL JOINT COMMITTEE ON LEARNING DISABILITIES 1981 DEFINITION

The first widely accepted revision of the definition of LD was developed in 1981 by the National Joint Committee on Learning Disabilities (NJCLD), a committee composed of the major professional organizations concerned with the LD. In the NJCLD definition, the term *learning disabilities* no longer refers just to children. This definition states

> Learning disabilities is a generic term that refers to a heterogeneous group of disorders manifested by significant difficulties in the acquisition and use of listening, speaking, reading, writing, reasoning or mathematical abilities. These disorders are intrinsic to the individual and presumed to be due to central nervous system dysfunction. Even though a learning disability may occur concomitantly with other handicapping conditions (e.g., sensory impairment, mental retardation, social and emotional disturbance) or environmental influences (e.g., cultural differences, insufficient/inappropriate instruction, psychogenic factors), it is not the direct result of those conditions or influences.

The NJCLD definition has come to the fore as a result of one of the recommendations of the Interagency Committee on Learning Disabilities (1987). This committee, established in 1986 as a result of legislation, recommended that the legislative definition of learning disabilities be revised for purposes of epidemiologic research, for diagnosis, and for other research studies. The committee recommended the adoption of the NJCLD definition with some modifications. A significant change for purposes of this discussion that would meet with considerable support from ACLD and VR, among others, was to include social skills as one of the areas of difficulty. Recognizing the effect of a learning disability on social competence and the need for assessment in this area were also highlighted by the revised definition of the Vocational Rehabilitation Services (see below). Since 1981, NJCLD has also published two major position papers on the impact of learning disabilities on adults and their needs. These statements (NJCLD, 1983, 1985) addressed the postsecondary educational, vocational, transitional, employment, and psychosocial/emotional problems of LD adults.

ACLD 1984 POSITION PAPER

A fuller elaboration of these needs, as well as an emphasis on the chronicity of learning disabilities, were highlighted in a position paper adopted September 22, 1984, by ACLD (ACLD *Newsbriefs*, 1985), which reads

Specific Learning Disabilities is a chronic condition of presumed neurological origin which selectively interferes with the development, integration, and/or demonstration of verbal and/or non-verbal abilities.
Specific Learning Disabilities exists as a distinct handicapping condition and varies in its manifestations and in degree of severity.
Throughout life, the condition can affect self esteem, education, vocation, socialization, and/or daily living activities.

In light of a major concern with diagnosis in LD adults, the acknowledgment that SLDs can affect "self-esteem, education, vocation, socialization, and/or daily living activities" and not just academic achievement was important (ACLD *Newsbriefs*, 1985).

VOCATIONAL REHABILITATION DEFINITIONS

RSA developed its own definition of learning disabilities for the VR program, which gradually was refined to include an employment dimension since the purpose of VR programs is to facilitate the employment of individuals whose handicap interferes with employability. The original definition of SLDs developed by the RSA (RSA, 1981) was criticized because it emphasized verbal/academic problems (Mulkey, Kopp, & Miller, 1984). According to this first definition

Individuals with SLD are those individuals who have a disorder in one or more of the psychological processes involved in understanding, perceiving, or using language or concepts—spoken or written—a disorder which may manifest itself in problems related to listening, thinking, speaking, reading, writing, spelling, or doing mathematical calculations (RSA, 1981).

The Vocational Rehabilitation Center (VRC) of Allegheny County, Inc., soon after amended this definition to include social competence and emotional maturity, two important areas of functioning for employability that can be affected by a learning disability (McCue, 1984). This definition states

Individuals who have a disorder in one or more of the central nervous system processes involving perceiving, understanding and/or using concepts through verbal (spoken or written language) or non-verbal means. This disorder manifests itself with difficulties in one or more of the following areas: attention, reasoning, memory, communicating, reading, writing, spelling, calculation, coordination, social competence and emotional maturity.

However, the effect of the learning disability on employment was omitted from this definition. In 1981 the VRC of Allegheny County revised the definition to include as the last sentence, "These disorders may constitute, in an adult, an employment handicap" (RSA, 1985). This VRC definition was promulgated by RSA as the national VR definition for program purposes for use by state VR agencies that had no written policy containing a definition of learning disabilities.

CALIFORNIA COMMUNITY COLLEGE 1987 DEFINITION

According to Kanter, Halliday, Mellard, and Howard (1987), in 1980, the California Community College (CCC) system came under the scrutiny of the State Department of Finance. Not only were the numbers of LD community college students rapidly increasing, there was inconsistency in the system. Because no standardized definition of learning disabilities and no uniformly adopted diagnostic procedures existed in the CCC system, a student could be diagnosed as LD and be eligible for services on one campus and not on another. The state agencies were aware of the complexity of the problems in the CCC student population and the difficulty in differentiating among the underprepared, underachieving, English-as-a-second-language speakers, and LD.

In 1982, the Department of Finance put a cap on expenditures for services to LD students in the CCC system. There were then 11,000 CCC LD students (Kanter, 1987). The cap was placed along with a mandate and funding to develop a definition, standardized diagnostic procedures, and eligibility criteria for CCC LD students. The following definition was developed in response to this mandate in accordance with the Title V regulations, the state education code, and state and federal legislative guidelines:

Learning disability in California Community College adults is a persistent condition of presumed neurological dysfunction which may also exist with other disabling conditions. This dysfunction continues despite instruction in standard classroom situations. Learning disabled adults, a heterogeneous group, have these common attributes:

1. Average to above-average intellectual ability,
2. Severe processing deficit,
3. Severe aptitude-achievement discrepancy or discrepancies,
4. Measured achievement in an instructional or employment setting,
5. Measured appropriate adaptive behavior in an instructional or employment setting.

A fundamental difference in the CCC definition as compared to the earlier definitions is that there is no exclusion clause nor a statement regarding the LD individual having other significant problems concomitantly. This aspect of the definition (by its omission) is meant to emphasize the underlying principle that "learning disabilities could exist across . . . disabling conditions" (Kanter, 1987).

Another aspect of the definition that reflects perhaps the provision of a more vocationally oriented curriculum in the CCC system (in addition to the liberal arts) is the inclusion of measured achievement and adaptive behavior in an instructional or employment setting. This reflects both the recognition that a learning disability can have a significant impact on functioning in achievement or adaptive behavior, in either an academic or employment setting, but also that there must be an indication of potential for college-level work. For example, measured academic achievement in reading, math, or spelling must be at or above the tenth percentile or the individual must have been employed for at least 6 consecutive months at least half-time in a competitive setting. In this way, it was argued, the LD can be differentiated from the low achiever who is not able to attend college.

DIAGNOSTIC PROCESS

The increased awareness of the continuing needs of LD adults reflected in the revised definitions, the burgeoning of support services in postsecondary settings, and the accessibility of VR services have all contributed to the significant increase in the number of adults referred for diagnosis to university and nonprofit clinics, licensed physicians, hospital evaluation centers, campus facilities, and private psychologists.

THEORETICAL CONSIDERATIONS

According to Johnson (1987, p. 9), diagnosis is "a complex process that involves a search for patterns . . . ongoing hypothesis testing, and decision making to determine the nature and scope of the problem." The examiner should integrate extensive information from a variety of sources into a meaningful whole. It is a problem-solving task, in that sometimes contradictory observations or data have to be interpreted and understood based on underlying theories of learning and how the brain takes in information and integrates, retains, and responds (Johnson & Myklebust, 1964). The diagnostic process relies heavily on theories such as Hebb's (1981) theory of semiautonomous systems for information processing, Luria's (1966) theory of simultaneous and successive processing of information, and task analysis (Johnson, 1987).

REASONS FOR REFERRAL

There are multiple reasons for an adult to be referred or to refer oneself for diagnostic evaluation, and these will differ based on the individual's setting, life stage, goals, and progress toward achievement of these goals. The basic reason that cuts across all of the above considerations, however, is to establish or verify a prior diagnosis of a learning disability to develop a plan of action that will enhance the individual's chances of achieving his or her goals. In some rare instances, establishing the diagnosis of a learning disability may be the sole reason for seeking a diagnostic evaluation. Such an individual may just want to know if a learning disability, in fact, is the cause of the multitude of problems experienced in the past and present. The desire to know one's own capabilities, limitations, strengths, degree of competence, and severity of deficits as compared with one's peers may be the sole purpose for requesting a diagnostic evaluation.

DIFFERENTIAL DIAGNOSIS

Integral to the diagnostic process is the task of differentiating learning disabilities in adults from other handicapping conditions that can result in language deficits, academic underachievement, nonverbal deficits, emotional and social/interpersonal difficulties, and functional limitations in daily living and employment. Adults who experience difficulties in the above aspects of functioning may not, in fact, be LD, but rather may have sensory impairments, below-average intelligence, lack of motivation, emotional disorders, lack of educational opportunities, or lack of English language proficiency. These aspects of functioning must be assessed in the diagnostic process to rule them out or to determine their contribution, if any, to the individual's present difficulties. Because differential diagnosis has already been discussed in Chapter 3, this discussion of the diagnosis of learning disabilities in adults addresses specific issues and concerns in the assessment of adults.

THE CLIENT-CLINICIAN RELATIONSHIP

In spite of the fact that the adult seeks the evaluation or is a willing participant in the process, there may be considerable wariness, anxiety, withholding, and perhaps even resistance to engaging in the tasks as they become more difficult. This is to be expected since the adult who has experienced difficulties in an academic setting or in employment has spent a great deal of psychic energy hiding these difficulties and developing compensatory strategies to bypass these deficits. Clients assume, and rightly so, that the examiner will want them to expose these weaknesses, will test to determine what they can and cannot do, and thereby expose those deficits that they have worked so hard to conceal.

A second factor that makes this exposure of deficit areas very painful is that adults who have experienced a series of failures throughout life inevitably suffer from low self-esteem. Their lack of self-confidence often leads to shyness and withdrawal from new people and different experiences, especially when performance in these tasks may have significant impact on the future.

The skillful clinician should try to shift the emphasis from right/wrong, good/bad, or passing/failing performance to information seeking, discovery, and problem solving. One of the most effective ways of accomplishing this has been the creation of a client-clinician partnership in the investigative/ diagnostic process. It is important to take ample time to explain the purpose for each test and to ask the client to reflect on the task, explain what made it easy or difficult, and describe the strategies used to respond or solve the problems. In this way, the clinician not only gains valuable insight, but the client realizes the process itself is significant, not just the response.

Another important ingredient in this process is acknowledging that some of the tasks will have to be performed under the pressure of time. Because many adolescents and adults are accustomed to requesting extended time on examinations as one of the reasonable and appropriate accommodations made for the LD, they may not readily understand the reason for adhering to time restrictions on specific measures. Moreover, they may misinterpret this practice as indicative of the examiner's lack of understanding and empathy, or insensitivity to their problem.

It is, therefore, important to explain to adult clients that the test must be administered the way it was standardized in order to determine how this individual compares with his or her peers. By giving the client the identical task untimed (e.g., a parallel form of a standardized reading comprehension test, given untimed), the clinician can then determine how much of the performance on a specific task is attributable to slow rate versus a specific difficulty in the area assessed.

RATE OF PERFORMANCE

When the client is given an untimed task, it is important to observe rate of performance. First, did the client respond impulsively, with little or no self-monitoring and checking of completed work, perhaps even in spite of instructions to do so? If so, it will be important to note that so an intervention plan can include a step-by-step sequence that will remind the individual to do the necessary reflection and monitoring.

On the opposite end of the continuum is the client who takes double, triple, or even ten-fold (though rare) the usual time for a specific untimed measure. Though this may indicate significantly high motivation in such individuals, it may also indicate a perfectionist tendency, lack of self-confidence, and the presence of significant physiologic problems. Such observations have implications for accommodations in postsecondary settings and employment since extreme slowness in rate of performance may exceed the limits of flexibility and accommodation in some job sites. Rate of performance, therefore, has significant implications for career choice and prognosis for success.

SITUATION-SPECIFIC FACTORS

During the diagnostic testing, the clinician attempts to create the ideal learning/testing environment to allow the client to perform at his or her best. The diagnostician has to consider environmental conditions (temperature, light, ventilation) as well as the client's motivation, anxiety, and fatigue. In addition, the examiner should test the same performance under different time constraints, with varying memory loads and retrieval demands, and with varying degrees of competing stimuli in the environment in an effort to simulate the conditions of learning/working environment in a postsecondary setting or job site. Creating and testing the client in these altered environments provide the clinician with direct observational data as to how the client responds to stress, performs when fatigued, and deals with frustration. For example, when frustrated, did the client resort to impulsivity, give up or persevere? In other words, what is the individual's level of psychological and physiologic resilience and stamina? If an individual has limited stamina, did he or she ask for a 10-minute break before reaching extreme fatigue? In this way, the clinician can determine the level of self-advocacy as well as stamina.

AREAS OF ASSESSMENT

Areas of assessment include the spectrum of functioning that has the potential to be affected by the learning disability (e.g., educational/academic functioning, social/interpersonal abilities, employment, and life skills). Underlying processing abilities that need to be continuously evaluated based on the nature of each task and response modality include attention, perception, integration, storage, and retrieval.

SOURCES OF INFORMATION

The NJCLD's most recent position paper (NJCLD, 1987) addressed the question of assessment and diagnostic issues of learning disabilities. The first area of importance listed was the understanding of learning disabilities as a lifelong condition. This position paper elaborates on the importance of understanding that the manifestations of a learning disability will vary over time based on the individual's age, developmental stage, and specific settings. Moreover, assessment procedures will vary accordingly and should not be limited to academic areas exclusively nor to available formal, standardized measures. They recommended that data be collected, if possible, from a variety of "on-site" locations, using direct observations, interviews, and, especially significant with LD adults, self-report.

A variety of sources of information provide insight into the individual's comprehension and expression of oral language, reading, written expressive language, mathematics, motor skills, and nonverbal/nonacademic areas such as visual/spatial abilities, directionality, and visual planning. Some of the most valuable information is provided by the adults themselves during the intake interview, or from questionnaires, rating scales, and check lists that they fill out. Other major sources of information are formal testing and observational data. However, due to the limited number of measures appropriate for LD adults and the desirability of approximating the demands of the settings in which the LD adult hopes to function, the diagnostician must devise informal tasks as well.

The area of written language expression provides a good example of the limitations of available standardized tests as compared to the writing demands of the college curriculum, on the one hand, and employment, on the other. Presently no standardized measures assess college-level essay writing competence, ability to proofread and revise, accuracy in copying, ability to fill out specific forms, or ability to write to dictation (as in taking telephone messages). To assess these aspects of functioning and others, the use of informal testing, work samples, on-site observations, and reports from instructors and supervisors in the academic or employment setting are essential. The diagnostician should, therefore, be trained in formal and informal assessment and interviewing techniques.

DEVELOPMENTAL HISTORY

The client and parent (if appropriate) are important providers of information and are often asked to complete forms that provide detailed information regarding developmental history, family background, incidence of learning disabilities and other related illnesses and disabilities in family members, birth and medical history, educational history, employment record, and self-perceived areas of strength and weakness, academic interest, and career/life goals.

After all of the above information is integrated, it is helpful to review the case history orally with the individual for further elaboration and clarification. With the client's permission, family members often can be invited to this meeting. Though they may have been reluctant to put in writing that the client's mother or father, a prominent doctor or artist, is LD, they often are willing to share that information in such a meeting. Or, in other instances, after an explanation to the individual and family of the rationale for inquiring about birth and medical history, the mother may recall a long-forgotten event, such as their child's mysterious "disappearance" immediately after delivery for a period of 24 hours, amnesia following a traumatic car accident, or a frighteningly high fever accompanied by convulsions. Obviously, the case history information includes selective remembrances, hopes, and fears that influence the recall of information, which can be of critical importance in the diagnostic process. Clients and families often benefit from assistance in this part of the process.

ASSESSMENT OF THE COLLEGE BOUND

Assessment of the college-bound should include those areas of functioning that have been observed to be residual problems in LD adults in college settings (Vogel, 1985) and that may affect success in college. Often included are measures of receptive and expressive oral and written language in the areas of semantics, syntax, and morphology; reading skills, including word attack and comprehension of single words and paragraphs read orally and silently, and reading rate; mathematics reasoning and computation; verbal and nonverbal concept formation; study habits and attitudes; and selected auditory and visual processing, including perception, discrimination, memory, sequencing, analysis, and synthesis. This latter part of the assessment provides important diagnostic teaching information for remediation, especially for the widespread and severe spelling disabilities that plague many LD adults.

An area of assessment in adults that is often neglected, yet highly indicative of success in higher education and in employment, is abstract reasoning (Stone, 1987). The presentation of novel tasks as described by Stone (1987) or the Analysis-Synthesis and Concept Formation subtests of the Woodcock Johnson Psycho-Educational Battery (WJPEB) provide the examiner with important observational data on the client's rate of comprehension, problem-solving strategies, and learning rate. Often another aspect of problem-solving behavior based on Luria's (1966) theories of simultaneous and successive processing can have a significant impact on performance. As the complexity of a task increases, and the client must hold in mind and manipulate one, two, three, or more organizational principles, adults suspected of having a learning disability may have more and more difficulty.

Some of the underlying reasons for difficulty with tasks requiring simultaneous processing seem to be oral language difficulties, organizational problems (Stone, 1987), rigidity of thinking, and memory deficits. Clients have been observed that succeed when only one abstract or organizing principle (e.g., size, shape, or color) has to be applied to solve a problem, but when two or more are introduced, they become confused. It is therefore important to use formal tests or design informal tasks that are sufficiently complex and that approximate the complexity of problem solving required in the anticipated postsecondary or employment setting.

ASSESSMENT FOR VOCATIONAL REHABILITATION

The diagnosis of SLDs according to the VR definition is a complex issue because although the definition is in terms of functional deficits, the determination of eligibility is in terms of the medical criteria of the *Diagnostic and*

Statistical Manual of Mental Disorders (3rd edition, revised) (DSM-IIIR) (American Psychiatric Association, 1987) or ICD-9 (U.S. Department of Health and Human Services, 1980). To overcome this inconsistency, the recommended practice has been to require a comprehensive assessment of all of the potential areas of deficit according to the RSA (1985) definition (attention, memory, communication, reading, writing, spelling, calculation, coordination, social competence, and emotional maturity). In addition, the assessment must provide sufficient evidence to establish a DSM-IIIR or ICD-9 diagnosis (McCue, 1987). Federal regulations also require that the diagnosis of LD must be made by a licensed physician or a licensed or certified psychologist, or both, skilled in the diagnosis/treatment of such disabilities.

To determine eligibility for VR services and to develop a suitable vocational plan, the examiner must also ascertain the client's strengths and functional limitations (Abbott, 1987). For each of the areas described in the definition, the question that must be addressed in diagnostic evaluation is what, if any, is the functional limitation in employment that results from deficits in these areas? For example, would a dyslexic adult have difficulty reading the classified ads, a job application form, or certain manuals necessary for job success? Informal testing would have to be designed using representative materials to answer these questions. In the math area, the questions may be related to measurement, whether liquid, dry, or linear, and the ability to handle money or keep track of time.

In the areas of underlying processing deficits, auditory perceptual problems may result in misperception of and resulting difficulty in comprehension following oral directions. Such problems are usually worsened by background noise and when the individual cannot see the speaker's face. Assessing receptive language in a quiet environment and then in an environment simulating a noisy office will provide valuable information for the client and vocational counselor. Likewise, for the client with attentional deficits, working in an open office area without protection from extraneous auditory and visual stimuli may significantly reduce performance level. Based on informal testing, self-report, and employers' reports, such problems can be ascertained and appropriate career choices and eventual placement decisions made.

An area of special significance incorporated into the revised definition of SLDs by the VRC of Allegheny County is the assessment of social skills. Situational assessment of performance on a day-to-day basis by employers and supervisors should provide input as to co-worker relations, supervisory relations, coping skills, response to criticism, ability to ask for help, group communication skills, and ability to deal with monotonous and frustrating aspects of work.

SOME OUTCOMES OF THE DIAGNOSTIC PROCESS

More often than not adults seek diagnostic evaluation because the information will lead to accommodations or modifications in their environment, provision of some special support services, remediation and vocational training, financial assistance to cover the costs of such services, or to become eligible for these services at no cost.

From the vantage point of the service provider, the diagnostic process will answer some basic questions about the intellectual, educational, behavioral, vocational, and social/emotional functioning of this individual. It will help the clinician to assist the LD adult set appropriate goals, enable the client and diagnostic team to assess together the appropriateness of those already made, and determine the prognosis for success in achieving those goals.

In considering alternative postsecondary settings, the diagnostic information can provide the basis for recommending appropriate settings, necessary support services, specific accommodations or compensatory strategies, and planning remedial and academic programs. In a VR setting, the diagnostic process provides information to assist the client with career exploration and decision making, to set career goals, to determine the overall vocational plan leading to employment, to project the appropriate length of service, to implement a job training program, and to provide follow-up, as needed (Abbott, 1987). For those individuals who have already determined their vocational or career goals, the diagnostic process can help determine both readiness and feasibility of attainment and if necessary develop a transition program to enhance success.

One additional specific outcome of the diagnostic process in the VR setting is the integration of the medical, vocation, social, educational, and psychological data into a prescriptive plan. Vocational rehabilitation services requires an individualized written rehabilitation program (IWRP) for each person determined eligible (Abbott, 1987). This has been referred to as the "prescriptive" function of assessment (McCue, 1987). The IWRP typically includes at least the following discrete information:

- Long-range rehabilitation goals

- Intermediate rehabilitation objectives

- Specific VR services to be provided with initiation and duration time lines

- Objective criteria, evaluation procedure, and schedule to determine if progress on achieving the objectives/goals is satisfactory

- Assessment of potential need for postemployment services

In determining the selection of the individual's goals/objectives and the services necessary to attain them, the information garnered from diagnostic evaluations plays a key role, particularly with regard to issues whether to remediate, compensate, or accommodate the functional limitations imposed on the person by the learning disabilities.

DETERMINING ELIGIBILITY

One of the most difficult tasks for the clinician and one of the major reasons for referring an adult for diagnosis is to determine if that individual is eligible for some special accommodations or support services (e.g., modified administration procedures for examinations, support services offered through the Office of Disabled Student Services, or VR services). In some instances, verification of the diagnosis of LD by providing a copy of the psychoeducational evaluation or individualized education program (IEP) is sufficient evidence to determine eligibility for accommodations.

With the increase in LD college students, the verification process may become more complex; the recently revised verification procedures of the College Entrance Examination board exemplify this change. Two alternative routes can be followed to arrange for nonstandard administration of the Scholastic Aptitude Test. The first requires providing a copy of the student's IEP that contains a statement of the nature and effect of the learning disability. The second alternative is to provide two letters dated within the last 3 years describing the learning disability and the tests used in diagnosis. These letters could be from a physician, psychologist, child-study team, or learning disabilities specialist. One of these letters must also confirm that the diagnosis is in compliance with the state guidelines for diagnosis of a LD. This latter requirement, though necessary for public school special education services, may place students who have attended private schools or received LD assistance outside of the public school setting at a disadvantage. The IEP or one of the letters must also state a need for modified examination procedures.

In some large public postsecondary institutions, the CCC system, and the California State University system, diagnostic and eligibility criteria have been or are being developed in an attempt to ensure greater uniformity and consistency across diagnosticians within the same institution or on different campuses within the same state. It is also interesting to note that the question of eligibility at the postsecondary level has only recently been addressed (Best, Howard, Kanter, Mellard, & Pearson, 1986; Kanter et al, 1987; Vogel, 1987b, 1988) but is a pressing and timely issue as the numbers of LD college students, VR clients, and costs increase, and funding becomes insufficient to meet the demand for services.

An important distinction, however, must be made between diagnostic and eligibility criteria. This distinction is important because it can explain how individuals can be diagnosed as LD in elementary and secondary school, or a previous college, and not be eligible for services at the college level or when applying for VR services (Abbott, 1987; Best et al, 1986; Kanter et al, 1987; Vogel 1987a) because they fall below or above a specific cutoff or criterion for IQ, aptitude-achievement discrepancy, intra-individual differences, or level of severity. These inconsistencies arise because of differences in definition; in the operationalization of the adopted definition; in state and federal mandates (e.g., entitlement versus eligibility); in situation-specific expectations, demands and available support services; and the interaction among these factors.

The eligibility model discussed below has three features: an ability cutoff score, intra-individual discrepancy among abilities (scatter), and aptitude/achievement discrepancy as measured by aptitude or intelligence tests as compared to academic achievement measures. In addition, in accordance with the NJCLD's recommendation on assessment and diagnosis (NJCLD, September 20, 1987), diagnosis and eligibility are not determined solely on the basis of quantitative data, standardized test results, or discrepancy formulas. In regard to each of these three features, there is a provision for override based on informal procedures, qualitative information, and professional judgment.

At the present time, the CCC system is the first and only formal model for diagnosing LD and determining eligibility for accommodations at the postsecondary level. This first model now used in most, if not all, of the CCC system was developed in response to a mandate from the California state legislature and chancellor of the CCC office (Best et al, 1986; Kanter et al, 1987).

THE CALIFORNIA COMMUNITY COLLEGE ELIGIBILITY MODEL

The California Assessment System for Adults with Learning Disabilities implemented in October 1987 was developed by the CCC system in conjunction with the Kansas Institute of Learning Disabilities over the last 5 years. It was designed as a data-based eligibility model that would provide guidelines for the diagnosis of LD in such a way as to minimize inequities and biases.

The system was developed with comprehensive input from college administrators, faculty, LD specialists, ancillary staff, students, the board of governors, legislators, and VR personnel. Experts from many fields including special education, measurement, psychology, policy analysis, decision theory, and speech and language composed task forces, responded to questionnaires, and became consultants on various aspects of the system. This is a highly complex model designed for implementation specifically within the community college population of California, a population that presents a significant diagnostic challenge.

The task was first one of differential diagnosis (i.e., differentiating LD students from low achievers; underprepared, non-native English speakers;

and slow learners). However, as discussed above, the LD definition developed, and as used in the CCC system, clearly includes LD non-native, underprepared students, and those with multiple handicaps. The second task was to establish the diagnosis of LD based on the operationalization of the CCC definition of LD. Last, eligibility based on the student's performance in relation to established criteria was to be determined.

The diagnostic and eligibility model was based on a survey of the literature and data from questionnaires given to LD professionals in the CCC system, as well as a national sample of LD experts and other service providers. Specific measures were identified that measured the identified characteristics of LD adults, and normative data were collected on a random stratified sample of 900 nonhandicapped CCC students and 900 previously clinically diagnosed LD students. These samples provided baseline data and allowed for data manipulation and computer simulations of alternative eligibility models. Statewide local norms were then generated from these data and cutoff scores selected, followed by trial implementation, revision, and finally implementation in October 1987.

The diagnostic model in use in 100 of the 106 CCCs as of July 1987 is based on quantitative data, self-reported information, and the clinical judgment of the LD diagnostician. LD professionals must be certified by the state of California as community college LD specialists and in addition must have completed 3 days of training specifically devoted to the implementation of this model (Halliday, 1987). Based on specific guidelines and the CCC definition of LD, the eligibility model relies on formal and informal evaluation procedures providing information on present problems; educational, family, medical, and vocational history; language abilities, academic and vocational achievement; expected achievement level; and academic-processing skills.

There are seven components to the CCC eligibility model using the above information and clinical judgment.

1. *Intake screening.* The first component is the intake screening during which the student provides information on questionnaires and in an interview regarding present difficulties, history, career goals, and employment experiences. During the interview, the diagnostician assesses the student's language proficiency, academic attributes, or skills based on self-report or prior testing (e.g., oral or written language abilities or the student's attitude toward these skills) (Kanter et al, 1987).

2. *Measured achievement.* The second component is to determine if the student has achieved a certain degree of success in either an academic or employment setting that would differentiate the LD individual from the low achiever. Performance below a certain level in academic achievement areas would indicate this student may not be able to benefit from the CCC curriculum even with LD support services. Measured achievement may be demonstrated on formal testing, college entrance or placement exams,

academic success in high school or college, or a successful employment experience at least half-time for 6 consecutive months.

3. *Adaptive behavior.* The third component, adaptive behavior, refers to the area of social competence and social maturity as reflected in the student's behavior in personal and professional life, whether within or outside the classroom. Measures used follow a self-report or interview format (e.g., Adaptive Behavior Scale and Scales of Independent Behavior).

4. *Ability level.* The fourth component provides an indication of sufficient intellectual ability to succeed in the community college setting. This aspect of the eligibility criteria follows the most widely accepted federal guidelines and includes individuals with an IQ of 80 or above on either verbal, performance, or full scale IQ of the Wechsler Adult Intelligence Scale—Revised (WAIS-R) or the broad cognitive ability full scale cluster on the WJPEB, part I. This component also allows for two groupings of subtests on the WAIS-R (perceptual organization and verbal comprehension factors) and the reading, math, or written language aptitude clusters of the WJPEB. Kanter et al. (1987) reported that 34 percent of the 900 randomly selected clinically diagnosed LD students on CCC campuses who provided the data base fell below the 78 IQ level (Mellard, 1987). This finding relates to the earlier statement regarding some of the reasons for determining definition, diagnostic procedures, and eligibility criteria.

5. *Processing deficit.* The fifth component evaluates the student's ability to acquire, integrate, store, retrieve, and express information as exemplified in the WAIS-R factor scores and WJPEB cluster scores. The specific discrepancies (i.e., strengths and weaknesses) among these grouped scores are used as the criteria for distinguishing low and underachievers from LD individuals.

6. *Aptitude-achievement discrepancy.* The sixth component is based on information and data collected while determining if the student has met some of the previous components. A significant discrepancy between aptitude and reading, math, or written language achievement is determined based on the local CCC norms generated from the data base. These norms take into account the correlation of subtests and regression effects and range in different age bands from 18 to 40 and over. In the development of these components, Mellard (1987) reported that this component was the most consistent descriptor of the 900 clinically diagnosed LD students as well as the best discriminator between the LD and randomly identified nonhandicapped sample. However, among the random sample, 32 percent also had met this criterion (i.e., one in three non-LD students had met the criterion as having a significant aptitude-achievement discrepancy) (Mellard, 1987). This finding confirms that if eligibility for service was based solely on a discrepancy formula, many non-LD individuals would be identified as LD and would be eligible for service (Mellard, 1987; Reynolds, 1985; Sinclair & Alexson, 1986).

7. Eligibility recommendation. At the completion of each step in the six components, there is a criterion component check, (i.e., the examiner must indicate whether the interview or test administration procedures, or both, are appropriate, as well as if they were valid and accurately completed) (Mellard, 1987). If not, the clinician has the option to use secondary procedures and in such cases must state why the primary procedures were invalid and describe the alternate method. Clinicians can use an alternate method no more than 0.1 percent of the total number of LD students on their campus. If that number is exceeded, the chancellor's office must be notified. This provision allows the chancellor's office to monitor problems that may arise in the eligibility model or in its implementation.

After completing the procedures for each component, the LD professional indicates whether the criterion has been met. In the seventh component, all of the information must be integrated and clinical judgment used to make a final determination, assuming the student met the criteria for each of the six components.

On the other hand, a student may meet all six component criteria and may not be diagnosed as LD and thus not be determined eligible for service (seventh component). This component acknowledges the importance of clinical judgment and that other factors could possibly account for a student having met the six components. The LD professional's judgment is heavily relied on at each step in the process, culminating in the seventh step. At each step and finally the seventh component, clinicians are held responsible and must certify and document their decisions.

THE VR SERVICES MODEL

The question of diagnosis to determine eligibility for VR services takes on a different urgency for the LD adult whose learning disability has interfered with employability. The VR services differ from those mandated by P.L. 94-142 in a fundamental way. Whereas P.L. 94-142 is an "entitlement" program (i.e., because an individual is LD, he or she is entitled to services), the VR program is an "eligibility" program (i.e., when an individual is diagnosed as LD, he or she may or may not be eligible for VR services). The individual must meet certain eligibility requirements. According to the *Federal Register* (January 19, 1981), the diagnostic evaluation for those suspected of being LD, as for all others with a handicapping condition, must indicate that the learning disability has caused the individual a substantial handicap to employment, and that VR services will benefit the individual in terms of employability.

Once found eligible for VR services, a person with LD may be faced with another barrier to the actual receipt of VR services, namely, the "order of selection" principle. The rationale was that if funding were insufficient to assist all eligible clients with SLDs, the most severely disabled would be given priority. At present, guidelines for determining severity level of eligible clients with SLDs are identical to those developed by RSA prior to the policy change of 1981. To determine a person with LD as being severely handicapped it must be documented that the individual has a substantial loss of functional capacity, has restriction of activity attributable to medical factors, and will normally require multiple VR services over an extended period of time. The problem in this regard for persons with LD is that the methodology developed by RSA and employed by many state VR agencies in determining the degree of severity of the handicap uses evaluative criteria more consistent with limitations associated with a physical disability (e.g., unable to climb a flight of stairs, not able to walk 100 yards on level ground without a pause). Because of this pressing concern for LD persons, various attempts have been made by RSA, the Pittsburgh RSA Project on SLDs, the Task Force of RSA Region IX on SLDs, and ACLD's Vocational Committee (Westhead & Duane, 1985) to develop guidelines for determining severity level for clients with SLDs. None have been promulgated as yet by RSA, though there is a concerted effort to validate several models and check lists (see samples in Zwerlein et al, 1984) that have been developed.

FUTURE RESEARCH DIRECTIONS

The recognition of the continuing needs of adults with learning disabilities is still in its infancy, and data-based research is sorely needed (Gray, 1981; Vogel, 1988). First, descriptive data are needed on the residual problems and characteristics of adults with learning disabilities whose formal education culminated prior to high school graduation, after high school graduation, or after completing vocational or technical training, a community college degree, a four-year degree, or a professional degree. This type of information will enable diagnosticians to identify more readily learning disabilities in individuals in different IQ ranges and different levels of severity and to use this information to set realistic goals and expectations. Based on studies of LD adults' educational attainments, it is hoped that successful employment patterns will emerge that can assist clients and clinicians in the decision-making process and in determining needed VR services and prognosis.

Studies are also needed to validate the diagnostic and eligibility criteria in use in the CCCs. In this way, the percent of adults with SLDs that have met each criterion in the various settings can be determined and compared to a normative control group. Through such studies with younger LD individuals and LD college students, it has been found that the previously widely used diagnostic criterion of a 15-point discrepancy between verbal and performance IQ is actually descriptive of only about 20 percent of the LD population (Sattler, 1982; Vogel, 1986, 1987), yet some colleges and universities in the process of developing eligibility criteria still include the 15-point discrepancy.

Other important areas to investigate are numerous: (1) What is the validity of neuropsychological measures presently in widespread use? (2) Are these instruments able to discriminate between LD and non-LD individuals, underachievers, underprepared, and slow learners? (3) What is the relationship between assessment and outcome? (4) What information or combination of information from formal and informal testing; developmental, educational, and vocational history; personality and motivational factors; and social and vocational competence will be the best predictors of successful outcome? (5) How can the predictive validity of the present diagnostic test batteries be improved? (6) How can new instruments best be developed and standardized to assess the effect of learning disabilities on social competence, emotional maturity, daily living, and employability? It is hoped that raising these questions becomes the first step toward a deepening dialogue among learning disabilities professionals and VR experts, and among diagnosticians, researchers, and service providers in both areas within and across state boundaries.

REFERENCES

Abbott, G. (1987, February). *Accessing vocational education and vocational rehabilitation training and employment programs.* Paper presented at the 1987 ACLD International Conference, San Antonio, TX.

ACLD. (1985). January–February *Newsbriefs.* Pittsburgh: ACLD.

American Psychiatric Association (1987). *Diagnostic and statistical manual for mental disorders* (3rd ed., revised). Washington DC: APA.

Best, L., Howard, R., Kanter, M., Mellard, D., & Pearson, M. (1986, April). *Program standards and eligibility criteria for learning disabled adults in California community colleges.* Paper presented at the 65th Annual Convention of the Council for Exceptional Children, New Orleans.

Blalock, J. (1982). Persistent auditory language deficits in adults with learning disabilities. *Journal of Learning Disabilities, 15,* 604–609.

Blalock, J. (1981). Persistent problems and concerns of young adults with learning disabilities. In W. Cruickshank & A. Silver (Eds.), *Bridges to tomorrow: The best of ACLD (Vol. 2)* (pp. 35–55). Syracuse: Syracuse University Press.

Brill, J. (1987). [Review of *A guide to colleges for learning disabled students, revised.*] *Learning Disabilities Focus,* 2(2), 127.

Cowen, S. (1986a). [Review of *Lovejoy's college guide for the learning disabled.*] *Learning Disabilities Focus,* 1(2), 120–121.

Cowen, S. (1986b). [Review of *Peterson's guide to colleges with programs for learning-disabled students.*] *Learning Disabilities Focus,* 1(2), 121–122.

Cox, S. (1977). The learning-disabled adult. *Academic Therapy,* 13, 70–86.

Critchley, M. (1973). Some problems of the ex-dyslexic. *Bulletin of the Orton Society,* 23, 7–14.

Dinklage, K. (1971). Inability to learn a foreign language. In G. Blaine & C. McArthur

(Eds.), *Emotional problems of the student* (2nd ed.). (pp. 185–206). New York: Appleton-Century-Crofts.

Federal Register. (1977, August 23). *Education of handicapped children: Implementation of part B of the Education of the Handicapped Act. Federal Register,* Part II. Washington, DC: U.S. Office of Education; U.S. Department of Health, Education and Welfare.

Frauenheim, J. G. (1978). Academic achievement characteristics of adult males who were diagnosed as dyslexic in childhood. *Journal of Learning Disabilities, 11*(8), 476–483.

Gerber, P. (1981). Learning disabilities and eligibility for vocational rehabilitation services: A chronology of events. *Learning Disability Quarterly, 4*(4), 422–425.

Gray, R. (1981). Services for the LD adult: A working paper. *Learning Disability Quarterly, 4,* 426–434.

HEATH Resource Center. (1986). *Information from HEATH, 5*(2). Washington, DC: HEATH.

Hebb, D. (1981). The semi-autonomous process: Its nature and nuture. *American Psychologist, 18*(1), 16–17.

Hopkins, C., & Sullivan, M. (1982). *Guide to college programs for learning disabled students.* Skokie, IL: National Association of College Admissions Counselors.

Interagency Committee on Learning Disabilities. (1987). *Learning disabilities: A report to the U.S. Congress.* Washington, DC: U.S. Department of Health and Human Services.

Johnson, D. (1987). Principles of assessment and diagnosis. In D. Johnson & J. Blalock (Eds.). *Adults with learning disabilities* (pp. 9–30). Orlando: Grune & Stratton.

Johnson, D., & Blalock, J. (Eds.). (1987). *Adults with learning disabilities.* Orlando: Grune & Stratton.

Johnson, D., & Myklebust, H. (1964). *Learning disabilities: Educational principles and practices.* New York: Grune & Stratton.

Kanter, M., Halliday, K., Mellard, D., & Howard, R. (1987). *What LD is, not what it isn't.* Paper presented at the 1987 AHSSPPE Conference, Washington, DC.

Liscio, M. (Ed.). (1986). *A guide to colleges for learning disabled students.* Orlando: Academic.

Luria, A. (1966). *Human brain and psychological processes.* New York: Harper & Row.

Mangrum, C., & Strichart, S. (1984). *College and the learning disabled student.* New York: Grune & Stratton.

Mangrum, C., & Strichart, S. (Eds.). (1985). *Peterson's guide to colleges with programs for learning disabled students.* Princeton NJ: Peterson's Guides.

Martin, E. (1987). Developing public policy concerning "regular" or "special" education for children with learning disabilities. *Learning Disabilities Focus, 3*(1), 11–16.

McCue, M. (1984, May). Assessment and rehabilitation of learning-disabled adults. *Rehabilitation Counseling Bulletin,* 281–290.

McCue, M. (1987, April). *The role of assessment in the vocational rehabilitation of adults with SLD.* Paper presented at the State-of-the Art conference on Learning Disabilities for the National Institute on Disability and Rehabilitation Research, Washington, DC.

Moss, J., & Fielding, P. (Eds.). (1984). *A national directory of four year colleges, two year colleges and post high school training programs for young people with learning disabilities* (5th ed.). Tulsa, OK: Partners in Publishing.

Mulkey, S., Kopp, K., & Miller, J. (1984). Determining eligibility of learning disabled adults for vocational rehabilitation services. *Journal of Rehabilitation, 50*(2), 53–58.

National Joint Committee on Learning Disabilities. (1983, January 30). *Learning disabilities: The needs of adults with learning disabilities.* A position paper of the National Joint Committee on Learning Disabilities. Unpublished manuscript.

National Joint Committee on Learning Disabilities. (1985, February 10). *Adults with learning disabilities: A call to action.* A position paper of the National Joint Committee on Learning Disabilities. Unpublished manuscript.

National Joint Committee on Learning Disabilities. (1987, September 20). *Issues in learning disabilities: Assessment and diagnosis.* Position paper of the National Joint Committee on Learning Disabilities. Unpublished manuscript.

Newill, B., Goyette, C., & Fogarty, T. (1984). Diagnosis and assessment of the adult with specific learning disabilities. *Journal of Rehabilitation, 50*(2), 34–38.

Rawson, M. (1968). *Developmental language disability: Adult accomplishment of dyslexic boys.* Baltimore: Johns Hopkins Press.

Rehabilitation Services Administration Program Information Memorandum No. 81–22. July 27, 1981.

Rehabilitation Services Administration. (1985). Program policy directive: Guidelines for determining severe handicap for individuals with SLD. Proposed policy change never promulgated.

Reynolds, C. R. (1985). Critical measurement issues in learning disabilities. *Journal of Special Education, 18,* 451–475.

Ridenour, D. & Johnston, J. (1981). *A guide to post-secondary educational opportunities for the learning disabled.* Oak Park, IL: Time Out to Enjoy.

Rogan, L., & Hartman, L. (1976). *A follow-up study of learning disabled children as adults. Final report.* (ERIC Document Reproduction Service No. ED 163-728.) Evanston, IL: Cove School.

Sanchez, S. (1984). Where do we go from here: A look to the future in rehabilitation of learning disabled persons. *Journal of Rehabilitation, 50*(2), 82–88.

Sattler, J. (1982). *Assessment of children's intelligence and special abilities.* Boston: Allyn & Bacon.

Scheiber, B., & Talpers, J. (1987). *Unlocking potential: college and other choices for learning disabled people—a step-by-step guide.* Bethesda, MD: Adler & Adler.

Sclafani, A., & Lynch, M. (1987). *College guide for students with learning disabilities 1987–88.* Farmingville, NY: Spedco.

Silver, A. A. (1969). More than 20 years after [Review of *Developmental language disability: Adult accomplishments of dyslexic boys*]. *Journal of Special Education, 3*(2), 219–222.

Silver, A. A., & Hagin, R. A. (1964). Specific reading disability: Follow-up studies. *American Journal of Orthopsychiatry, 34,* 95–102.

Simpson, E. (1979). *Reversals: A personal account of victory over dyslexia.* Boston: Houghton Mifflin.

Sinclair, E., & Alexson, J. (1986). Learning disabilities discrepancy formulas: Similarities and difference among them. *Learning Disabilities Research, 1,* 112–118.

Skyer, R., & Skyer, G. (1982). *What do you do after high school?* Rockaway Park, NY: Skyer Consultation Center.

Skyer, R., & Skyer, G. (1986). *What do you do after high school?: The nationwide guide to residential, vocational, social and collegiate programs serving the adolescent, young adult, and adult with learning disabilities.* Rockaway Park, NY: Skyer Consultation Center.

Stone, A. (1987). Abstract reasoning and problem solving. In D. Johnson & J. Blalock (Eds.). *Adults with learning disabilities* (pp. 9–30). Orlando: Grune & Stratton.

U.S. Department of Education. (1987). *Ninth annual report to congress on the implementation of the Education of the Handicapped Act.* Washington, DC: U.S. Department of Education & U.S. Office of Special Education and Rehabilitative Services.

U.S. Department of Education. (1980). Rehabilitation Services Administration. Task Force on Learning Disabilities. *Action plan on learning disabilities.* Washington, DC: U.S. Department of Education.

U.S. Department of Health and Human Services. (1980). *The international classification of diseases. 9th revision, clinical modification* (2nd ed.). Washington, DC: U.S. Government Printing Office.

Vocational Rehabilitation Center of Allegheny County. (1983). *Specific learning disabilities: A resource manual for vocational rehabilitation.* Pittsburgh: VRC of Allegheny County.

Vogel, S. (1987b). Eligibility and identification considerations. In S. Vaughn & C. Bos (Eds.), *Research in learning disabilities: Issues and future directions* (pp. 121–137). Boston: College-Hill.

Vogel, S. (1988). Learning disabled college students: Current research and application for program managers. *1987 AHSSPPE Proceedings.*

Vogel, S. (1986). Levels and patterns of intellectual functioning among LD college students. *Journal of Learning Disabilities, 19*(2), 71–79.

Vogel, S. (1982). On developing LD college programs. *Journal of Learning Disabilities, 15,* 518–528.

Vogel, S. (1987a). Response to [A shared attribute model of learning disabilities] by Barbara Keogh. In S. Vaughn & C. Bos (Eds.), *Research in learning disabilities: Issues and future directions* (pp. 13–18). Boston: College-Hill.

Vogel, S. (1985). *The college student with a learning disability: A handbook for college LD students, admissions officers, faculty, and administrators.* Lake Forest, IL: Vogel.

Westhead, E., & Duane, D. (1985). *Positions re eligibility of SLD adults for rehabilitation services and definition of "severity."* A report to ACLD. Unpublished paper.

Zwerlein, R., Smith, M., & Diffley, J. (1984). *Vocational rehabilitation for learning disabled adults: A handbook for rehabilitation professionals.* Albertson, NY: National Center on Employment of the Handicapped at Human Resources Center.

CHAPTER 5

The Gifted Learning Disabled Student

PRISCILLA L. VAIL

The many problems involved in agreeing to a definition of learning disabilities as well as the criteria selected for diagnosis are compounded when dealing with the individual who is learning disabled and of superior intellectual ability. Priscilla Vail first discusses the special issues in identifying and working with the gifted student. She then focuses on the gifted student who is learning disabled.

The literature on the gifted learning disabled student is not extensive. Priscilla Vail shares her personal perspective on and experience with these students.

Giftedness and learning disabilities may conceal one another. This results in the paradox of the average student who is not an average thinker. These students' innate cleverness helps them develop compensations that keep them academically afloat, but the underlying problem keeps them from getting to the top. Unrecognized disabilities steal power from performance. As curriculum demands increase in rate, complexity, variety of disciplines, and levels of abstraction, the student finds it increasingly difficult to sustain the effort required for success. These students may appear to be dropping dramatically, when in fact they are holding their own. External demands gallop past them; early compensations may no longer suffice. The "residual learning disabled" may not even show up until junior high school. Evaluators must be on the alert for camouflage in the middle group.

Fox (1984) has noted that gifted children with learning disabilities do not appear gifted on group IQ tests and may not be below grade-level placement academically in regular class; thus, they are often missed. These children often create coping strategies for academic tasks allowing them to compensate for their weaknesses and to obscure their difficulties (Whitmore & Maker, 1985). Waldron, Saphire, and Rosenblum (1987) have noted that gifted children with learning disabilities are more quiet or withdrawn; thus, they are not noticed. They may even be at the top of the class.

When students with unrecognized learning disabilities keep up with high academic performers, their achievement may come at the expense of emotional comfort and physical peace. Parental, academic, or self-imposed pressure to stay at the top may cause emotional, social, or family problems. Emotional symptoms may include irritability, tearfulness, fear, anger, apparent passivity, fatigue, loneliness, dependence, or intolerance. In the academic/intellectual domain, unwillingness to risk, rigid thinking, adherence to the "right idea," intense competition, or the temptation to quit may be seen. Since the physical, emotional, and intellectual selves can only be separated artificially, it is not surprising that symptoms in the three realms overlap, interconnect, even become one another's cause and effect.

Special issues relating to the gifted child are discussed first, then issues relating to the gifted child who is learning disabled follow. To diagnose the gifted child accurately, one needs to consider traditional and nontraditional ways of identifying or recognizing giftedness.

My personal bias is born of many years of testing, observing, and teaching students in classrooms and of listening and talking to parents. My idea of giftedness runs counter to the daisy petal–plucking exclusive/inclusive model: you are either gifted or you are not. Many students with clusters of the characteristics attributed to the gifted and talented will flourish or not depending on their surroundings. Many adults in the full flower of human and professional development, whose abilities in their chosen fields are outstanding but whose performance in other areas is mediocre or below average, were "hidden in plain sight" in school. Certain talents, particularly those in mathematics and music, develop early. Others unfold slowly, reaching their peak only when the person attains adult levels of psychological growth.

Unfortunately, some skillful test takers can hit a numerical bull's eye. They may absorb facts and formulas precociously, yet be rigid thinkers. Experience shows that not all high scorers are gifted and talented and not all gifted and talented are high scorers.

The term *identification* leans to the exclusive/inclusive model, implying that the existence of specific objective components and designated numerical scores leads to a diagnosis that is both verifiable and replicable. How convenient it would be to say that the presence of factors x, y, and z and the absence of factors a, b, and c result in a combination called G. Any and all people with x, y, and z and without a, b, and c are G. No people without x, y, and z and no people with a, b, and c are G. But giftedness and talent, by nature idiosyncratic, resist formulae and overflow restrictions.

The term *recognition* encourages true looking. It allows for the combination of surprise and delight (or shock and horror), with which genuine originality is usually met. Which groups of people are most accurate at recognizing giftedness? Studies presented at the World Conference on Gifted Children in London in 1975 (Gibson & Chennells, 1975) give the blue ribbon to parents and second place to peers, and show that children are also accurate self-observers.

That teachers missed more frequently than parents and other children comes as no surprise if we consider two things. First, teachers are trained to use numerical scores for final assessment. Second, the traits and characteristics of gifted or talented children are frequently inconvenient in traditional classrooms.

Next, ten current models for identifying the gifted child are explored briefly. Each has its strengths and weaknesses.

MODELS FOR IDENTIFYING GIFTEDNESS

INTELLIGENCE QUOTIENT

In local and state programs (in both independent and public education) the qualifying IQ score may range from a low of 120 to a high of 135. Some programs require that either the verbal IQ or the performance IQ be at this level. Others focus on the full-scale IQ.

Discussion

Opponents call an IQ score unfair, citing examples of obvious cultural bias. Furthermore, the type of test is important. An individually administered, skillfully interpreted IQ test will provide more valid information than modified or group-administered instruments.

When the final number is the criterion for including or excluding a child, a one-point difference wields inappropriate power. It is reminiscent of "Off with her head," the cry of *Alice in Wonderland's* White Queen. Several years ago a mother approached me with tears in her eyes. "In our state, any 120 must be serviced." I winced at the omission of the word *child*, and the use of the verb *serviced*. She continued, "Amy only got 119, so she couldn't be with her friends. She had retesting rights, and they did her [note the verb!] the day before Christmas vacation. She was 119 again. I don't think she'll ever be the same. She just gave up on herself." How ridiculous. How terrifying.

IQ is one valuable element in assessing a child's probable comfort level in a program designed for gifted students, but it is only one element. In spite of negative possibilities, valuable insights are gained by looking for the diagnostic watchword discrepancy, or scatter, among the interior scores. A discrepancy of more than 15 points between verbal and performance deserves close attention, and the discrepancy or scatter among the whole set of interior subtest scores should be studied, watching for patterns of power and weakness. Patterns tell more than individual numbers. In addition to looking at function in the traditional verbal and performance categories, recategorization of scores as sequential, conceptual, and spatial adds another dimension to the picture (Vance & Singer, 1979), as does arranging the scores by the student's own high, average, and low, noting what skills were required to perform each subtest.

Advantages

An IQ score is considered by many to be impartial and objective.

Disadvantages

The final number is a composite score made up, in turn, of other composites. Therefore, it may flatten high performance in certain areas, disguising extraordinary abilities and concealing specific deficits.

STANDARDIZED ACHIEVEMENT AND APTITUDE TESTS

The results of standardized achievement and aptitude tests are reported in percentiles or stanines.

Discussion

Because gifted learning disabled children may do poorly on such tests, they should not be used as the only instruments for identification, but they can be used to advantage with some students. For example, Julian Stanley at Johns Hopkins runs programs for mathematically precocious youth (MPY) and verbally precocious youth (VPY). Seventh graders who score above a certain percentile on specified sections of the college boards are eligible for his programs. He feels that this is a valid identification tool and that it is critical to find these gifted youngsters and offer them accelerated fare.

Advantages

These tests attempt to measure the level of actual learning as opposed to theoretical aptitude. They can be a clean measure of how much information a student has acquired so long as the child is from a good school and has a background culturally compatible with the test.

Disadvantages

The ruminative thinker, the overthinker, the culturally different, the residual dyslexic, the undereducated, and the bruised test taker may not do well on this type of pencil-paper, time and power, group-administered, multiple-choice test.

RENZULLI: MODELS OF IDENTIFICATION AND TEACHING

Joseph Renzulli, professor of educational psychology and director of the Teach the Talented Program at the University of Connecticut in Storrs, is an advocate and designer of pullout programs that fall under his umbrella of school-wide enrichment (Renzulli, 1986; Renzulli & Reis, 1986).

Discussion

Renzulli is the originator of the three-ring conception of giftedness (Fig. 5-1).

Advantages

This model offers flexibility for both student selection and scheduling, and philosophically leans to inclusion.

Disadvantages

Opponents say the fare is diluted and that programs based on exclusivity foster deeper, higher learning.

GARDNER: THEORY OF MULTIPLE INTELLIGENCES

Howard Gardner describes seven separate intelligences: linguistic, musical,

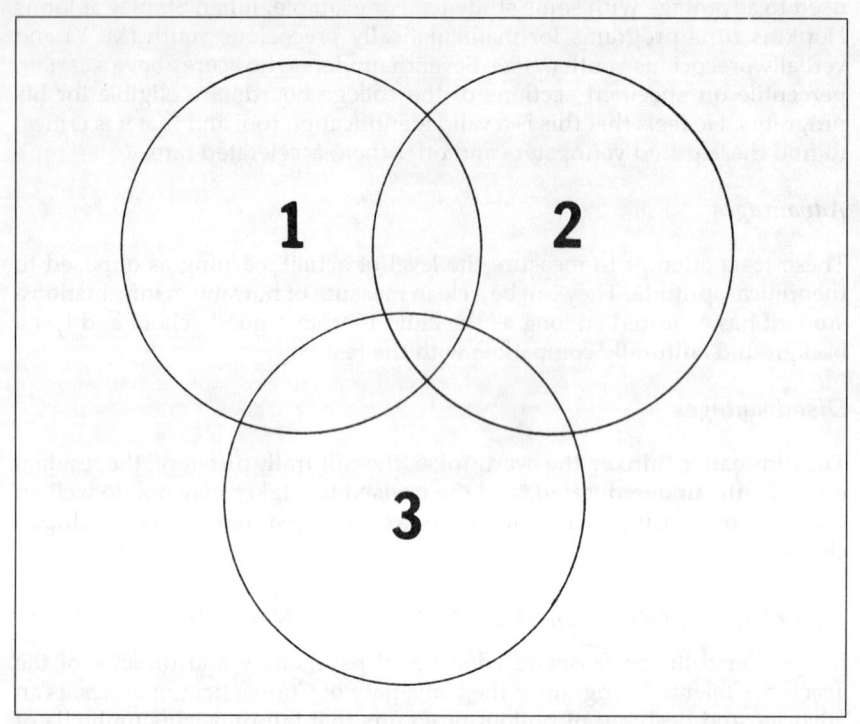

Fig. 5-1. Renzulli's three-ring conception of giftedness. 1 = above average ability; 2 = creativity, and 3 = task commitment. (Redrawn from J. Renzulli (1986). The three ring conception of giftedness; a developmental model for creative productivity. In R. J. Sternberg and J. E. Davidson (Eds.), *Conceptions of giftedness.* New York: Cambridge University Press.)

logical/mathematical, spatial, bodily/kinesthetic, interpersonal, and intrapersonal (1983).

Discussion

Evident as these abilities are in many major thinkers and contributors to our civilization, they may not raise a student's grade point average, and many of these intelligences go hand in hand with school failure. Gardner provides a scientifically respected way of seeing where a child is "at promise" as well as at "at risk." Drawing from anthropology and the arts, as well as from education and science, he offers a generous way of looking at human beings.

Advantages

Gardner's work offers an expanded view of intelligence and giftedness. It is inclusive, innovative, and judged scientifically sound by his peers in medicine, science, and education.

Disadvantages

There is no test at this time, so the interested observer/diagnostician must read Gardner's book and then judge for him- or herself. Shortcut seekers will find this disappointing.

STERNBERG: TRIARCHIC THEORY OF HUMAN INTELLIGENCE

Discussion

Robert J. Sternberg's triarchic theory combines assessment of the following elements: componential (internal), experiential (internal and external), and contextual (external). Each of these, in turn, is built from its own three subsets. Componential combines metacomponents, performance, and knowledge/acquisition. Experiential combines novelty, automatization, and motivation. Contextual combines adapting to environments, shaping environments, and selecting environments. Sternberg believes that giftedness shows in superior skill in insight and the ability to deal with novelty (Sternberg, 1985; Sternberg & Kolligian, 1987). The complexity inherent in his model allows for a positive, enthusiastic interpretation of those behaviors and thought patterns that may be at variance with traditional academic expectations.

Advantages

Sternberg's complex and erudite work allows for the inclusion of common sense and "street smarts" in measuring intelligence. His model can be used to account for and explain the existence and perpetuation of learning disabilities, and it increases the opportunities and ways a person may show intelligence. Thus his bias is toward inclusion. His interpretation of both giftedness and learning disabilities implies that some people will fit both categories at once.

Disadvantages

As with Gardner, at this writing no test is available commercially.

KAUFMAN ASSESSMENT BATTERY FOR CHILDREN (K-ABC)

The K-ABC, developed by Alan and Nadine Kaufman, is normed for children from age 2½ to 12½. It is based on the work of the Russian neurologist A. R.

Luria and on the Kaufmans' experiences working with David Wechsler on the development of his tests (K-ABC, 1984). The test is designed to distinguish between simultaneous and sequential thinking and learning.

Discussion

The K-ABC results add a heretofore missing dimension to the evaluation and discussion of an individual's learning style. The spontaneous, intuitive learner may do poorly in a bottom to top, sequentially organized curriculum. The child with weak rote memory who prefers manipulatives to symbols may have severe academic problems and still be very intelligent. This instrument allows such discrepant patterns to emerge.

Advantages

This test can be given by a tester who need not be a certified psychologist. It can precede or follow a Wechsler assessment without duplication or contamination, and the design and results of the subtests dovetail well. Many students who do poorly on rote memory tasks in school show similar patterns on the K-ABC, but they also have a chance to demonstrate companion strengths on other subtests.

Disadvantages

Because this test is less than 10 years old, not enough time has passed for a large body of interpretive data to develop. It takes over an hour to administer the whole battery, several subtests are culturally biased, and the achievement sections are inferior to the rest of the instrument.

TEACHER NOMINATION
Discussion

As will be seen shortly, the collection of traits associated with giftedness are both a bane and a blessing, and many of them create friction in traditional classrooms.

Advantages

Teacher nomination allows for assessing the child in the context of daily learning, in a group as well as individually. The alert, intuitive teacher has access to observations no one else can make.

Disadvantages

Teachers are human and may not be able to be objective. The well-behaved child may have an unfair advantage; the original thinker may be an inconvenience and hence be misinterpreted or overlooked in the search for the perfect gifted child.

PARENT NOMINATION

Discussion

Although parental nomination may be an important part of the process, it cannot be the whole process.

Advantages

Parents are their children's first and lifelong advocates. Joined by genetics, daily living, and intense interest, they often recognize patterns of behavior the rest of us do not see.

Disadvantages

All parents see gifts in their children. How can parental assessment be objective? Some parents proclaim their children gifted because they themselves are vicariously competitive. Others fear their child's estrangement from friends, which often follows the identification of a child as gifted.

SELF-NOMINATION

Discussion

Self-nomination should be allowed whenever possible because it is an excellent barometer of interest. This coordinates with Renzulli's inclusion of task-commitment in the three circles.

Advantages

To know one's own strengths and weaknesses is a cornerstone of maturity.

Disadvantages

This opportunity may reward the braggart, paralyze the insecure, or perplex the ambivalent.

VAIL: TEN TRAITS*

The Vail model of identifying gifted students looks for certain characteristics of traits (Vail, 1987). While these traits invigorate learning, they may also create friction in the classroom or in the home. In fairness to the students evaluators are trying to understand, it needs to be acknowledged that singly, or in combination, these traits can be both blessings and burdens.

Discussion

1. *Rapid grasp of concepts.* Gifted people grasp concepts so quickly it seems as if the knowledge has been inside them all along, waiting to be awakened simply by being mentioned. Although such "instant learning" can be stimulating, it can also be unsettling to classmates, teachers, and the student. Classmates may resent a peer who learns without apparent effort, and teachers may resent students who learn without explanations. Students themselves are often perplexed by their talent for "instant learning." They may enjoy the excitement but wonder whether it is dishonest—a sort of intellectual shoplifting—and worry whether knowledge that arrives without effort might vanish without warning. Some gifted students who learn quickly think easy learning does not count, and they develop a cynical attitude toward schooling in general.

2. *Awareness of patterns.* Gifted people are unusually alert to patterns. They recognize symmetry in nature, in seashells, or in leaves, and in such humanmade creations as architecture and art. They notice patterns of interval and repetition in mathematics and music, frequently relating the one to the other. They understand abstract conceptual patterns that may connect such seemingly different disciplines as science and art and, through language, they recognize the psychological patterns in literature that parallel those in daily living. Thinking in patterns is a way of thinking in analogy, the foundation of much higher-level academic work. But it is not always easy for others to understand the patterns the gifted student sees. Adults or peers may think the child is being purposely obscure, just as he or she may become annoyed by their apparent slow wit.

3. *Energy.* Intellectual and psychological energy levels may exceed a gifted person's level of physical energy. Physical energy is more evident to the casual observer than the other two, but these energies of the mind are the fuel for abstract exploration and discovery. Unfortunately, an uncertain or weary adult may misinterpret a student's high intellectual energy as a personal challenge instead of recognizing it as the urge to pursue a problem longer and more deeply than other persons. The student who persists with,

---

*This description initially appeared in P. L. Vail (1987). *Smart Kids with School Problems; Things to Know and Ways to Help* (pp. 2–6). New York: Dutton.

"But have you stopped to think about . . ." or "I know something else about that that no one else thought of . . ." is sometimes an unwelcome challenge.

4. *Curiosity.* Curiosity spurs vigorous investigation of physical, intellectual, or psychological realms. It is as natural a force to gifted thinkers as physiologic hunger and thirst. Questions of "why?" "how come . . .?" "where did . . .?" "when was the first . . .?" "what is . . . made of?" have led to great discoveries, but such questions are not always welcome in school. They may take time from the matter at hand and are seen as diversions. Sadly, too, teachers who are uncomfortable not knowing an answer resent students with wide, deep curiosity. When a student of any age finds curiosity unwelcome in school, the temptation is to save it for extracurricular endeavors.

5. *Concentration.* Many gifted people can focus their intellectual energies for long periods of time. Although the ability to concentrate is admirable and deserves exercise, it is often at odds with academic schedules and family living. Big ideas need generous pieces of time if they are not to be lost, but school schedules are built of 40-minute class periods, and the clock governs such family activities as car pools, soccer practices, music lessons, and dentist appointments, or mealtimes. The gifted may need large unstructured periods of time.

6. *Exceptional memory.* The gifted person may have an encyclopedic memory for people, events, and emotions both in their experiences and from their reading. A student may have a vivid recollection of the blue front door to his grandmother's house that he has not seen since the age of 4. Paradoxically, this same student may forget last week's spelling rule, the multiplication tables, or the capital of North Dakota. This discrepancy between a powerful experiential memory and a weak memory for specific factual information may create an incorrect impression of a kid who "doesn't care," "hasn't studied," or "only learns what he feels like learning."

7. *Empathy.* The gifted person is often highly sensitive to the feelings of others. Students who feel welcome in school can use their empathetic skills positively, enhancing the quality of everyone's life in the classroom, lunchroom, and halls or on the athletic field. The unwelcome gifted thinker whose traits create friction in conventional academic settings may choose to use this empathy negatively, knowing just how to gain attention or make trouble.

8. *Vulnerability.* A young poet creating new patterns or metaphors may be stubbornly innovative and invulnerable to the criticisms of an unimaginative teacher. This same young poet, however, is often socially and emotionally more vulnerable than his or her peers, particularly to loneliness that comes from the knowledge of being different. A look at real children shows that intellectual strength confers no immunity to emotional pain.

9. *Heightened perception.* Like the other traits, heightened perceptions complicate life for gifted people. They focus on beauty and also on ugliness, on joy and also on pain, on the attainable and on the unattainable. These

perceptions cast a mercilessly bright light on the discrepancies between reality and the ideal, sometimes throwing the perceiver off balance. For example, young children with heightened perceptions often become intellectually aware of the idea of death before knowing how to make emotional peace with its inevitability. The knowledge arrives spontaneously, pushing the child into a period of distress aroused by heightened perceptions but not alleviated by them.

10. *Divergent thinking.* Divergent thinkers who enjoy open-ended questions see problems and situations from unusual angles and can tolerate the ambiguity of seeing things from several different points of view. They are willing to wrestle with "what if . . ." and are happiest exploring questions that have no verifiable answers in the back of the book. Their ability to recognize patterns, combined with their heightened perceptions, often lead them to insights that may be bewildering to the rest of us or that seem "off the track" or "beside the point." This kind of originality can create friction between a gifted student and the kind of teacher who wants everyone in the class to use identical procedures.

Advantages

This is an inclusionary point of view. Diagnosticians, educators, and parents who use it feel it stands up well.

Disadvantages

There is no test to validate a hunch. Altogether this approach may help in recognizing giftedness, it does not focus on the gifted learning disabled as such.

CLASSIFICATION OF GIFTEDNESS

When used as a label, the word *gifted* can be cruel, inaccurate, or confusing. The numerical criteria vary in an unsettling way from community to community as well as from state to state. In concluding one section of a workshop I gave recently, I asked if there were questions. "Should I move?" asked a mother. I thought her chair was perhaps uncomfortable. "Sure there are plenty of chairs in front," I replied. "No. No. I mean sell my house and move." "Why?" I asked. "Because you see in our town you have to be 125 to be gifted, and my kid is 123. But two towns away you only have to be 120. See? Should I move?"

The criteria also shift according to M & Ms, and this does not mean little chocolate candies, but rather *marks and money.* How surprising that when a certain sum is allocated for a program for the gifted in a community or district, an exactly fitting number of gifted children float to the surface. But what happens if the funds dry up? A 10-year-old friend of mine told me proudly, "I'm gifted." I saw him 2 years later when half of the funding was gone. "How are you, Sam?" "Not good. Not good at all. They dropped me out of gifted. I guess I'm not smart any more." He had gone from gifted to dysgifted. Now if the school administrators in his district could get an increased budget, would he become re-gifted? It sounds funny until we realize that it happened to a real child. Real children's sad feelings are never funny.

As a label, the word *gifted* also creates at least three problems. It implies its own opposite; if you are not gifted, what are you? Worthless, a slug from the garden, or, as the kids would say, "a retard"? Second, the label may be worn as a highly visible addition to the parental feather bonnet, and worst of all, it can spawn the kind of competition that sets learners against each other instead of joining them in the common pursuit of knowledge.

Accurate diagnosis of giftedness in a child or adult will encompass the points of view implicit in the ten models cited above, although the emphasis can differ depending on the reason for needing the word. Is it to qualify for a postdoctoral program in physics? Is it to earn a spot in a pull-out program twice a week for an hour each time in an elementary school? Is it to qualify to enter a separate school or section of a school? Is it to gain permission to participate in a 6-weeks' enrichment program? Is it to get into a Saturday club to learn card tricks and become a junior magician? Is it for a summer program? Or is it needed to highlight the painful discrepancy between high conceptual levels and weak mechanical skills through the use of superficially antithetical terms: gifted learning disabled?

GIFTED LEARNING DISABLED

Having considered ten different models of giftedness, the combination of giftedness and learning disabilities should be explored.

What are these gifted learning disabled kids like? As seen in the comments from the report cards, they may be students who relish thinking and problem solving but have poor organizational skills. Some are imaginative, verbal students whose written work is poor. Others remember their experiences, persons, and emotions but cannot seem to memorize school work. Some have trouble listening and following directions. Others do not seem to harness their intelligence. Or they may be young people who welcome challenge outside of school but avoid it in the classroom.

Studies focused on identifying the gifted learning disabled have shown the inherent difficulties (Daniels, 1983; Elkind, 1973; Senf, 1983). The same problem may exist in identifying gifted children in general (Fox, Brady, & Tobin, 1983).

A gifted learning disabled child shows depressed academic skills combined with personality or behavior disturbances. Waldron, Saphire, and Rosenblum (1987) have shown that the gifted and the gifted learning disabled student present with different classroom and home behaviors. The gifted students are more disruptive, less respectful toward the adults, and less respectful toward the property of others. In contrast, the gifted learning disabled students were quieter with more passive or asocial behavior. The only gifted learning disabled students identified by the schools in the study were those with disruptive behavior, often associated with possible attention deficit hyperactivity disorder. The more passive students requiring equal attention go unidentified. For these reasons, the models for identification must assess intelligence, achievement, and behavioral characteristics.

A word of caution is that unreadiness for formal academics may sometimes masquerade as a learning disability. The intelligent developmentally unready child (Jansky, 1975) needs to be given extra time. Advanced verbal skills in a kindergartener, for example, may conceal overall unreadiness (Vail, 1978; Elkind, 1987). By overlooking the underlying immaturity, the child is being set up for school problems that usually start to surface in third grade. Grade-placement decisions must be based on wider criteria than chronologic age (Grant, 1987; Ames 1978). The more intelligent the child is, the more important it is to remember the category of "superior immatures" and to recognize that apparent learning disabilities can be created just as genuine disabilities can be inherited (Vail, 1987).

Emotional vulnerability goes hand in hand with giftedness, and confusion and self-doubt may accompany learning disabilities. When both sets of emotions are combined, the power of the double burden the child carries can be seen, and educators have a double obligation to recognize, diagnose, and prescribe.

WHAT DO THE GIFTED LEARNING DISABLED NEED?

The needs of the gifted learning disabled are three. First, these boys and girls—and the adults they will become—need to experience that social and emotional growth that leads to psychological equilibrium and self-acceptance. The human being arrives on earth with a capacity for language that when nourished, grows into the ability to communicate, moving from inner language to genuine dialogue (Vygotsky, 1962). Then through listening and responding, the child connects with peers and the adult world (Welty, 1983), while moving toward autonomy.

Children who know their own strengths, limits, and compensations are ready to meet the rest of the world on an optimistic, friendly basis because they are friends with themselves. But social/emotional stability may be elusive for these children because their giftedness sets them apart initially;

they feel different. They may require practice in making friends just as other children must practice to learn their math facts. To be both learning disabled and gifted makes a double difference. These children need warmth and wisdom from adults in their lives to attain social/emotional maturity and to avoid the haunting call of the British poet Stevie Smith, "I was too far out all my life and not waving but drowning."

Second, these children need intellectual challenge that offers opportunity for success. Because it is so easy to see what they *cannot* do, particularly in the early years, it takes discipline on educators' parts, along with heightened awareness to see the errors, and then to find what the child is particularly good at. It is important to notice and remark where the child is, in Howard Gardner's words (1983) "at promise" as well as "at risk."

Gardner (1986) suggests that each evaluation of a child, whether it be a school conference, report card, or comprehensive pyschoeducational workup, should begin with a "propensities report." Looking at the child through the lens of Gardner's multiple intelligences will give a clear indication of what chrysalid abilities need to be developed. While untended weaknesses ache, unexercised talents itch.

Finally, gifted learning disabled children need an honest and realistic interface with the outside world, built on mutual respect. The child who is helped to meet the first two needs is ready and equipped for this one. Honest interface means providing the necessary support to compensate for the disabilities so the child can go on with the business of living in spite of them. At the very least, like everyone else, these children need to be able to read the warnings on the medicine bottle, understand the directions on a tax form, and complete a job application or write a business letter without looking foolish. These take work and training, but they can be done.

Young children judge their own competence as learners (which they often equate with their worth as human beings) by success or failure in initial experiences with reading, writing, spelling, and pencil-paper arithmetic (Eisenberg, 1975). We have only to look at the studies correlating juvenile crime and learning disabilities (Hogensen, 1974) to see the urgency for providing early preventive measures. We have only to look at the tragedy of and increase in juvenile suicide to see that school problems can be unbearable. And we have only to reflect on the traits of giftedness to understand the extra pain resulting from the combination of giftedness and learning disabilities. To meet the need for honest interface with the world, these students need the specific kinds of support that will turn them from learned helplessness (Seligman, 1975) to learned competence.

Home life and school life should offer similar emotional support but different types of experience. At home, parents can offer the assurance of love in spite of academic problems. Through daily living, by allying themselves with what the child does well, they can give evidence of faith and good humor. Parents also need to be encouraged to "find a pro you trust and then trust the pro," relieving themselves of guilt and providing privacy for the student who is learning to overcome difficulties.

To outline productive strategies, some components of the students' academic life should be considered: the options, types of setting, types of work, measures of mastery, and teacher's personal qualities. Which emotions and experiences the school is trying to foster and provide need to be determined.

OPTIONS IN EDUCATION

In educating the gifted, the options are to separate, accelerate, enrich, or ignore.

In fairness to the student, there must be a separation between remedial support and intellectual expansion: They cannot come in the same package. When the classroom or discipline-specific teacher is untrained in working with either learning disabled or gifted students, the youngster must receive alternative support, perhaps in a resource room, sometimes in a pull-out program, sometimes in private tutoring.

Acceleration of the gifted has its devotees (Stanley, 1977), but too many instances of brittleness, unhappiness, and even intellectual and emotional paralysis result from trying to raise a "one-minute kid" (Vail, 1976). Certainly talent in math and music (which peak early) needs vigilant support. But as seen in Bloom's studies on what produces great skills (1976), lateral expansion, parental interest, and an affectionate relationship with the teacher matter more in the formative years than vertical growth and high-powered demands.

When enrichment permeates a whole school, academic life becomes more interesting for all students, not to mention their teachers. The Renzulli model (1986b) illustrates that this depends more on a point of view than a specific dollar amount and can flourish in schools with modest budgets. By offering ceilingless activities in reading, writing, math, science, or the arts, the teacher encourages students with particular propensities to soar, perhaps taking others along in a contagion of enthusiasms. In this setting, the more pedantic student is still free to work along at a measured pace, and no student needs to feel either repressed or pressured. Enrichment is an automatic companion of those methods and materials that honor originality over conformity.

Sadly, because gifted learning disabled students are inconvenient, their needs are often ignored. When educators do not know how to provide for specific needs, they are apt to duck the question by denying the existence of the problem (back to hidden in plain sight). Most educators, benevolent by nature, are increasingly willing to acknowledge a problem when a solution is possible and affordable.

The ideal strategy is to train classroom teachers at every grade level to recognize the learning disabled and to use multisensory teaching techniques on a regular basis (Traub & Bloom, 1975; Enfield, 1987). This approach is more cost effective than hiring enough special educators to teach every child in need. It also reduces the chance that the clever young child will slip between the cracks because the difficulty is not crippling enough to keep him or her 2 years behind grade level, the qualifying criterion for extra help in many school systems. Although, of course, some children need special training and support services in addition to the teaching they receive in the classroom, putting special education techniques in regular classrooms creates continuity and consistency between how children are taught in class and the extra support they get on the side. Using resource teachers to train faculty members in diagnosis and remediation expands the benefits of specialized knowledge, empowers teachers, helps students, and saves money.

Administrators have the double power to hire and require. By hiring teachers who also have training in special education, by encouraging and rewarding teachers who seek out such training, and by restructuring the role of the resource teacher, an administrator can build a whole faculty of proud professionals qualified to handle a problem instead of denying or ignoring its existence. Denial steals energy and breeds resentment.

Types of Settings

Gifted learning disabled students need to work in three different types of setting: with the whole class, in small groups, and alone. They need to do some things with the whole group because they have excellent contributions to make, and they need to be woven into the fabric of the class. They need to work in small groups sharing a particular interest or in small groups that combine divergent talents. When a shy artist, a skillful wordsmith, an inventive musician, a nonacademic athlete, an average kid, and a class leader cooperate on a project, be it dinosaurs or colonial American culture, the result will be richer than anything each could produce alone. These students also need to work alone on independent projects. Sometimes they work much more quickly than other students, but frequently they work more slowly, partly because of their learning disabilities, partly because their levels of interest run deep. They need the luxury of time to penetrate far below the surface in their explorations, to see the connections and patterns that bring high delight to them and new insights to the rest.

Types of Work

These students need three different types of work: factual, aesthetic, and imaginary. But much traditional education only focuses on the first. Certainly gifted learning disabled students need a solid body of reliable factual information to serve as the skeletal structure for their thinking and subsequent learning. We cannot afford the "planned amnesia" E. D. Hirsch decries in *Cultural Literacy*. It is not only contemporary voices that speak to this point. Louis Pasteur said, "Chance favors the prepared mind."

In addition to acquiring facts, these students need aesthetic opportunities to develop the patterns and connections mentioned here and to connect what they are learning with what stirs in their souls. Studies of the relationship between the limbic system and higher cortical function demonstrate that positive emotional engagement enhances the entire learning process (Restak, 1984). Thus neurology joins with literature in urging aesthetic and intellectual fusion; in *Howard's End*, the novelist E. M. Forster pleads, "Only connect."

Gifted students, learning disabled students, and particularly students who are both gifted and learning disabled need imaginary work. They deserve to move beyond other persons' discoveries. The utilitarian educator, the modern day equivalent of Dickens' Gradgrind, may dismiss imaginary work as frivolous. But the imaginations and dreams of gifted thinkers have given society its richest treasures. A student cannot be told to "Put your imagination in the freezer until you have graduated from school, and then put it in the microwave to start it up again." Children must be helped to keep their imaginations sparkling and working all the way along. Pie in the sky from an idealist? Hardly. Albert Einstein, whose quiddity may have lain in his combination of giftedness and dyslexia, wrote, "The gift of fantasy has meant more to me than my talent for absorbing positive knowledge."

Measures of Mastery

Standardized tests, oddly enough, can protect creativity. A strong objective profile can free a teacher to use projects and creativity as well as workbooks and basals. When standardized test scores are low or average, as they often are for the gifted learning disabled student, they should be kept in proper proportion, offering other measures in the student's cumulative dossier.

Children come alive in narrative reports; they vanish in check lists. Although comments are time consuming for a teacher to write, educators owe personalized evaluation to students and their parents. Numerical or letter grades are a fact of life, but they need to be balanced by other measures.

The materials used and the ways educators assess mastery reflect their priorities. Theodore Sizer, former dean of the Harvard Graduate School of Education and author of *Horace's Compromise: the Dilemma of the American High School*, urges educators to move far beyond the traditional written book report and blue book exam. He must have had gifted learning disabled students in mind when he described alternative "exhibitions": models, art projects, original drama, simulation games, photography, or documented science experiments. The list is only limited by the breadth and depth of one's imagination.

Teachers' Personal Qualities

Who should teach these children, and what specific stores of knowledge do these teachers need? Certainly anyone teaching learning disabled students needs solid grounding in multisensory techniques and the strategies for special education. If these were part of every teacher-training institution and graduate school, education would be more effective across the board (Enfield, 1987). But the interested administrator can make this knowledge available to teachers who can also find it on their own.

From the educational research, psychological studies, and personal experience, the personal qualities in a teacher that matter to a child are known. In her many years of offering training, Katrina deHirsch has said, "Children move from learning to love to loving to learn." Struggling learning disabled students, frustrated gifted thinkers, or intellectual adventurers frightened by their own power need strong supportive adult presence to maintain internal stamina.

In a 5-day seminar at Wellesley College for leaders in elementary education, the participants were asked for the personal qualities of teachers they remembered best. Over and over, they responded fair, demanding, humorous, tough, supportive, intellectually awake, curious, warm but not permissive, honest, intelligent, and knowledgeable in subject matter. Brilliant was seldom mentioned. Granted, these were not post-doctoral fellows in physics. They were elementary educators, but the later learner is only an extension of the beginner.

EDUCATORS' GOALS

My view of the emotions and experiences schools should hope to offer forms the body of this paper, not simply a personal wish list but a model of benevolent and powerful education, drawn from the practical experience and musings of giants in education and medicine.

Ned Hallowell, instructor in psychiatry at Harvard Medical School and school psychiatrist at Fessenden School and Brookwood School, spoke at a conference entitled "Anarchy, Discipline, and Moral Behavior in the Middle School" in January 1986. He is quoted in the October 1986 issue of *Independent School:* "Remember that time of life, that state of mind, when you were lord of all the fields and king or queen of all the stars and feel now how much your will to love and dream and risk and create depends on your having had that once, having had that time when everything was new and possible and impossible all at once."

Realistically, do educators go forward with pessimism or optimism? Pessimism wins out if some of the current cries for educational reform are listened to. Pressure for higher test scores will constrict the originality of many creative thinkers. Raising standards without increasing support runs the risk of crushing the undiagnosed gifted learning disabled student. Encouraging imaginative men and women into teaching and then burying them in bureaucracy rewards the pedant and punishes the potential star. Charting children by numbers promotes ridiculous policies. In one instance a gifted dyslexic had remedial help withdrawn because she improved so much that she was no longer 2 years below grade level and therefore could not be "serviced" (that verb again). She was too weak to reach her potential without support and too strong to win the numbers game by losing it.

The gifted learning disabled student who is understood and helped faces short-term periods of discomfort and hard work as well as times of great satisfaction. But the student who is not diagnosed and helped faces short-term academic discomfort snowballing into long-term self-doubt, a poor education, diminished professional opportunities and, often, an unfulfilled life.

But in spite of the problems, there are solid grounds for hope. The education field is literally exploding with new, solid knowledge about learning levels and patterns. Intelligent, dedicated educators are working to liberate the gifted, the learning disabled, and those who fit both categories. Increasing numbers of reliable lenses are available through which to look at how, why, and when children learn.

Excellent and inexpensive printed materials and games for teaching the mechanics of reading, writing, and spelling are also available. Electronic saviors are rescuing poor spellers or good thinkers with illegible handwriting. There are tantalizing manipulative materials for teaching math. More and more, these materials are making their way into classrooms all over the country. At conferences, educators have opportunities to see, hear, and touch what is new and what is good that is not new.

Perhaps as exciting as any other development is the willingness of some of the most prestigious colleges and universities to acknowledge the presence of gifted learning disabled students on their campuses and their dedication to bending some of the academic machinery in accommodation (Brown, 1985). When such institutions as Brown, Dartmouth, Stanford, and Harvard proudly claim these students, it helps other institutions feel they belong to a noble tradition.

Openness from gifted learning disabled students themselves helps others see the complexity and the power these people offer. In addition to the examples from the past, Bruce Jenner, Susan Hampshire, and now Whoopi Goldberg, to mention three celebrities, are highly visible models of successful young people living rich, productive lives in spite of, and because of, the paradox of their learning styles.

Gifted learning disabled students have always been among us, but have often been misunderstood, undervalued, and forced through a system they could neither escape nor conquer. Now educators have the knowledge to make a differential diagnosis and the lenses through which to see gifted dyslexics for what and who they are. They are no longer hidden in plain sight.

REFERENCES

Bloom, B. S. (1976). *Human characteristics and school learning*. New York: McGraw-Hill.
Brown University. (1985, June). *Dyslexics at Brown: A Student Perspective*. One of a series of occasional publications of the Office of the Dean of the College, Providence, RI.
Daniels, P. R. (1983). *Teaching the gifted/learning disabled child*. Rockville, MD: Aspen.
Eisenberg, L. (1975). *Psychiatric aspects of language disability, reading, perception and language* (pp. 215–229). Baltimore: York.
Elkind, D. *Miseducation: Pre-schoolers at risk*. (1987). New York: Knopf.
Elkind, J. (1973). The gifted child with learning disabilities. *Gifted Child Quarterly, 20*, 478–490.
Enfield, M. L. (1987). *A cost-effective classroom alternative to "pull out" programs. Intimacy with language*. Baltimore: Orton Dyslexia Society.
Fox, L. H., Brady, I., & Tobin, D. (1983). *Learning-disabled gifted children: Identification and programming*. Baltimore: University Park.
Fox, L. H. (1984). The learning-disabled gifted child. *Learning Disabilities: An Interdisciplinary Journal, 8*:117–128.
Gardner, H. (1983, 1986). *Frames of mind: The theory of multiple intelligences*. New York: Basic.
Gibson, J., & Chennells, P. (Eds.). (1975). Gifted children; Looking to their future. *Proceedings of the World Conference For Gifted Children*. London: Latimer with National Association for Gifted Children.
Grant, J. *I hate school*. (1987). Rosemont, NJ: Modern Learning.
Hallowell, N. (1986, October). Anarchy, discipline, and moral behavior in the middle school. *Independent School*.
Hirsch, E. D. (1987). *Cultural literacy*. Boston: Houghton Mifflin.
deHirsch, K. (1977). *Interactions between educational therapist and child*. Orton Monograph No. 53. Baltimore: Orton Dyslexia Society.
Hogenson, D. (1974). Reading failure and juvenile delinquency, Orton Monograph No. 63. Baltimore: Orton Dyslexia Society.
Jansky, J. J. (1975). The marginally ready child. Orton Monograph No. 68. Baltimore: Orton Dyslexia Society.
K-ABC. (1984, Fall). Special Issue; *Journal of Special Education, 18* (3).
Kolligian, J., Jr., & Sternberg, R. J. (1987, January). Intelligence, information processing, and specific learning disabilities: a triarchic model. *Journal of Learning Disabilities, 20*(1), 8–17.
Renzulli, J., (1986). The three ring conception of giftedness; a developmental model for creative productivity. In R. J. Sternberg, & J. E. Davidson (Eds.), *Conceptions of giftedness*. New York: Cambridge University Press.
Renzulli, J., & Reis, S. M. (1986). *The schoolwide enrichment model*. Mansfield Center, CT: Creative Learning.
Restak, R. (1984). *The brain*. New York: Bantam.
Seligman, M. E. P. (1975). *Helplessness: On depression, development and death*. San Francisco: Freeman.
Senf, G. W. (1983). The nature and identification of learning disabilities and their relationship to the gifted child. In L. H. Fox, L. Brady, & D. Tobin (Eds.), *Learning-disabled gifted children: Identification and programming*. (pp. 37–49). Austin, TX: Pro-Ed.

Sizer, T. R. (1984). *Horace's compromise: The dilemma of the American high school.* Boston: Houghton Mifflin.
Stanley, J., George, W. C., & Solona, C. (1977). *The gifted and creative; a 50 year perspective.* Baltimore: Johns Hopkins Press.
Sternberg, R. J. (1985). *Beyond I.Q.: A triarchic theory of human intelligence.* Cambridge, England: Cambridge University Press.
Traub, N., & Bloom, F. et al. (1975). *Recipe for reading.* Cambridge, MA: Educator's Publishing.
Vail, P. L. (1987). *Gifted, precocious or just plain smart?* New York: Programs for Education.
Vail, P. L. (1987). *Smart kids with school problems; Things to know and ways to help.* New York: Dutton.
Vail, P. L. (1986). The one minute kid. (pp. 15–18). *Independent School.*
Vail, P. L. (1979). *The world of the gifted child.* New York: Walker.
Vail, P. L. (1978). The gifted child; Common sense, uncommon needs. *Independent School.*
Vance, H. B., & Singer, M. G. (1979). Recategorization of WISC-R subtest scaled scores for learning disabled children. *Journal of Learning Disabilities, 12*(8), 63–66.
Vygotsky, L. (1962). *Thought and language.* Cambridge: M.I.T. Press.
Waldron, K. A., Saphire, D. G., & Rosenblum, S. (1987). Learning disabilities and giftedness: Identification based on self-concept, behavior, and academic patterns. *Journal of Learning Disabilities, 20:*422–427.
Welty, E. (1983). *One writer's beginnings.* Cambridge: Harvard University Press.
Whitmore, J. R. (1980). *Giftedness, conflict, and underachievement.* Boston: Allyn & Bacon.
Whitmore, J. R., & Maker, C. J. (1985). *Intellectual giftedness in disabled persons.* Rockville, MD: Aspen.

SUGGESTED READING

Ames, L. B. (1978). *Is your child in the wrong grade?* Rosemont, NJ: Modern Learning.
Anderson, R. C., Heibert, E. H., Scott, J. A., & Wilkinson, I. A. G. (1985). *The report of the commission on reading: Becoming a nation of readers.* Washington, DC: The National Academy of Education, The National Institute of Education, The Center for the Study of Reading.
Ansara, A. (1972). Language therapy to salvage the college potential of dyslexic adolescents. *Orton Monograph* No. 78. Baltimore: Orton Dyslexia Society.
Blachman, B. A. (1983). Are we assessing the linguistic factors critical in early reading? *Annals of Dyslexia 33;* 91–109.
Bloom, B. S. (1976). *Human characteristics and school learning.* New York: McGraw-Hill.
Bowlby, J. (1980). *Loss, sadness, and depression.* New York: Basic.
Bright, G. (1970). The adolescent with scholastic failure. *Orton Monograph* No. 33. Baltimore: Orton Dyslexia Society.
Brown University. (1985, June). *Dyslexics at Brown: A Student Perspective.* One of a series of occasional publications of the Office of the Dean of the College, Providence, RI.
Brutten, M., Richardson, S. O., & Mangel, C. (1979). *Something's wrong with my child.* New York: Harcourt, Brace, Jovanovich.
Clarke, L. (1973). *Can't read, can't write, can't talk too good either.* New York: Penguin.
Cordoni, B. (1982, November). A directory of college LD Services. *Journal of Learning Disabilities. 15*(9), 529–534.
Cowin, P., & Graff, V. (1977). Comprehensive treatment of the older disabled reader. *Orton Monograph* No. 28. Baltimore: Orton Dyslexia Society.
Cox, A. R. (1967, 1969, 1974). *Structures and techniques. Remedial language training; Multisensory teaching for alphabetic phonics.* Cambridge: Educator's Publishing Service.

Critchley, M. (1981). *Dyslexia research and its application to education.* London: Wiley.
Daniels, P. R. (1983). *Teaching the gifted learning disabled child.* Rockville, MD: Aspen.
Denckla, M. B., & Rudel, R. G. (1974). Rapid 'automatized' naming of pictured objects, colors, letters and numbers by normal children. *Cortex, 10,* 186–202.
Denckla, M. B. & Rudel, R. G. (1976). Rapid 'automatized' naming (R.A.N.): Dyslexia differentiated from other learning disabilities. *Neuropsychologia, 14,* 471–479.
Eisenberg, L. (1975). Psychiatric aspects of language disability. *Reading, Perception and Language,* 215–229. (Baltimore: York, 1975).
Elkind, D. (1981). *The hurried child.* Reading, MA: Addison-Wesley.
Elkind, D. (1987). *Miseducation: Pre-schoolers at risk.* New York: Knopf.
Erikson, E. H. (1950). The eight ages of man. In *Childhood and society.* New York: Norton.
Erikson, E. H. (1968). *Identity: Youth and crisis.* New York: Norton.
Featherstone, H. (1980). *A Difference in the family.* New York: Basic.
Feldman, D. H. (1986). *Nature's gambit: Child prodigies and the development of human potential.* New York: Basic.
Fraiberg, S. H. (1959). *The magic years.* New York: Scribner's.
Galaburda, A. M. (1985). Developmental dyslexia: A review of biological interactions. *Annals of Dyslexia, 35,* 21–33.
Gallagher, J. (1975). *Teaching the gifted child.* (2nd Ed.). Boston: Allyn & Bacon.
Gardner, H. (1983). *Frames of mind: The theory of multiple intelligences.* New York: Basic.
Geschwind, N. (1984). The brain of a learning disabled individual. *Annals of Dyslexia 34,* 319–327.
Geschwind, N. (1982). Why Orton was right. *Annals of Dyslexia, 32,* 13–30.
Gillespie, J. (1982, November). The pushouts: Academic skills and learning disabilities in continuation high school students. *Journal of Learning Disabilities, 15,*(9), 539–540.
Grant, J. (1986). *I hate school.* Rosemont, NJ: Programs for Education.
Hampshire, S. (1982). *Susan's story.* New York: St. Martin's.
Healy, J. M. (1987). *Your child's growing mind: A parent's guide to learning.* New York: Doubleday.
Heath, D. (1977). Academic predictors of adult maturity and competence. *Journal of Higher Education, 48,* 613–632.
Heath, D. (1976). Adolescent and adult predictors of vocational adaptation. *Journal of Vocational Behavior, 9,* 1–19.
Heath, D. (1977). Some possible effects of occupation on the maturing of professional men. *Journal of Vocational Behavior, 11,* 263–281.
Heath, D. (1978). Teaching for adult effectiveness. *Journal of Experiential Education, 1,* 6–11.
Hernstein, R. J., & Wilson, J. Q. (1985). *Crime and human nature.* New York: Simon & Schuster.
Hinds, K. (1985, January). Dyslexia. *Brown Alumni Monthly.* Providence, RI: Brown University.
deHirsch, K. (1977). Interactions Between Educational Therapist and Child. *Orton Monograph* No. 53. Baltimore: Orton Dyslexia Society.
deHirsch, K. (1984). *Language and the developing child.* Baltimore: Orton Dyslexia Society.
Hirsch, E. D. (1987). *Cultural literacy.* Boston: Houghton Mifflin.
Hogenson, D. (1974). Reading failure and juvenile delinquency. *Orton Monograph* No. 63. Baltimore: Orton Dyslexia Society.
Howe, B. (1982, November). A language skills program for secondary LD students. *Journal of Learning Disabilities, 15*(9), 541–544.
Jansky, J. J. (1975). The marginally ready child. *Orton Monograph* No. 68. Baltimore: Orton Dyslexia Society.
Johnson, D. J., & Myklebust, H. R. (1971). *Learning disabilities: educational principles and practices.* New York: Grune & Stratton.
K-ABC. (1984, Fall). Special Issue; *The Journal of Special Education, 18*(3).

Kagan, J. (1984). *The nature of the child*. New York: Basic.
Kastein, S., & Trace, B. (1966). The Birth of Language. Springfield, IL: Thomas.
Keogh, B. K. & Pelland, M. (1985, April). Vision training revisited. *Journal of Learning Disabilities. 18*(4), 228–236.
Kesselman-Turkel, J., & Peterson, F. (1981). *Study smarts*. Chicago: Contemporary.
King, D. H. (1986). *Keyboarding*. Cambridge: Educator's Publishing Service.
Lash, J. P. (1980). *Master and teacher, the biography of Helen Keller*. New York: Delacorte.
Levine, M. D. (1987). *Developmental variation and learning disorders*. Cambridge: Educator's Publishing Service.
Levinger, L. (1977). The intellectually superior child. In Call, J., Noshpitz, J., Berlin, I., Cohen, R. (Eds.), *Basic handbook of child psychiatry*. New York: Basic.
Lieberman, S. (1984, March). Visual perception vs. visual function. *Journal of Learning Disabilities, 17*(3), 180–181.
Liscio, M. A. (Ed.). (1985). *A guide to colleges for learning disabled students*. Orlando, FL: Academic/Grune & Stratton.
Luria, A. R. (1987). *The mind of a mnemonist*. Cambridge: Harvard University Press. (Originally published New York: Basic, 1968.)
Masland, R. H. (1976). The Advantages of Being Dyslexic. *Orton Monograph* No. 72. Baltimore: Orton Dyslexia Society.
MacCracken, M. (1976). *Turnabout children*. Boston: Little Brown.
McGuinness, D. (1986). *When children don't learn*. New York: Basic Books.
National Association of Secondary School Principals. College Study Skills Program, Reston, VA (1979). Developed by Milton Academy and Harvard University.
Oliphant, G. (1976). The lens of language. *Bulletin of The Orton Dyslexia Society, 26*, 49–62.
Orton Dyslexia Society. (1987). Intimacy With Language. *Proceedings of the ODS Symposium*. Airlie, VA.
Passow, A. H. (1987). Issues and trends in curriculum for the gifted. *Gifted International, 4*(2). New York: Trillium.
Plunkett, M. (1967). *A writing manual for teaching the left-handed*. Cambridge: Educator's Publishing Service.
Rawson, M. B. (1978). *Adult accomplishments of dyslexic boys*. Cambridge: Educator's Publishing Service.
Rawson, M. (1977). Dyslexics as adults; the possibilities and the challenge. *Orton Monograph* No. 22.
Rawson, M. B. (1974). Self concept and the cycle of growth. *Orton Monograph* No. 62.
Renzulli, J. (1986). The three ring conception of giftedness; a developmental model for creative productivity. In R. J. Sternberg & J. E. Davidson (Eds.), *Conceptions of giftedness*. New York: Cambridge University Press.
Renzulli, J. & Reis, S. M. (1986). *The schoolwide enrichment model*. Mansfield Center, CT: Creative Learning.
Reichman, J., & William C. H. (1983, May). Conductive hearing loss involving otitis media. *Journal of Learning Disabilities, 16*(5), 272–278.
Rosner, J. (1979) *Helping children overcome learning difficulties*. New York: Walker.
Ste. Exupery, A.(1943). *The little prince*. New York: Reynal & Hitchcock.
Selfe, L. *Nadia*. (1979). New York: Harcourt Brace Jovanovich (by arrangement with Academic, London).
Seligman, M. E. P. (1975). *Helplessness: On depression, development and death*. San Francisco: Freeman.
Silva, P. A., Kirkland, C., Simpson, A., Stewart, I. A., & Williams, S. M. (1982). Some developmental and behavioral problems associated with bilateral otitis media with effusion. *Journal of Learning Disabilities, 15*(7), 417–421.
Silver, L. (1984). *The misunderstood child*. New York: McGraw-Hill.

Simpson, E. (1979). *Reversals: A personal account of victory over dyslexia.* Boston: Houghton Mifflin.
Sisk, D. (1987). *Creative teaching of the gifted.* New York: McGraw-Hill.
Sizer, T. R. (1984). *Horace's compromise: The dilemma of the American high school.* Boston: Houghton Mifflin.
Smith, S. L. (1979). *No easy answers: The learning disabled child at home and at school.* New York: Bantam.
Stanley, J., George, W. C., & Solona, C. (1977). *The gifted and creative; a 50 year perspective.* Baltimore: Johns Hopkins Press.
Sternberg, R. J., & Kolligian, J., Jr. (1987, January). Intelligence, information processing, and specific learning disabilities: a triarchic model. *Journal of Learning Disabilities, 20*(1).
Strauss, R. (1978). Richard's Story. *Bulletin of The Orton Dyslexia Society, 28,* 181–185.
Terman, L. M. (Ed.). (1925). *Genetic studies of genius: Mental and physical traits of a thousand gifted children.* Palo Alto, CA: Stanford University Press.
Thompson, L. J. (1969). Language Disability in Men of Eminence. *Orton Monograph* No. 27. Baltimore: The Orton Dyslexia Society.
Torrance, E. P. (1965). *Gifted children in the classroom.* New York: Macmillan.
Traub, N., Bloom, F., et al. (1975). *Recipe for reading.* Cambridge: Educator's Publishing Service.
Vail, P. L. (1981). *Clear and lively writing: Language games and activities for everyone.* New York: Walker.
Vail, P. L. (1978). Limerence, language and literature: an essay. *Orton Monograph* No. 77.
Van Tassel-Baska, L. J., & Olszewski, P. (1985). Towards development of an appropriate math/science curriculum for the gifted learner. *Journal for the Education of the Gifted, 8,* 257–272.
Vellutino, F. R. (1977). *Alternative conceptualizations of dyslexia: Evidence in support of a verbal-deficit hypothesis.* Cambridge: Harvard Educational Review, A Special Issue: Reading, Language, and Learning.
Vogel, S. A. (1982, November). On developing LD college programs. *Journal of Learning Disabilities, 15*(9), 518–528.
Vygotsky, L. (1962). *Thought and language.* Cambridge: M.I.T. Press.
Weiner, N. (1953). *Ex-prodigy: My childhood and youth.* New York: Simon & Schuster.
Welty, E. (1983). *One writer's beginnings.* Cambridge: Harvard University Press.
Whitmore, J. R. (1980). *Giftedness, conflict, and underachievement.* Boston: Allyn & Bacon.
Wiig, E. H. & Semel, E. M. (1976). *Language disabilities in children and adolescents.* Columbus, OH: Merrill.

RESOURCES

The Alexander Graham Bell Association for the Deaf, 3417 Volta Place N.W., Washington, DC 20013 offers many materials that are suitable for students with marginal to moderately severe problems with auditory learning, as well as those whose hearing is severely impaired. Their catalogue is free.
The American Association for Gifted Children, 140 East Monument Ave., Dayton, OH 45401.
American Speech, Hearing, and Language Association, 10801 Rockville Pike, Rockville, MD 20852
Association for Children and Adults with Learning Disabilities, 4156 Library Rd., Pittsburgh, PA 15234.

The Association for the Gifted (TAG), c/o Council for Exceptional Children, 1920 Association Dr., Reston, VA 22091
Books On Tape, P.O. Box 7090, Newport Beach, CA 92660
Council for Exceptional Children, 1920 Association Dr., Reston, VA 22091
Council for Learning Disabilities, Education Building, University of Louisville, Louisville, KY 40292
Educator's Publishing Service, 75 Moulton St., Cambridge, MA 02238
The Foundation for Children with Learning Disabilities, 99 Park Ave., New York, NY 10016
International Reading Association, P.O. Box 8139, Newark, DE 19711
Literacy Volunteers of America, whose tutors are trained to work with adults, has branches all over the country. Their main headquarters is 404 Oak St., Syracuse, NY 13203
The National Association of Independent Schools, 18 Tremont St., Boston, MA 02108
National Institute of Dyslexia, 3200 Woodbine St., Chevy Chase, MD 20815
The Orton Dyslexia Society, 724 York Rd., Baltimore, MD 21204
World Council for Gifted and Talented Children. Papers from their annual conference are published yearly by the Trillium Press, Box 921, New York, NY 10159

CHAPTER 6

Challenges for the Future

WILLIAM M.
CRUICKSHANK

> Dr. Cruickshank shares his ideas of the future in special education and presents a series of challenges for the profession.

The problems of the present are clear. The lack of a uniform definition of learning disabilities and criteria for operationalizing that definition has resulted in each school system in the United States doing what it believes to be best. However, in some cases, the decisions may be based on what is best for the budget rather than what is best for the child or adolescent.

The profession of education and especially that component of education that is concerned with students who have learning disabilities must address critical issues. These challenges are present and cannot be avoided.

CHALLENGE NUMBER 1

The profession is challenged to adopt a historically and professionally honest and accurate definition of learning disabilities.

Contained in this challenge are, among others, three significant factors: (1) the acknowledgment of the neurologic basis of all learning and the neurologic dysfunction (actual or authoritatively assumed) in learning disabled people; (2) the recognition that learning disabilities respect no specific intelligence level but are found within the entire intelligence range; and (3), from (1) and (2) above, perceptual processing deficits develop out of which academic, social, and emotional failures multiply.

CHALLENGE NUMBER 2

The profession is challenged to recognize that two disparate groups of children are too often combined in public and private school classrooms (i.e., learning disabled children [as partially defined in Challenge No. 1] and children with problems of learning that are environmentally determined who do not have neurophysiologic dysfunction).

If this challenge is accepted, then schools must have two separate approaches to education for children too often seen as a single group and placed together in classrooms. The schools would have a rich program of structure and developmental education for the learning disabilities group and a rich program of remediation for those with environmentally produced problems of learning. What is needed educationally for one group is almost diametrically the opposite of what is needed for the other group. They cannot effectively be educated together.

CHALLENGE NUMBER 3

The U.S. Department of Education is challenged to stimulate a competent epidemiologic research program, to develop an accurate definition of learning disabilities (Challenge Number 1), and to fund a thorough epidemiologic assessment and study of a population of a minimum of 100,000 children to definitively ascertain the number of learning disabled children in the school-age population.

What is involved in this challenge? First, the cooperation would be needed of a sociologically determined typical American city in which every child of school age, except for those in the highest grade, would be evaluated. Second, the assessment would include accurate tests of auditory perception, visual perception, tactile perception, intelligence, and gross and fine motor development; an appropriate neurophysical developmental scale (e.g., that developed by Dr. Melvin Levine or Dr. Richard Galpin); an educational assessment; and other appropriate diagnostic information (Levine & Saltz, 1984; Galpin, 1971). This is not a matter of wishful thinking; it can be accomplished with skilled personnel within a reasonable period and for a reasonable cost. The profession has struggled with guess work, supposedly accurate estimates, poor definitions, and misunderstandings for too long. It is time that accurate and specific data on incidence and prevalence be obtained and used as a basis for school programming.

CHALLENGE NUMBER 4

The U.S. Department of Education or the National Institute for Mental Health is challenged to undertake a longitudinal study of the effectiveness of one or more educational methodologies recommended for accurately defined learning disabilities in identified children and youth.

I have strongly recommended a five-part program of structure for many years, a program that has proved effective with small groups of children. With several hundred clinical case records as confirmation, the significance of structure for as long as it is needed is seen. On the other hand, there may well be other effective teaching procedures for these children, and they should be studied longitudinally. Too much theory and insufficient corroborated longitudinal research are available to current educators in this significant aspect of the study of learning disabilities and child development.

CHALLENGE NUMBER 5

All teachers of LD children are challenged to read "A New Perspective in Teacher Education: The Neuro-Educator" (Cruickshank, 1981) and to pursue suggestions made there to bring their understanding of learning disabilities and their expertise into harmony with an accurate definition of the problem.

Too many teachers have received their professional preparation at the hands of college or university faculty members who themselves have had limited professional preparation in this area of exceptionality, who have had little or no direct clinical experience with these students, who know little of the neurology of learning disabilities, and who have completed little or no significant research in the field. As a result, the profession is characterized by too many poorly prepared teachers who attempt to use teaching programs that are either inappropriate or, at best, poor. Further professional exposure to courses and faculty members directly involved on the cutting edge of learning disabilities is mandated if the field is to serve these young people.

CHALLENGE NUMBER 6

Every school superintendent, elementary school and secondary school principal, school psychologist, and director of special education is challenged to enroll in and to attend at least one introductory course in higher education dealing with learning disabilities and to read and to discuss the topics that are addressed with their staffs.

Too many administrators who are in positions to make decisions regarding placement and curriculum are unsophisticated regarding learning disabilities, have had no orientation to this significant problem, and, in some cases, actually deny the fact of learning disabilities. The needs of these students cannot be met in the face of ignorance or lack of professional preparation.

In addition, all pediatricians and pediatric neurologists are challenged to become fully aware of the implications of developmental medicine in their practices because they are the first medical professionals to see LD children. Although learning disabilities is in part a medical problem, it is also an educational problem. Physicians must learn to accept educators as equals among equals in the development of a therapeutic regimen for these children; there is no professional hierarchy in learning disabilities.

CHALLENGE NUMBER 7

Educators at every level are challenged to reflect seriously on the proposition that children and youth with perceptual processing deficits (based on neurophysiologic dysfunctions) cannot be effectively placed in integrated or mainstreamed classrooms of this nation.

The learning characteristics of most of these children indicate that they cannot effectively change failure into success in the regular grades even with the supposed support of a resource room. The regular classroom cannot be modified sufficiently to meet the structured needs of those with learning disabilities; if well-intentioned general educators do so, they violate the nature and needs of pupils with normal neurologic development.

CHALLENGE NUMBER 8

The proliferation and continuance of commercial companies dedicated to the production and manufacture of untested teaching and learning materials supposed to be beneficial to the LD child are challenged.

In attending conferences, both large and small, much of what is supposed to be appropriate to LD children or youth is alarming. When commercial representatives are approached and questioned regarding the statistical or research base on which the materials are founded, the honest representative too often states that "only experience has demonstrated the effectiveness of these materials." Expensive, expendable, and often with no orientation to the nature of perceptual processing deficits, these materials constitute a disservice to teachers and students when they are misrepresented by their mere presence at a conference focusing on learning disabilities. Indeed, it is felt that if the number of these companies were reduced by half, there would still be too many vying inappropriately for the scarce dollars of teachers, parents, and school boards.

CHALLENGE NUMBER 9

The concept of least restrictive environment (LRE) for not only those with learning disabilities but also any type of child with physical or mental disability is challenged.

LRE is the popularization of a concept that flies in the face of a total educational plan for any state or province. This problem has been addressed before, but it needs to be constantly stressed. Every educational community, be it state, county, or large city, needs all types of quality educational programs—quality and excellent residential facilities, quality and excellent special classes (here particularly for those with perceptual processing deficits), quality and excellent resource rooms, quality and excellent home teaching, and quality and excellent programs of normalization within the regular classrooms.

CHALLENGE NUMBER 10

The editor and the consulting editors of *LD Focus* and the executive and professional advisory boards of the Council for Exceptional Children's

Division on Learning Disabilities are challenged to produce a journal that is continually accurate and beneficial to practicing educators and thereby beneficial to the children whom these educators serve.

In the same vein, the authors of future articles are challenged to produce writings germane to accurately defined LD children and youth that can assist others in providing realistic and absolutely honest educational programs to those with learning disabilities.

An issue not mentioned in the *Learning Disabilities Focus* article pertains specifically to dyslexia but is also significant for all other types of youths with learning disabilities. This pertains to the remarkable neuro-anatomic research being sponsored by the Orton Society on Dyslexia and being carried out by Dr. Albert Galaburda (and the late Dr. Norman Geschwind) of the Neurology Department of Harvard University Medical School. The meticulous studies of the brains of individuals who during life were diagnosed accurately as having had dyslexia are going to prove of value to the better understanding of all subtypes of learning disabilities as well. In the years to come, Galaburda's work (Galaburda et al, 1985) and that of his associates will have equal value and reputation to that of Gall, Broca, Wernicke, Flourens, and other eighteenth- and nineteenth-century investigators. However, the Galaburda studies being undertaken with all of the twentieth and twenty-first-century technologic attributes, will, of course, outshine these early, halting investigations. Galaburda is remarkable in his understanding of the learning problems of those to which he brings his neuroanatomic skills. We need to know his writings and research. This work offers hope that someday we will have a better and more complete understanding of dyslexia and learning disabilities.

REFERENCES

Cruickshank, W. W. (1981). A new perspective in teacher education: the neuro-educator. *Journal of Learning Disabilities, 14*, 337–341.

Cruickshank, W. W. (1985). Learning disabilities: A series of challenges. *Learning Disabilities Focus, 1*, 5–8.

Galaburda, A. M., Sherman, G. F., Rosen, G. D., Abuitiz, F., and Geschwind, N. (1985). Developmental dyslexia: four connective patients with cortical anomalies. *Annals of Neurology, 18*, 222–233.

Galpin, R. R. (1971). Developmental evaluation of learning problems in children. Unpublished. Information available from the Neuro Education Center, William Beaumont Hospital, 3203 Coolidge Highway, Royal Oak, MI 48072.

Levine, M. D., & Saltz, P. (1984). *Middle childhood: Development and dysfunction* (p. 521). Baltimore: University Park.

Author Index

Abbott, G., 123, 124, 126
Abele, E., 99
Abuitiz, F., 166
Adelman, H. S., 23, 75
Aiken, L. R., 102
Alexson, J., 128
Algozzine, B., 13, 74
American Psychiatric Association, 113, 123
Anderson, R. C., 90
Ansara, A., 102
Applebee, A., 83
Argonowitz, 50, 60
Asher, S. R., 91
Ashlock, R., 94
Association for Children with Learning Disabilities, 114, 115
Athey, I., 89
Ausubel, D., 81

Bader, M. S., 92
Bain, A. M., 101
Baker, L., 100, 101
Baroody, A., 86
Bauer, J. N., 14
Belmont, L., 81
Berk, R. A., 12, 14, 15
Best, L., 125, 126
Binet, A., 4
Birch, H., 81

Blalock, J., 112
Blalock, J. W., 80, 82
Blank, M., 89
Blankenship, C. S., 100
Bloom, B. S., 150
Bloom, F., 151
Boder, E., 93
Bond, G. L., 13
Boodoo, G. M., 12, 14, 15
Boshes, B., 74
Bradley, L., 84
Bradley, M., 86
Brady, I., 147
Bredekamp, S., 52
Breen, J. J., 74
Bricker, D. D., 28, 39
Brill, J., 112
Brown, A. L., 100, 101
Brown University, 154
Bruner, J. S., 79, 94
Bryan, T., 88, 97
Bryant, P., 84, 86
Burris, N. A., 85, 92
Burrows, A. T., 91–92
Busby, 50, 53
Busse, L. A., 81

Cable, B. A., 80
Calfee, R., 91
Carlisle, J. F., 90, 91
Carnine, D., 100

167

Carroll, S., 79, 80
Carter, B., 81, 84
Cawley, J. F., 93, 94
Chalfant, J. C., 4, 5, 6, 12, 15, 16, 21, 28, 43
Chall, J. S., 83–84, 90, 91
Chapman, R. S., 83
Chennells, P., 137
Cicci, R. L., 80
Clay, M., 92
Clements, S. D., 5
Cobb, G., 39
Cohen, J., 87
Cone, T. E., 12, 13, 15
Cooley, S., 14, 15
Cowen, S., 112, 113
Cox, J., 12, 14, 15
Cox, S., 112
Crais, E. R., 83
Critchley, M., 112
Crouse, M. A. B., 90
Cruickshank, W. M., 5
Cullinan, D., 88, 96

Daniels, P. A., 147
Danielson, L. C., 14
Darch, C., 91, 100
Davidson, L. A., 3
de Hirsch, K., 76, 83, 84, 88, 153
Denhoff, E., 80
Derr, A. M., 89
Deshler, D., 14, 15
Diffley, J., 113, 130
Dinklage, K., 112
Dobson, L. N., 93
Dodds, J., 80
Dominic, J. F., 86
Downing, J., 83
Duane, D., 130
Durkin, D., 78

Ehri, L., 89
Eisenberg, L., 149
Elkanin, D., 81

Elkind, D., 148
Elkind, J., 153
Elkins, J., 34
Elliot, L. L., 81
Embry, D., 60
Enfield, M. L., 151, 153
Englert, C. S., 100
Epstein, M. H., 88, 96
Erikson, E. H., 87, 97
Erickson, M. T., 14

Feagans, L., 23
Ferreiro, E., 83
Fielding, P., 113
Fischer, F. W., 81, 84
Fleischer, J., 86
Fogarty, T., 113
Forgnone, C., 13
Forness, S. R., 96
Fox, B., 84
Fox, L. H., 136, 147
Frankenburg, W., 80
Frauenheim, J. G., 112
Frederiksen, C. H., 86
Freebody, P., 90
Friedman, J., 82
Frith, U., 85

Gajar, A. H., 99
Galaburda, A. M., 166
Gallagher, J., 43
Gallagher, J. J., 23, 24
Gallagher, J. M., 89
Galpin, R. R., 163
Ganschaw, L., 102
Gardner, H., 98, 139–140, 149
Gardner, J., 39
Garnett, K., 86
Garvey, C., 79
Garwood, G., 28
Gelman, R., 89
Gentry, J. R., 93
Gerber, M. M., 89
Gerber, P., 113

Geschwind, N., 166
Gesell, A., 80
Gibson, J., 137
Gillam, R. B., 83
Ginsburg, H., 86
Giordano, G., 92, 93
Glover, A. T., 35, 40, 43
Goyette, C., 113
Graden, J., 74
Grant, J., 148
Graves, D. H., 92
Gray, R., 130
Greenfield, P., 78
Greenwood, J. A., 103
Gresham, F., 88, 97
Gresham, F. M., 87
Grosbang, C., 82
Gutkin, T. B., 12, 14, 15

Hagin, R. A., 112
Hainsworth, M., 80
Hainsworth, P., 80
Hallahan, D. P., 23
Hallau, M. G., 60, 62
Halliday, K., 116, 126, 127, 128
Halliday, M., 82
Hallowell, N., 153
Halstead, W. C., 3
Hammer, M. A., 81
Hammill, D., 86
Hanna, J. S., 85
Hanna, P. R., 85
Harris, A., 13
Hartman, L., 112
Hassan, R., 82
Hazel, J. S., 87, 88, 98
HEATH Resource Center, 112
Hebb, D., 117
Hedders, J. W., 96
Hinshelwood, J., 3, 29
Hirsch, E. D., 152
Hodges, L., 5
Hodges, R. E., 85
Hogenson, D., 149

Hopkins, C., 112
Howard R., 116, 125, 126, 127, 128
Hresko, W., 84

Inglis, J., 74
Interagency Committee on Learning Disabilities, 114

Jackson, D. C., 91–92
James, H. J., 91
James, K., 82
Jansky, J., 76, 79, 83, 84
Jansky, J. J., 148
Johnson, D., 76, 77, 84, 112, 117
Johnson, D. J., 5, 12, 13, 82, 89
Johnson, M. B., 82
Johnston, J. R., 83

Kameenui, E. J., 91, 100
Kamii, C., 82
Kanter, 116
Kanter, M., 116, 125, 127, 128
Kauffman, J. M., 23
Kavale, K. A., 23
Kavale, K. H., 74
Keogh, B. K., 23, 35, 40, 43, 75
Kirk, S., 43
Kirk, S. A., 4, 12, 28, 43, 50, 53
Kolson, C., 13
Kopp, K., 115
Kose, L., 102

Larsen, S. C., 77
Larson, R., 86
Laurie, T. E., 96
Lavatell, C., 82
Lawson, J. S., 74
Lehtinen, L., 79, 80, 81
Lerner, J., 28
Lerner, J. W., 5, 13
Levin, E., 96
Levine, M. D., 163
Lewis, A., 79

Lewkowitz, N. K., 100
Liberman, I. Y., 81, 84
Licht, B. G., 99
Liscio, M., 113
Litowitz, B., 83
Lloyd, J. W., 88, 96
Loban, W., 82
Lomax, R. G., 100
Luick, A., 50, 53
Luria, A., 117, 122
Luria, A. R., 3
Lynch, M., 113
Lyon, G. R., 23

Maker, C. J., 136
Mangrum, C., 112, 113
Mann, L., 12, 14, 15
Martin, E., 113
McCarthy, J., 34, 36
McCarthy, J. M., 28, 54
McCue, M., 113, 115, 123, 124
McCune-Nicolich, L., 79, 80
McEntire, E., 102
McGee, L., 100
McGue, M., 74
McKinney, J. D., 23
McLarnon, L. D., 88, 97
McLeod, J., 13, 14
Mellard, D., 14, 15, 125, 126, 127, 128
Menyuk, P., 82
Mercer, C., 13
Meyen, E. L., 16
Miller, J., 115
Miller, S. E., 94
Minskoff, E. H., 16
Minskoff, J. G., 16
Moats, L. C., 93
Morocco, C. C., 92, 102
Moss, J., 113
Moulton, J. R., 92
Moultrie, R., 16
Mulkey, S., 115
Myklebust, H., 86, 117

Myklebust, H. R., 74
Mykelbust, H. S., 5, 13

Nathan, R. B., 85, 92
National Joint Committee on Learning Disabilities (NJCLD), 114, 120, 126
Neuman, S. B., 92, 102
Newill, B., 113

Oka, E., 83, 88
Okola, C. M., 96
Orton, S. T., 3, 29

Page, E. B., 12, 14, 15
Pearson, M., 125, 126
Penfield, W., 3
Perfett, C. A., 100
Peterson, N. L., 28
Piaget, J., 80, 81, 89
Piercy, M., 81
Pihl, R. O., 88, 97
Piontkowski, D., 91
Podhajski, B., 83
Poggio, J., 14, 15
Pysch, M. V., 16

Rawson, M., 112
Read, C., 85
Rehabilitation Services Administration (RSA), 115, 123
Reid, D., 83
Reid, D. K., 89
Reis, S. M., 139
Reisman, F. K., 94
Reitan, F. M., 3
Renzulli, J., 139, 140, 150
Reschley, D. J., 87
Restak, R., 152
Reynolds, C. R., 12, 14, 15, 128
Rice, M. L., 82
Richey, L., 74
Richgels, D. J., 100

Index

Roberts, L., 3
Rogan, L., 112
Rose, S. A., 89
Rosen, G. D., 166
Rosenblum, S., 136, 148
Rosenshine, B. V., 90
Roth, S., 100
Routh, D. K., 84

Saltz, P., 163
Salvia, J., 77
Sameroff, A., 79
Saphire, D. G., 136, 148
Sattler, J., 131
Saunders, D. O., 91–92
Savin, H. B., 84
Scheffelin, M. A., 5
Scheiber, B., 45
Scholl, G. T., 77, 88
Schumaker, J. B., 87, 88, 89
Sclafani, A., 113
Seligman, M. E. P., 149
Semel, E., 99
Semel, E. M., 90, 99
Senf, G. W., 147
Shankweiler, D., 81, 84
Sharma, M. C., 102, 103
Shaw, R. A., 102
Sheard, C., 100
Shepard, L. A., 75
Sherman, G. F., 166
Shinn, M., 74
Siegler, R. S., 99
Silver, A. A., 112
Silverman, R., 77
Simpson, E., 112
Sinclair, E., 128
Singer, M. G., 138
Sitlington, P., 96
Sizer, T. R., 152
Skyer, G., 113
Skyer, R., 113
Smith, M., 113, 130
Smith, M. L., 75

Smith, S., 33
Snyder, L., 82
Spearman, C., 4
Spector, J., 91
Spiro, R. J., 100
Stanovich, K. E., 89, 100
Steeves, K. J., 94
Sternberg, R. J., 141
Sticht, T. G., 91
Stone, A., 122
Stone, C. A., 98, 99
Strauss, 29
Strauss, A., 28, 29, 81
Strichart, S., 112, 113
Sullivan, E., 81
Sullivan, M., 112

Tallal, P., 81
Talpers, J., 112
Taylor, J., 3
Taylor, L., 23, 75
Taylor, R. L., 77, 88
Teberosky, A., 83
Temple, C. A., 85, 92
Teulings, L. H., 85
Thomas, C. C., 100
Thomassen, A., 85
Thurstone, G., 4
Thurstone, L., 4
Tinker, M. A., 13
Tobin, D., 147
Torgesen, J. K., 23, 99
Traub, N., 151
Trifiletti, J., 13

Underhill, B., 94
Underhill, R. B., 94

Vail, P. L., 144, 148, 150
Vallecorsa, A., 77
Valus, A., 74
Varce, H. B., 138
Vausha, R. W., 5
Vellutino, F. R., 81

Vocational Rehabilitation Center of Allegheny County, 113
Vogel, S., 112, 122, 125, 126, 130, 131
Vygotsky, L., 148

Waldron, K. A., 136, 148
Walker, J. A., 60, 62
Wallace, G., 77
Weaver, S. J., 77
Weller, C., 23
Welty, E., 148
Werner, H., 29
Wernicke, C., 3
Wechsler, D., 4, 81–82
Westhead, E., 130
White, S. H., 81

Whitmore, J. R., 136
Wigfield, A., 91
Wiig, E. H., 90, 99
Williams, J. P., 84
Wilson, L. R., 12, 13, 15
Wilson, V. L., 12, 14, 15
Winne, P. H., 97
Wons, B. Y. L., 89, 97, 98
Woodcock, R. W., 82
Woodlands, M. J., 97
Woolf, C., 83

Ysseldyke, J. E., 74, 77

Zaporozhets, A., 81
Zigmand, N., 77, 94, 96
Zirkelbach, T., 103
Zwerlin, R., 114, 130

Subject Index

Achievement level expectancy formulas, for diagnosing LD students, 13–14
ACLD, 5
Adolescence, assessment of learning disabilities in, 95–103
　language development in, 99
　mathematical skills and knowledge, 102–103
　reading skills in, 99–101
　social and cognitive development in, 96–99
　written expression, 101–102
Adults, learning disabilities in college, 112, 122
　definition of LD, 113–117
　　ACLD position paper, 114–115
　　California Community College definition, 116–117
　　NJCLD definition, 114
　　vocational rehabilitation definitions, 115–116
　diagnosis of, 117–125
　　assessment, areas of, 120
　　client-clinician relationship, 118–119
　　college-bound, assessment of, 122
　　developmental history, 121–122
　　differential diagnosis, 118
　　information, sources of, 120–121
　　outcomes of, 123–125
　　rate of performance, 119
　　reasons for referral, 117–118
　　situation-specific factors, 120
　　theoretical considerations of, 117
　　vocational rehabilitation, assessment for, 122–123
　eligibility, determining, 125–130
　　California Community College eligibility model, 126–130
　　for vocational rehabilitation services, 113, 129–130
　future research in, 130–131
　Rehabilitation Act of 1973 (section 504), response to, 112–113
Age-related effects, heterogeneity/homogeneity due to, 61–62
Alexia, 3
Aphasia, 3
Aptitude-achievement discrepancy, as component of California Community College model for eligibility, 128
Assessment and marker variables for preschool LD children, 39–50
　assessment of preschool children, 41–42

173

Assessment and marker variables for preschool LD children—*continued*
  developmental inventories, 48–49
  in diagnosis of, 43, 44–47
Association for Children and Adults with Learning Disabilities (ACLD), 30, 31, 36
  1984 position paper on LD, 114–115
Association for Children with Learning Disabilities, 5

Behavioral adjustment of middle school children, 88
Behavioral symptoms of LD students, observing and recording, 10–11
Between-group variance in SLD preschool population, 61

California Assessment System for Adults with Learning Disabilities, 126–127
California Community College (CCC) 1987 definition of LD, 116–117, 125
  eligibility model, 126–129
  components of, 127–129
Children, assessment of. *See* Early childhood, assessment in; Middle school children, assessment of; Preschool children, specific learning disabilities in; School-age children, assessment of
Client-clinician relationship in adults with LD, 118–119
Cognitive development
  of adolescents, 96–99
  of middle school children, 88–89
  in young children, 81–82

College, adults with LD and, 112, 122
College-bound adults with LD, assessment of, 122
Congenital word blindness, 3
Cultural factors in diagnosing LD students, 9–10
Curriculum and instruction for teaching preschool children with SLD, 55, 60–61
  age-related effects, 61–63
  analysis of, 65–66
  learning principles of, 63–67
  population, heterogeneity of, 61

Decision-making in determining services, 17–18
"Developmentally Appropriate Practice" document, questions raised on SLD preschool children in, 55, 60, 62
Deviation component, 40, 43
Diagnostic criteria for entry and exit from services
  administrative procedures for, 15–20
  decision-making procedures, 17–18
  formal procedures for identifying high-risk students, 16–17
  regular education prereferral activities, 15–16
  transitioning and exiting procedures, 18–20
  identification, criteria for, 6–15
  discrepancy criterion, 12–15
  etiologic criterion, 7
  exclusionary criterion, 7–10
  failure to achieve, 6–7
  psychological process criterion, 10–12
  origins of, 1–6

Index

neurology, contributions from, 2–4
psychology, contributions from, 4–5
parent movement, contributions from, 5–6
status and needs, statement of, 21–24
  areas of consensus, 21–22
  areas of divergence, 22–23
  future of, 23–24
Diagnostic process for adults with LD. *See* Adults, learning disabilities in, diagnosis of
Discrepancy component, 40
Dismissal criteria for LD students, specific, 20–21
Divergent thinking, 146
Dyslexia, 3

Early childhood, assessment in
  cognitive development, 81–82
  graphic representation, 85–86
  language development, 82–83
  mathematics development, 86–87
  motor development, 80
  perceptual development, 80–81
  reading assessment, 83–85
  social development, 79–80
  specific LD, diagnosis of, 78–79
  writing, assessment of, 85–86
Education for All Handicapped Children Act. *See* Public Law 94–142
Educator of LD students, goals of, 153–155
Eligibility of adults with LD, determining, 125–130
  California Community College model, 126–129
  for vocational rehabilitation services, 129–130
Enrichment for gifted LD, 150

Entering services, administrative procedures for, 15–18
  decision-making processes, 17–18
  formal procedures for identifying high-risk students, 16–17
  regular education prereferral activities, 15–16
Environmental factors in diagnosing LD students, 9–10
Exiting or dismissal criteria, specific, 20–21
Exiting services, administrative procedures for, 15–21
  decision-making processes, 17–18
  transitioning procedures, 18–21

Future, challenges for
  courses in higher education, need for, 164
  definition, need for, 162–163
  groups of LD children, need for recognition of, 162
  journal, need for accurate and beneficial, 165–166
  least restrictive environment, concept of, 165
  materials, learning and teaching, 165
  methodologies, study on effectiveness of, 163
  perceptual processing deficits, need to recognize characteristics of students with, 164–165
  teachers, need for understanding of LD by, 163–164
Future, in field of LD identification, 23–24

Gardner theory of multiple intelligences, 139–141

Gifted LD student, 136–137, 147–153
  educational settings for, 151
  educator's goals for, 153–155
  measures of mastery in, 152
  needs of, 148–153
  options in education for, 150–151
  resources for, 162–163
  teachers of, 153
  types of work for, 151–152
Giftedness
  classification of, 149–150
  models for identifying, 137–147
    Gardner theory of multiple intelligences, 139–141
    intelligence quotient, 137
    Kaufman Assessment Battery for Children (K-ABC), 141–142
    parent nomination, 143
    Renzulli models, 139
    self-nomination, 143
    standardized achievement and aptitude tests, 138–139
    Sternberg's triarchic theory, 141
    teacher nomination, 142–143
    Vail's ten traits, 138–139
  recognition of, 137
  studies on, 136–137
Grade level discrepancy model, use of to diagnose LD students, 12–13
Graphic representation in young children, 85–86

Hearing impairment, as exclusionary criteria for diagnosis of LD students, 8
High-risk students, formal procedures for identifying, 16–17

Identification of LD students, criteria for
  discrepancy criterion, 12–15
  etiologic criterion, 7
  exclusionary criterion, 7–10
  failure to achieve, 6–7
  psychological process criterion, 10–12
Individualized written rehabilitation program (IWRP), 124
Infants and toddlers, assessment of
  family service plan for, individualized, 51–52
  typical profiles of preschoolers with SLDs, 50, 53, 54–55
Informal estimates, use of to diagnose LD student, 12
Informal task-process assessment, 11
Intake screening, as component to the California Community College eligibility model, 127
Intelligence, concept of, 4–5. *See also* Giftedness, identifying
Intelligence quotient, as model for identifying giftedness, 137–138
Interagency Committee on Learning Disabilities (ICLD), 32
  definition of LD, 33

K-ABC. *See* Kaufman Assessment Battery for Children
Kaufman Assessment Battery for Children (K-ABC), 54, 56–57, 141–142

Language development, assessing
  of adolescents, 99
  of middle school children, 89–90
  of young children, 82–83
Learning disabilities
  and ACLD position paper, 114–115

Index

definition of, need for accurate, 162, 163
definition of by California Community College system, 116–117
definition of by NJCLD, 114
definition of by vocational rehabilitation programs, 115–116
diagnosis of adults with. *See* Adults, learning disabilities in
and giftedness. *See* Gifted LD student.
Learning for preschool children with SLDs, principles of, 63–64, 67
analysis of, 65–66
Learning problems, possible causes of, 38–39
Least restrictive environment, concept of, 165
Literature for defining characteristics of children with SLD, 33–38

Marker Variable Project, 35–36
Mathematical skills and knowledge, assessing
in adolescents, 102–103
in middle school children, 93–94
in young children, 86–87
McCarthy Scales of Children's Abilities, 55, 58–59
Measured achievement, as component to California Community College eligibility model, 127–128
Mental retardation, as criteria for diagnosing LD students 8–9
Metacognitive strategies, 100
Methodologies, study of effectiveness of, 163

Middle school children,
assessment of, 87–95
behavioral adjustment in, 88
cognitive development in, 88–89
language development in, 89–90
mathematical knowledge, assessing, 93–94
reading skills, development of, 90–91
social development in, 87–88
written expression, assessing skills of, 91–93
Motor and health impairment, as criteria for diagnosing LD students, 8
Motor development of young children, 80
Multidisciplinary team and decision-making processes for diagnosis of LD students, 17–18

National Joint Committee on Learning Disabilities 1981 definition of LD, 114, 126
Neurology, contributions from in diagnosis of LD students, 2–4

Parent movement, contributions from in diagnosis of LD students, 5–6
Parent nomination, 143
Perceptual development of young children, 80–81
Perceptual processing deficits, need to recognize, 164–165
Play, as academic learning, 79–80
Preschool children, specific LD in
assessment and marker variables of, 39–50
assessment of preschool children, 41–42

Preschool children, specific LD in, assessment and marker variables of—*Continued*
  developmental inventories, 48–49
  marker variables appropriate in diagnosis, 43, 44–47
curriculum and instruction, 55–67
  age-related effects, heterogeneity/homogeneity due to, 61–63
  Kaufman Assessment Battery for Children, protocol of, 56–59
  learning, principles of, 63–67
  McCarthy Scales of Children's Abilities, 58–59
  questions raised by, 55, 60–61
  population, heterogeneity of, 61
critical issues of, 31–38
  characteristics, subtype literature for identifying, 33–38
  definitions, 32–33
  etiology of, 38–39
  history of, 28–29
  infants and toddlers, assessment of, 50–55
    family service plans for, 57–58
    profiles of, 50, 53, 54–55
  recent events focusing on, 29–31
Processing deficit, as component of California Community College eligibility model, 128
Psychology, contributions from in diagnosis of LD students, 4–5
Public Law 91–230 (The Specific Learning Disabilities Act of 1969), 5, 29
Public Law 94–142 (The Education for All Handicapped Children Act), 5, 18, 29, 40, 113–114, 129
  and discrepancy criterion, 12–15
  and definitions of LD, 32–33
  guidelines in states, 8–10
  psychological process criterion and, 10–12
  and transitioning procedures, 18–19
Public Law 99–457 (Education of the Handicapped Act Amendments of 1986), 29, 50, 55
  and assessment of infants and toddlers, 50, 51–52, 64, 67

Reading assessment
  of adolescents, 99–101
  of middle school children, 90–91
  of young children, 83–85
Regression model, use of to identify LD students, 14–15
Regular education prereferral activities, 15–16
Rehabilitation Act of 1973, Section 504 of, 112–113
Renzulli
  models of identification and teaching, 139
  three-ring conception of giftedness, 140
Research directions for adults with LD, future of, 130–131

School-age children, assessment of
  adolescence, 95–103
    language development in, 99
    mathematical skills and knowledge, 102–103
    reading skills in, 99–101
    social and cognitive development in, 96–99

Index

written expression, skills in, 101–102
conclusions on, 103–104
early childhood, 78–87
  cognitive development in, 81–82
  graphics, functions of, 85–86
  language development in, 82–83
  mathematics development in, 86–87
  motor development in, 80
  perceptual development in, 80–81
  reading assessment in, 83–85
  social development in, 79–80
  writing, functions of, 85–86
literature on, 74–78
middle childhood, 87–95
  behavioral adjustment in, 88
  cognitive development in, 88–89
  language development in, 89–90
  mathematical knowledge, assessing, 93–94
  reading skills, development of, 90–91
  social development in, 87–88
  written expression, assessing skills of, 91–93
Section 504 of the Rehabilitation Act of 1973, response to, 112–113
Self-nomination, 143–144
SLDS. *See* Specific learning disabilities
Slow learning rate, as diagnostic criteria for LD student, 9
Social development
  of adolescents, 96–99
  in early childhood, 79–80
  of middle school children, 87–88
Social/emotional maladjustment, as criteria for diagnosing LD student, 9
Specific learning disabilities (SLDs). *See also* Preschool children, specific LD in
  definition of, 32–33, 115
Specific Learning Disabilities Act of 1969, 5, 29
Standard score discrepancy models, use of to identify LD students, 14
Standardized achievement and aptitude tests, 138–139
Standardized tests, use of to diagnose LD student, 11–12
Sternberg's triarchic theory of human intelligence, 141
Streptosymbolia, 3
Students with LD, criteria for identifying. *See* Identification of LD students, criteria for.
Subtype studies
  analysis of, 68–70
  for defining characteristics of children with SLDs, 33–38

Teacher consultant model, 16
Teacher intervention approach, 16
Teacher nomination, 142–143
Teacher support teams model, 16
Teachers, need for understanding of LD students by, 163–164
Teacher of LD students, personal qualities of, 153
Team teaching model, 16
Ten traits (Vail) model of identifying gifted students, 144–146
Thirteenth Annual Report of the U.S. Department of Health and Human Services, data from, 30–31

Toddlers, assessment of. *See* Infants and toddlers, assessment of
Transitioning procedures in identification of LD students, 18–19
Trial placements, use of in dismissal or exiting, 20

University of California, Los Angeles (UCLA) Marker Variable Project, 43
U.S. Department of Education, future challenge for, 162, 163
U.S. Department of Health and Human Services, 113

Vail model of identifying gifted students, 144–146
Visual impairment, as criteria for diagnosing LD student, 8
Vocational rehabilitation for adult with LD, assessment of, 122–123
Vocational Rehabilitation Center (VRC) of Allegheny County, Inc., 115–116, 123
Vocational rehabilitation definitions of LD, 115–116
Vocational rehabilitation services model of determining eligibility of adult with LD, 129–130

Wechsler Adult Intelligence Scale—Revised (WAIS-R), 128
Wechsler assessment, 142
Wechsler Intelligence Scale for Children (WISC) profiles, 34, 54
Wechsler Preschool and Primary Scale of Intelligence (WPPSI), 35
Woodcock Johnson Psycho-Educational Battery (WJPEB), 122, 128
Word blindness, 3
Work, types of for gifted LD students, 151–152
WPPSI. *See* Wechsler Preschool and Primary Scale of Intelligence
Written expression, assessment of skills of
 in adolescents, 101–102
 in early childhood, 85–86
 in middle school children, 91–93

Young children, assessment of, 78–87
 cognitive development, 81–82
 graphics, functions, 85–86
 language development, 82–86
 mathematics development, 86–87
 motor development, 80
 perceptual development, 80–81
 reading assessment, 83–85
 social development, 79–80
 writing, functions, 85–86